ANGELS and
DEMONS

Angels and Demons

Perspectives and practice in diverse religious traditions

Edited by Peter G. Riddell *and* Beverly Smith Riddell

APOLLOS

APOLLOS (an imprint of Inter-Varsity Press)
Norton Street, Nottingham NG7 3HR, England
Email: ivp@ivpbooks.com
Website: www.ivpbooks.com

First published 2007

British Library Cataloguing in Publication Data
A catalogue record for this book is available from the British Library.

ISBN 978-1-84474-182-3

Set in Monotype Garamond 11/13pt
Typeset in Great Britain by Servis Filmsetting Ltd, Manchester
Printed and bound in Great Britain by Ashford Colour Press Ltd, Gosport, Hampshire

Inter-Varsity Press publishes Christian books that are true to the Bible and that communicate the gospel, develop discipleship and strengthen the church for its mission in the world.

Inter-Varsity Press is closely linked with the Universities and Colleges Christian Fellowship, a student movement connecting Christian Unions in universities and colleges throughout Great Britain, and a member movement of the International Fellowship of Evangelical Students. Website: www.uccf.org.uk

CONTENTS

CONTRIBUTORS

Dr Allan Anderson is Professor of Global Pentecostal Studies at the University of Birmingham.

Andrew G. Bannister teaches Philosophy and Islamic Studies at London School of Theology, where he is completing a PhD programme.

Dr Ruth Bradby recently completed a PhD programme at the University of Liverpool.

Dr Keith Ferdinando has served for many years in theological education in Africa, recently taught Missiology at London School of Theology, and is now working at the Rwanda Faculty of Evangelical Theology.

Dr Theodore Gabriel is Emeritus Senior Lecturer and Honorary Research Fellow in Theology and Religious Studies at the University of Gloucestershire.

Professor Chris Gananakan is the Head of Pastoral Theology at the South Asia Institute for Advanced Christian Studies (SAIACS) in Bangalore, India.

Revd Dr William K. Kay is Director of the Centre for Pentecostal and Charismatic Studies and Reader in Practical Theology, School of Theology and Religious Studies, University of Wales, Bangor.

Dr Bill A. Musk is Vicar at Holy Trinity & St Matthias Church in Tulse Hill, London.

Dr Martin Parsons took his PhD at London School of Theology and has served with Christian organizations and churches in South Asia.

Professor Christopher Partridge is Professor of Contemporary Religion at the University of Chester. From September 2007 he will be Professor of Religious Studies at Lancaster University.

Professor Peter G. Riddell is Director of the Centre for Islamic Studies and Muslim-Christian Relations at the London School of Theology.

Dr Nigel Scotland is Chair of Theology and Religious Studies at the University of Gloucestershire.

Revd Amy Summers-Minette is a graduate of Columbia Theological Seminary and currently serves as Associate Pastor at Covenant Presbyterian Church in Staunton, Virginia.

The co-editor, *Beverly Smith Riddell* studied theology at the United Theological College, Sydney, and has extensive editing experience in the corporate world.

GLOSSARY AND ABBREVIATIONS

AIC	African Independent 'Spirit' Church
amandawa	Spirit possession (TAR/Zulu)
amandiki	Spirit possession (TAR/Zulu)
ANE	Ancient Near East
ashram	Hindu monastery
atman	The universal Self (Hinduism)
avatar	Bodily manifestation of a higher being/deva (Hinduism)
avidya	Ignorance (Hinduism)
bhut	Ghosts (Islam)
channelling	The belief that humans can act as sources of information from the supernatural
charismata	Spiritual gifts
DDD	*Dictionary of Deities and Demons in the Bible*, 2nd rev. edn (Leiden: Brill, 1998)
diviner	A shaman who diagnoses spiritual origins of tribulations and prescribes remedies (TAR)
EI²	*Encyclopedia of Islam*, new edn (Leiden: Brill, 1960–)
glossolalia	Speaking in tongues
hadith (pl. *ahadith*)	Prophetic traditions (Islam)
hanif	Pre-Islamic Arabian monotheists
henotheism	Focusing on one god but allowing for the existence of others
isra'iliyyat	Popular Islamic stories deriving from Judaism or Christianity

JAPS	*Journal of Applied Psychological Studies*
jinn	Genies, spirits (Islam)
JRA	*Journal of Religion in Africa*
JSS	*Journal of Semitic Studies*
kraal	Rural village (South Africa)
kshatriya	Warrior king (Hinduism)
liminal	Only marginally perceptible
magick	The change in situations or events in accordance with one's will, which would, using normally accepted methods, be unchangeable (Satanism)
majnun	Affected by *jinn*; crazy
malak	Angel (Islam)
manthiravadi	Traditional spiritual healer (Hinduism)
mantra	Incantation (Hinduism)
maya	Illusion (Hinduism)
modalism	The view that Father, Son and Spirit are modes of being, rather that persons, thus denying personal distinction in the Trinity
moksha	Liberation from the cycle of death and rebirth (Hinduism)
monism	A philosophical term which holds that all things are merely manifestations of the One reality, that reality being God
NBD²	*New Bible Dictionary*, 2nd edn (Leicester: Inter-Varsity Press, 1982)
NCB	*The Holy Bible: New Century Version*, Ervin Bishop et al. (Fort Worth: Worthy Publishing, 1987)
NICOT	*New International Commentary on the Old Testament*, ed. Robert L. Hubbard (Grand Rapids: Eerdmans, 1990–)
NIDNTT	*New International Dictionary of New Testament Theology*, ed. Colin Brown (Grand Rapids: Zondervan, 1986)
NSBM	National Socialist Black Metal
peey	Capricious spirits (Tamil)
phanerosis	Normal manifestations of spiritual life

prakriti	Materiality (Hinduism)
prana	One unifying vital life force (Hinduism)
purusha	Soul (Hinduism)
qarinat	Twin spirit for each human (Islam)
qussas	Popular storytellers (Islam)
RSV	Revised Standard Version of the Bible
RT	*Redemption Tidings* (Assemblies of God denominational magazine)
samsara	The cycle of rebirth (Hinduism)
sat/asat	Being/non-being (Hinduism)
SJT	*Scottish Journal of Theology*
SLSW	Strategic level spiritual warfare
suniakaran	Practitioner of black magic (popular Hinduism of south India)
Sunna	The way/model of the Prophet Muhammad (Islam)
svadharma	True nature (Hinduism)
tafsir	Exegesis of the Qur'an (Islam)
TAR	Traditional African religions
TB	*Tyndale Bulletin*
Third Wave	Those who embraced baptism of the Spirit but did not belong to formal Pentecostal/Charismatic groups
UFO	Unidentified flying object
ukuthwasa	Spirit possession (TAR/Nguni)
wahy	Inspiration (Islam)
xeper	I have come into being (Temple of Set)
ZCC	Zion Christian Church (South Africa)

INTRODUCTION: ISSUES IN ANGELOLOGY AND DEMONOLOGY ACROSS DIVERSE RELIGIOUS TRADITIONS

This volume explores the spiritual realm, that netherworld between humans and God, and how followers of different faith traditions view the inhabitants therein. There is a delightful variety in this human perception of the divine, and yet so much that is similar between faiths and cultures.

The Religion, Culture and Communication Group of the Tyndale Fellowship provides a meeting forum for Christian scholars interested in the study of diverse religious traditions. It has met annually for conferences since 1996. The 2004 and 2005 conferences produced most of the chapters of this book.

The particular interest of the two conferences fell on the spiritual realm: in particular, how angelic and demonic concepts were overtly expressed, or were more obliquely reflected, in different religions. We were fortunate in gathering together researchers who were interested in the study of traditional African religions (Ferdinando), charismatic Christianity (Anderson, Kay, Scotland, Parsons), Hinduism (Gabriel, Gnanakan, Bradby in part), Islam (Riddell, Bannister, Musk), and post-Christian New Age spiritualities (Bradby, Partridge). The chapters in this present volume represent revisions of those conference papers, supplemented by the chapter by Summers-Minette on the Judeo-Christian roots of the concepts of angels and demons, and how their portrayal has changed in recent years in the popular media. Although a broad spectrum of faiths is represented in this volume, we acknowledge the absence of some other religious traditions, such as Catholic Christianity, present-day Judaism, Buddhism and Sikhism, caused not by a lack of interest in these faiths but rather by the absence of relevant specialists in our group of scholars.

The contributors mostly write as detached observers of the religious traditions they are describing. Nevertheless, authors of this volume do not shy away from taking a stand on controversial issues. For example, Nigel Scotland's preferences are clear in his typology of charismatic streams of thought; he manifests some scepticism about the group he terms 'expansive charismatics' and about deliverance ministry in general. In contrast, Martin Parsons' chapter is informed by personal experience with deliverance ministry. Parsons is a scholar and minister who has hands-on experience with binding and evicting demons. His contribution to this volume explores scriptural references to demons in general, and to specific demons he has encountered.

Furthermore, the chapter by Andy Bannister challenges fundamental Muslim beliefs about the divine source of the Qur'an, asking questions which Muslim scholars are reluctant to ask themselves, especially suggesting that popular storytellers may have been sources of some Qur'anic content. Hence, Muslim readers may feel some discomfort with this approach, which belongs squarely within the Western scholarly tradition of subjecting all claims to critical scrutiny.

Moreover, Ruth Bradby's detailed examination of *A Course in Miracles* skilfully mixes description with critique. The latter is particularly evident in the conclusion, when Bradby asks some hard questions of the relevance of the *Course in Miracles*, challenging the usefulness of New Age theology to the starving, oppressed and war-affected people in many parts of the world.

Two appendices have been included to assist readers in negotiating their way through a maze of terms. These appendices present a list of spirits in traditional African religions, and a list of gods in Hinduism.

Edited volumes which emerge from conferences often struggle to achieve coherence. The decision to focus on the spiritual realm in this present book overcomes that challenge. Indeed, a significant number of specific themes provide a web binding the various chapters together. The remainder of this introduction will survey these themes.

The spiritual battle

The concept of the spiritual battle – angels and demons fighting it out on behalf of their masters for dominion over the earth and the souls of the multitudes – appears in several faith traditions. Kay talks about the concept of spiritual warfare in the Pentecostal tradition, from the early days of Pentecostalism through to today's spiritual crusades led by Billy Graham and his family. Kay explains how novels by Frank Peretti popularized the concept of troops of angels battling a network of demons, and how some Pentecostal believers see much of human behaviour as the result of this spiritual conflict. Scotland's chapter introduces Strategic Level Spiritual Warfare – the battle carried out by charismatic Christians, involving intercessory prayer, deliverance and/or exorcisms. In Gnanakan's chapter, describing the Hindu tradition in South India, the manthiravadi is a warrior-healer who personally battles the demons on behalf of the afflicted person. The manthiravadi is often wounded in the process of providing healing. Musk describes the battles in folk Islam that are fought between evil jinn and angels who would protect us. Summers-Minette describes how, in Western popular culture, the spiritual battle provides a setting for dramatic conflict. Demons and angels wage war with each other as in the ancient Jewish and Christian traditions, although the battle is often depicted as internal to the warriors, in addition to the war they wage externally. In Gabriel's chapter, the author describes the cosmic battle between the suras and the asuras, representing – to a greater or lesser extent – Good and Evil. Although many faith traditions incorporate the concept of spiritual warfare and the epic battle of good versus evil, there is great diversity in how the spirit beings are presented and the consequences of the conflict on individuals and humankind.

Spirit beings

A key question posed by the contributors relates to debates about the origin of evil. Some of the religious traditions examined see God as the author of evil, as a way of affirming the overall sovereignty of a creator God. This is especially the case within Islamic orthodoxy. Other religious traditions see evil as emerging from within; Gabriel argues that the Hindu texts portray evil as a product of the human self. Still others consider environmental factors to be central to this question. The *Course in Miracles* discussed by Ruth Bradby denies the existence of evil at all. Neither do New Age practitioners have the concept of angels acting as advocates for them, because they see the distance between themselves and God as artificial, and seek always and only to bridge the gap.

A further theme emerging from the chapters relates to the vast distance perceived between the supreme deity and the lived world of creatures. This gap is filled by spirits, or angels and demons, in diverse religious traditions. This notion was encapsulated by Paul Hiebert in his 'flaw of the excluded middle', first articulated in a journal article in 1982. The chapters which most overtly engage with this idea are those by Parsons, Gnanakan, Bannister and Musk, respectively representing Christianity, Hinduism and Islam. However, Kay argues that a trinitarian theology provides a personalization of the Christian experience of God through the Holy Spirit, and that concentrating on angels and demons can serve to move focus away from God.

In popular culture it tends to be assumed that angels represent good and demons represent evil. However, a theme which emerges from several of the chapters is that some angels can be bad and some demons good. Ferdinando provides evidence of this in traditional African religions (TAR), where there is a blurring of boundaries between the physical and the spiritual as well as between the positive and negative spiritual entities. Kay and Scotland draw our attention to the notion of fallen angels in Christianity (although Kay points out that in Pentecostal Christianity a very clear distinction is drawn between angels and demons); and Summers-Minette describes the conflicted nature of spiritual beings that are being portrayed in today's popular books, movies and television shows. Demons with a soft spot and angels who fall from grace are concepts that are echoed in the exploration of Hindu traditions of sura and asura as described by Gabriel. He provides a powerful argument for the blurring of stereotypical views of spiritual beings, especially in the primary texts.

Various chapters consider the roles played by both angels and demons. Angelic roles are quite varied; in Islam, according to Riddell and Bannister, angels serve Allah as messengers, while also praising Allah, leading souls on the Day of Judgment, fighting alongside the righteous, and so forth. Summers-Minette writes that in the Judeo-Christian traditions and traditional Western popular culture, angels are seen as messengers and as our protective allies. Demonic spirit roles differ according to faith tradition. Ferdinando shows that spirits in TAR compromise the well-being of a person (through illness or injury). In the New Testament, however, evil spirits essentially draw a person away from God and subject him or her to temptation in addition to inflicting pain and/or misfortune. In different religious traditions spirits may take the form of ancestors. Ferdinando emphasizes this in the context of TAR; Musk makes the same point regarding folk Islam, while Anderson points out that Pentecostals and charismatics reject ancestor practices, believing the ancestor spirits have no power over Christians (yet such a belief in itself implies the existence of ancestor spirits.)

The physical appearance of angels to people is a theme that recurs in both Christianity and Islam. In the case of the former, Genesis 16 provides a scriptural context for this motif, with the Angel of the Lord appearing to Hagar. In the modern day, William Branham's vision of an angel is described by William Kay, while Muhammad's vision of an angel forms a central part of the revelatory claims of the Qur'an.

Responding to spirit beings

Another issue to emerge from the chapters is that human suffering is widely understood in spiritual terms. Ferdinando, Anderson, Gnanakan and Musk highlight this in their examination of their respective faith traditions, with Gnanakan commenting importantly that 'sickness is understood as a form of evil with spiritual causes'. Indeed, sickness and suffering can be seen as the outward manifestations of spiritual battles and warfare; this is a prominent theme in the chapters by Parsons and Musk.

Human suffering from spiritual causes can be addressed, however, according to the various contributions in this volume. The existence of specially gifted people who can connect with the spirit world provides the answer. Thus Ferdinando writes of the shamanistic diviner in TAR; Gnanakan gives a detailed description of the manthiravadi in popular Hinduism; Musk speaks of skilled Muslim practitioners who claim to counter the effects of evil spirits. Charismatic Christianity has developed the practice of deliverance ministry for the exorcism of evil spirits; Parsons provides a first-hand account of this in his chapter.

Another theme common to several religious traditions is that women are often perceived as having special spiritual powers which can be used for good (or evil). Hence it is often the case that the specially gifted people referred to in the previous paragraph are women, as witnessed in TAR, Islam and New Age spiritualities. Within folk Christianity the prevalent notion of female witches is also relevant here. And, as Summers-Minette notes, some of the most powerful forces in the spiritual battle within Western popular culture are females (often played by beautiful actresses).

In some traditions the shaman heals people of their illnesses by transferring demons from sufferers via himself, with resulting pain for himself. Both Gnanakan and Musk provide testimony to this phenomenon in Hinduism and Islam respectively. Again this notion bears some parallels with Christianity, especially the belief in Christ suffering on the cross himself to relieve human suffering.

The human response to the work of spirits is diverse, according to our contributors. The chapters provide examples of spirit appeasement, exorcism and accommodation. as seen in the chapters by Ferdinando, Gnanakan (with the medical workers in South India aiming for holistic treatment), and Musk. A particular kind of response is the use of talismans. These are referred to by both Gnanakan and Musk, the latter of whom reports that amulets are very common in non-literary religions, with the default religious position being that people can trap power with words and things. Scotland and Parsons describe charismatic Christian responses to demons, including spiritual attack by prayer and exorcism.

Other issues

Several of the chapters provide evidence of religious traditions referring to their sacred texts to determine or validate belief in the spirit world. Kay demonstrates how Pentecostal angelology is deduced from accounts of angelic activity in the biblical materials; Gabriel draws on the Vedas to present his portrait of suras and asuras; Bannister turns to the pages of the Qur'an and Hadith to provide core material for his discussion. Parsons links the demons he has personally experienced with the biblical texts describing them.

Another common feature across the chapters is emphasis upon the practical outworking of belief in angels/demons/spirits, rather than pure text-based theorizing. In other words, the various religions meet people where they are in terms of their felt needs. As Musk writes, 'pragmatism determines peoples' practices'.

Finally, these chapters reject a monolithic view of particular faiths or streams of faith. The notion of diversity within each faith is present within each chapter, but especially in those by Ferdinando, Gabriel, Bannister, Bradby and Partridge. In the context of post-Christian religious innovations in the West, we should note the contrast between Bradby's New Age groups, which interpret all in a positive light and reject demons, with the Satanism described by Partridge, which elevates and lauds the demonic. Hence we should avoid seeing New Ageism as monolithic; it is highly fragmented.

Variety in the spirit world

Spirit beings are fascinating. They can be wicked, good, conflicted, or non-existent. They announce, accompany, heal, injure, sway, charm, fight, tempt and judge. They can bring us closer to or distract us from God. Inside this volume you will see angels and demons in various faith traditions through the eyes of thirteen authors. You will find a great diversity of thought, some striking thematic similarities, and a fascinating view of worlds far divorced from our experience. Enjoy!

Peter G. Riddell
Beverly Smith Riddell

Variety in the spirit world

1 THE SPIRITUAL REALM IN TRADITIONAL AFRICAN RELIGION

Keith Ferdinando

The media have periodically introduced the British public to aspects of the African worldview of which they were apparently ignorant. Cindi John, for example, reported for the BBC on 3 June 2005: 'The conviction of three Angolans on child cruelty charges raised concerns about exorcism practices among some African communities.'[1] She then quoted the pastor of the French Christian Community Bethel (CCFB) near Harlesden: 'We know that *ndoki* [witchcraft] does exist. Back home and everywhere else too there are people who are used by the devil to bring a curse or bad luck to other people's lives, even to kill them.' Journalists have expressed amazement that people should believe in such things, but in reality 'it is not the presence of such beliefs that is odd or unusual but their absence'.[2] Much of the world thinks, and has always thought,

1. Cindi John, 'Exorcisms are part of our culture', <http://news.bbc.co.uk/1/hi/uk/4596127.stm>.
2. I. M. Lewis, *Social Anthropology in Perspective* (Cambridge: Cambridge University Press, 1985), p. 33.

in this way, and the traditional African spirit world is still richly populated.

However, it should be noted at the outset that any discussion of African religion as *one* phenomenon is disputable. There are hundreds of African ethnic groups, and some writers contest the legitimacy of a pan-African approach, referring instead to African traditional *religions*.[3] It is nevertheless not implausible to take a contrary approach, and many have done so: 'Behind the various rituals, gods, practitioners, and spirits in all these local religions lies a remarkable uniformity in the various peoples' understanding of the nature of the world, the nature of human beings and their place in the world, and the nature of evil.'[4] The issues are too large to debate here but, while the following discussion assumes the validity of the singular usage, what is said may not necessarily be applicable to all African ethnic groups.

The physical and spiritual worlds

In traditional Africa there is no dichotomy between the visible and invisible worlds, which form an indissoluble whole. The spirit world constitutes an integral part of human life, and people feel themselves to be in the presence of invisible realities no less real than the visible ones. They live in close proximity with spirits which communicate with them through dreams, through animals,[5] and through illness. Thus, African languages have no word for 'religion', since the spirit domain is part of a single, total reality: 'For Africans, the whole of existence is a religious phenomenon; man is a deeply religious being living in a religious universe.'[6]

---

3. Cf. J. Ferguson and R. Finnegan, *Aspects of African Religion* (Milton Keynes: Open University Press, 1977), p. 9.
4. R. C. Mitchell, *African Primal Religions* (Niles, IL: Argus Communications, 1977), p. 21.
5. A.-I. Berglund, *Zulu Thought-Patterns and Symbolism* (London: C. Hurst, 1989 [1976]), p. 94.
6. J. S. Mbiti, *African Religions and Philosophy* (Oxford: Heinemann, 1969), p. 15.

Accordingly, 'secular' activities – hunting, travelling, cultivating – are seen from a perspective that integrates spiritual and empirical dimensions and, particularly significant here, afflictions are also understood in spiritual terms and not as merely physical phenomena. They may be attributed to a spirit's agency or to a human witch but, whatever the source, according to the Zulu proverb, 'There is always somebody.'[7] Nevertheless, pursuit of spiritual causation of suffering does not imply ignorance of the obvious empirical factors involved, including germs or viruses. The empirical element explains *how* an event happened; but the pursuit of a spirit or sorcerer responds to the deeper, more unsettling question of *why* it happened – why to this person and at this time?

This in turn explains the pivotal role of diviners in African society, since it is they who diagnose the spiritual origins of tribulation and identify appropriate remedies. As a diviner explained: 'People come to me to find out what is causing their problems. It is my work to divine the cause of the evil, to figure out the source of the immorality that is provoking the problem. Once the immorality is identified then the person can take steps to neutralize it.'[8] Diviners use various techniques – mechanical devices, animal sacrifice and augury, and spirit familiars – to penetrate the spiritual world. Besides their mystical paraphernalia they also proceed by astute questioning of enquirers and a solid knowledge of their own communities. Whatever the means employed, 'the divinatory consultation is the central phase or episode in the total process of coping with misfortune, and it looks both backward to causation and forward to remedial measures'.[9] Traditionally the diviner is perhaps *the* most important human link with the invisible domain.

---

7. Berglund, *Zulu Thought-Patterns and Symbolism*, p. 270.
8. M. C. Kirwen, *The Missionary and the Diviner* (Maryknoll: Orbis, 1987), p. 29.
9. V. W. Turner, *The Forest of Symbols* (Ithaca: Cornell University Press, 1967), p. 361.

God and the spirit world

Some early Western travellers claimed that Africans had no conception of a Supreme Being; a few even denied the presence of any religious belief or activity. Such observations have since proved to be totally unfounded, but the nature of traditional African concepts of God remains controversial. Discussion focuses on the extent to which God was considered to be involved in the visible world and actively worshipped. Certainly he was often recognized as creator and sustainer of the cosmos. According to the Yoruba, Olodumare controlled the gift of life, and the Igbo and Akan peoples had similar beliefs.[10] Moreover, God was understood to be source of the force which pervades the universe and empowers both humans and spirits. However, for most peoples, with notable exceptions, God was a remote and almost unapproachable being, rarely the object of cultic activity. More rarely still did he intervene in human affairs.[11] 'As ultimate principles, many supreme gods are like African sacred kings: they reign but they do not rule ... [they] remain in the background of religious life.'[12] Much African mythology confirms this impression, with accounts of a primeval rupture between the Creator and humanity.

There have been numerous explanations of God's absence from traditional religious activity. Some argue that, in conformity with African social convention, he is indeed the object of cultic attention but that it is mediated through powerful but subordinate spirits, including ancestors. However, such an interpretation may be a rationalization of what was going on in the minds of those

---

10. E. B. Idowu, *Olodumare, God in Yoruba Belief* (London: Longmans, 1962), p. 169; A. J. Shelton, 'The Presence of the "Withdrawn" High God in North Ibo Religious Belief and Worship', *Man* 65 (1965), pp. 15–18; E. I. Metuh, 'Religious Concepts in West African Cosmogonies', *JRA* 13 (1982), p. 19.
11. E. G. Parrinder, *African Traditional Religion* (London: Sheldon Press, 1974), pp. 38ff.
12. B. C. Ray, 'African Religions: An Overview', in M. Eliade (ed.), *Encyclopaedia of Religion*, 1 (New York: Macmillan, 1987), p. 64.

who approached spirits and ancestors. In the case of ancestor veneration, Triebel argues,

> They feel, even more, that they know that they themselves depend on the ancestors, who are the guarantors of life. They are expecting life and the fullness of life . . . from the ancestors and from no one else. Because the ancestors cause misfortune on the one hand and because on the other hand only they can grant fortune, wellbeing, life, and a good living – that is, fullness of life – they alone are venerated.[13]

An alternative and perhaps more plausible interpretation of divine remoteness is that God is perceived to be too great to be concerned with human life. There is 'a dependence upon lesser spiritual causalities because there is no adequate recognition that the great power of the one God could really be concerned with this or that side of one's own small life'.[14]

However one interprets the 'absence' of God in traditional religion, it had significant implications for notions of the spirit world in two critical respects.

First, it meant that the spiritual domain was a chaos of competing forces, unrestrained by the presence of a sovereign God. This is especially apparent when traditional African conceptions are compared with that of the biblical writers, whose monotheism eclipses lesser spiritual causalities which, while real, take a secondary place. In contrast, adherents of African religion face an uncontrolled and threatening spirit world. While they may at times be able to negotiate potentially advantageous transactions with the spirits, there is nevertheless constantly impending danger.

Second, God's effective absence renders problematic the moral evaluation of spirits. Comparison with the biblical perspective is again instructive, for there the generally clear-cut distinction

---

13. J. Triebel, 'Living Together with the Ancestors: Ancestor Veneration in Africa as a Challenge for Missiology', *Missiology* 30 (April 2002), p. 193.
14. A. Hastings, *African Christianity* (London and Dublin: Geoffrey Chapman, 1976), p. 74.

between angels and demons derives from their contrasting relationships with Yahweh. By contrast, the anthropocentric criterion of evaluation, which shapes African approaches to the spirit world, means that it is rarely possible to speak simply of angel or demon. Spirits are morally ambivalent: they threaten and so may be demonic, but through appropriate ritual they might be rendered propitious. Both feared and welcomed, their presence and activity are constantly negotiated and renegotiated.

Nevertheless, there are rare cases of apparent moral dualism in the spirit world. Witchcraft spirits are always evil, although the criterion is again anthropocentric. Among the Xhosa, the spirit *umTyholi* is creator of evil things and source of bad dispositions among humans.[15] Particularly interesting is the contrast between the Dinka divinities, Macardit and Flesh. Dinka say,

> 'Macardit is bad', 'Macardit kills people', 'Macardit does not treat people with respect (kindness)' and 'Macardit is stupid' . . . Macardit is the final explanation of sufferings and misfortunes which cannot be traced to other causes more consonant with Dinka notions of divinity as just . . . Macardit presides over the ending of good things, the inevitable and sometimes brutal curtailment of human life and fertility.[16]

By contrast, Dinka pursue the presence of Flesh and 'tend to discuss it in subdued tones not noticeable when they talk of Divinity and other divinities'.[17]

Conceptual variety in the spirit world

There is huge variation in African conceptions of the spirit world. Here we consider a few widespread categories.

---

15. J. Hodgson, *The God of the Xhosa* (Cape Town: Oxford University Press, 1982), pp. 95–96.
16. G. Lienhardt, *Divinity and Experience: The Religion of the Dinka* (Oxford: Clarendon Press, 1961), p. 81.
17. Lienhardt, *Divinity and Experience*, p. 138.

Divinities

Many peoples, especially in West Africa, believe in powerful spirits immediately below the Supreme Being, generally termed divinities in English. They include the Yoruba *orisa*, Igbo *alusi* and Akan *abosom*; in Uganda the *balubaale* and *bacwezi* have similar status in the cosmologies of the Ganda and Nyoro. They 'are nearer to God and have a wider sphere of effectiveness than spirits',[18] possessing qualities that Christianity and Islam attribute to God himself. Historically there has been some transfer between the categories of Supreme Being and divinity, reflecting the amorphous, fluid quality of African religion.[19] Indeed, the Supreme Being seems sometimes simply a 'first among equals'.[20]

Yoruba believe in hundreds of *orisa*, offspring or emanations of Olodumare, the Supreme Being. All are morally ambiguous, some especially so, and all are feared. Orisa-nla is the supreme divinity, responsible for the creation of the world including humanity. He is also the source of human deformities – hunchbacks, cripples, albinos – the occurrence of which may be attributed to breach of taboo, but may equally reflect Orisa-nla's freedom to act as he pleases. Orunmila is the oracle divinity, whose cult is associated with *Ifa* divination, which is found all over Yorubaland. Esu, like Satan in Job, tests human sincerity, and myths speak of him as mischief-maker. Yoruba dread his malice and attribute human wickedness to him, saying of an evil-doer, 'It is Esu who stirred him.' Nevertheless, he is also worshipped and Yoruba have faith in his protective capacities. Ogun, a hunter and warrior, owns all iron, and users of tools or weapons depend on him. Sango is associated with natural disasters, particularly as god of thunder, but is also

18. T. Sundermeier, *The Individual and Community in African Traditional Religions* (Hamburg: Lit, 1998), p. 149.
19. N. S. Booth, 'God and the Gods in West Africa', in N. S. Booth (ed.), *African Religions: A Symposium* (New York: Nok Publishers, 1977). P. J. Ryan, '"Arise, O God!" The Problem of "Gods" in West Africa', *JRA* 11 (1980) pp. 161–171, gives a contrary view.
20. E. G. Parrinder, *West African Religion* (London: Epworth Press, 1949), pp. 16, 33ff.

regarded as an apotheosized human king. Sopona is divinity of the earth, especially associated with smallpox; implacably vengeful, much effort is spent in propitiating him.

Somewhat similar are the Dinka divinities. 'Free-divinities' correspond to fields of human experience: 'that imaged by DENG includes the phenomena of the sky associated with rain, that imaged by ABUK is the life of the gardens and the crops, and that imaged by GARANG . . . includes the heat of the sun and certain heated conditions of the human body'.[21] Humans often seek to regulate their relationships with nature through such divinities; Ganda fisherman depend on Mukasa, lord of the lake, and agricultural peoples often venerate an earth goddess.[22] Reflecting again the unity of visible and invisible dimensions, it is through these spirits that harmony with the physical environment is sought and maintained.

Divinities may also stand in a special relationship to certain clans. Dinka 'clan-divinities' are tutelary spirits of descent groups. The *bacwezi* are revered as spirits of the legendary founders of the ruling Nyoro dynasty, although subsequently identified with particular natural features.[23] Such beings are among the most powerful of the spirits of the human dead.

Ancestors

While many peoples do not recognize divinities, few are without an ancestor cult, and for many it is the primary religious focus: 'Lugbara religion comprises several cults, that of the dead being the most important. Most sacrifices are made to the dead.'[24] However, the category must be carefully defined. First, some prefer to speak of 'shades' or 'living dead', since the term 'ances-

---

21. Lienhardt, *Divinity and Experience*, pp. 159–160.
22. Cf. J. S. Ukpong, 'Sacrificial Worship in Ibibio Traditional Religion', *JRA* 13 (1982), pp. 165–166.
23. J. H. M. Beattie, 'Initiation into the Cwezi Spirit Possession Cult in Bunyoro', *African Studies* 16 (1957), pp. 150–161.
24. Cf. J. Middleton, *Lugbara Religion* (Washington DC, and London: Smithsonian Institution Press, 1987 [1960]), p. 25.

tors' risks 'limiting the concept unnecessarily, since there are spirits and living-dead of children, brothers, sisters, barren wives and other members of the family who were not in any way "ancestors"'.[25] Lugbara ancestors include 'all the dead and living forebears of *ego's* lineage . . . male and female . . . those who have begotten or borne children and also those who have died childless'.[26] Nevertheless, second, not all the dead are necessarily ancestors. Only those Yoruba dead who lived good lives, had children, and reached old age, became objects of cultic activity. Among the Zulu 'all human beings are potential shades. But the importance attached to a particular shade varies very much, depending on social status, and the age and number of children a man may have had prior to departure from the physically living.'[27] Third, the cult may be observed at different levels. The Gikuyu recognize three groups: the spirits of father and mother, clan spirits, and age-group spirits.[28] Finally, one must not equate ancestor cults with concern for ghosts. The !Kung fear and invoke the dead, but 'the concept of having special relations with their ancestors or of worshipping them is lacking'.[29] Similarly Nyoro 'say that when people die they cease to think of their living relatives as "theirs". By this they mean that ghosts no longer acknowledge the ties of affection and obligation which they felt when they were alive.'[30]

The ancestor cult 'represents the hierarchical social system carried over into the spirit world; it validates the traditional political structure; it ensures fertility, health, prosperity, and the continuity of past and future in family life; it is a sanction for the respect of the

---

25. Mbiti, *African Religions and Philosophy*, p. 85.
26. Middleton, *Lugbara Religion*, p. 33.
27. E. B. Idowu, *African Traditional Religion* (London: SCM Press, 1973), p. 187; Berglund, *Zulu Thought-Patterns and Symbolism*, p. 119.
28. J. Kenyatta, *Facing Mount Kenya* (London: Heinemann, 1979 [1938]), pp. 266–267.
29. L. Marshall, '!Kung Bushman Religious Beliefs', *Africa* 32 (1962), p. 241.
30. J. Beattie, *Bunyoro: An African Kingdom* (New York: Holt, Rhinehart and Winston, 1960), p. 76.

living elders'.[31] Such cults thus have pivotal importance in the lives of their adherents. A MoLuba 'is wholly devoted to the intercourse with the dead, and there is not a single feature of his life which is not affected by it', and the same is true of their communal life. 'Their familial, social and political authority and organization are based on the dead. Chiefs, clan leaders, and family heads all derive their power from the ancestors. Divination occurs through the dead, who either possess or speak to mediums.'[32] Ancestors communicate with their descendants through dreams and affliction, to guide, warn, reproach and punish. For some peoples ancestor veneration has also been a critical element in preserving ethnic identity through crisis: for the Herero following the early twentieth-century genocide, or the Gikuyu during the *mau mau* revolt and its suppression.[33] Similarly, the Zimbabwe liberation struggle was sustained by spirit mediums of the *mhondoro*, the Shona royal ancestors.[34]

Nevertheless, ancestors require attention from their posterity for their continued existence: they 'need descendants to perform the ritual services that confer, and maintain them in the state of ancestorhood'.[35] The living maintain the ancestors' strength by remembering their names and offering sacrifice. So, if their progeny depend on the ancestors' blessings and guidance, the ancestors in turn depend on their progeny's ritual activity. As ancestors' names are forgotten they cease to be 'living dead' and enter a state of 'collective immortality'. For the BaKongo, 'successive "deaths" of the dead reduce their mobility, their individuality,

---

31. D. B. Barrett, *Schism and Renewal in Africa* (Nairobi, Addis Ababa, Lusaka: Oxford University Press, 1968), p. 120.
32. W. F. P. Burton, quoted in C. Vecsey, 'Facing Death, Masking Death, in Luba Myth and Art', *JRA* 14 (1983), p. 26.
33. C. Elkins, *Britain's Gulag: The Brutal End of Empire in Kenya* (London: Jonathan Cape, 2005), pp. 171, 174.
34. D. Lan, *Guns and Rain: Guerrillas and Spirit Mediums in Zimbabwe* (London, Berkeley and Los Angeles: James Currey and University of California Press, 1985).
35. M. Fortes, *Religion, Morality and the Person: Essays on Tallensi Religion* (Cambridge: Cambridge University Press, 1987), p. 95.

and their ability to participate directly in the affairs of the living'.[36] Thus the relationship between ancestors and their descendants is reciprocal and subject to ongoing negotiation, as expressed in this Turu invocation: 'We have come here to provide you with a hide for your bed; now please stop causing distress to your *mwipwa*, Lisu, or we'll dig you up and throw you into the lake!'[37]

The Turu invocation also suggests the danger that ancestors represent for living kin. They share in the ambiguity that characterizes the African spirit world in general, and so arouse ambivalent attitudes. For many peoples they are a constant menace, punishing breaches of tradition and taboo, as well as kinship division and any failure to offer appropriate honour. They may bless their descendants but also punish, often savagely. 'The Luba respect their dead, even venerate them; but they also fear them.'[38] Among the Lovedu, 'Ancestors are appealed to and thanked for good crops, fertility, plenty, and all manner of good fortune and success.' However,

> Ancestors are capricious: their complaints as seen in the divining bones are usually about being neglected; but they cause illness to those they love most in order to receive recognition, have their name perpetuated, or their beads worn. They are said to 'hold' the woman experiencing difficult labour, to afflict children with sore eyes, and even to prevent the queen from making rain. Their complaints need imply no omission or neglect on the part of the afflicted, but merely some special desire that could not have been anticipated.[39]

This does not mean that ancestors are seen as wicked; they are kin and represent a people's most cherished ideals. However, their

---

36. W. MacGaffey, *Religion and Society in Central Africa* (Chicago: University of Chicago Press, 1986), p. 75.
37. H. K. Schneider, *The Africans: An Ethnological Account* (Englewood Cliffs, New Jersey: Prentice-Hall, 1981), p. 218.
38. Vecsey, 'Facing Death, Masking Death, in Luba Myth and Art', p. 27.
39. J. D. and E. J. Krige, 'The Lovedu of the Transvaal', in D. Forde (ed.), *African Worlds* (London: Oxford University Press, 1954), pp. 62–63.

proximity is threatening since its consequences are frequently negative. Accordingly, 'The food and libation given to the living-dead are paradoxically acts of hospitality and welcome, and yet of informing the living-dead to move away. The living-dead are wanted and yet not wanted.'[40] Similarly, funeral rites seek both to integrate the deceased into the community and yet to maintain a distance:

> The dead are dispatched to the other world, and then brought back ritually into the compound. They must be close at hand, so as to support the lives of those who come after. They take their allotted place. But not everything concerns them. Too much of their presence disturbs everyday life. The message of the [funeral] rituals is that life cannot be relied on, and that the ancestors are not always well-disposed towards the living.[41]

Are ancestors 'worshipped'? Some argue that ancestor cults should be seen in sociological rather than religious terms; they are just being treated as those members of the extended family who through age and wisdom deserve the most honour.[42] Speaking of the BaKongo, MacGaffey contends that the 'similarity between "worship" of the ancestors and etiquette addressed to the elders . . . supports Kopytoff's argument that the term "worship" should not be used to imply that, for Central African peoples, "ancestors" are radically different from living elders'.[43] However, the issue may be more complex than this dichotomistic approach suggests. Ancestor veneration might indeed reflect the social structure extended beyond death but still constitute 'worship', especially given the inseparability of 'religion' from the rest of human reality. The ritual terminology some peoples use suggests that ancestors are indeed distinguished from living elders: Yoruba use the same word, *bo*, to refer to worship of Olodumare and divinities, and of ancestral libations, while in their morning rite

---

40. Mbiti, *African Religions and Philosophy*, p. 84.
41. Sundermeier, *The Individual and Community in African Traditional Religions*, p. 91.
42. Mbiti, *African Religions and Philosophy*, pp. 8–9.
43. MacGaffey, *Religion and Society in Central Africa*, p. 148.

Igbo offer kola nuts to ancestors as well as to Chukwu and Ala (the earth goddess).[44]

Nor, as noted above, is it easy to argue that ancestors are simply approached as mediators with God. In the annual Bakossi feast of the ancestors, 'the prayer is addressed to Ngoe, the primeval ancestor. Other ancestors are named as intermediaries. The chain is unbroken with Ngoe as the ultimate point. He is not understood in the text as providing contact with God. There is no thought of God in this festival . . . The ancestors dispense blessings. They are responsible for the well-being of their successors.'[45]

Spirits

African cosmologies abound in other notions of spirit. There are human spirits not integrated into the ancestor cult, including those who received no proper burial, perhaps because they were identified as witches or died away from home. Among the BaKongo, 'witches become "ghosts," not "ancestors," and are condemned to anonymous wanderings in the trackless and infertile grasslands that lie between the forests and cultivated valleys'.[46] There are spirits of dead animals; when a Nyoro hunter first kills a hippopotamus, a rite is performed to ensure that its spirit will not haunt him.[47] Mandari believe in vengeful *nyok* – spirits of animals slain by humans, of deformed babies exposed to die, and of homicide victims.[48] There are spirits created as such and associated with mountains, trees and waterfalls, or which wander unattached. Spirits are sometimes linked with a piece of land, and propitiated

---

44. Idowu, *African Traditional Religion*, p. 183; E. G. Parrinder, *Religion in Africa* (Harmondsworth: Penguin, 1969) p. 69.
45. Sundermeier, *The Individual and Community in African Traditional Religions*, pp. 124–125.
46. MacGaffey, *Religion and Society in Central Africa*, p. 73.
47. J. H. M. Beattie, 'Spirit Mediumship and Hunting in Bunyoro', *Man* 63 (1963), pp. 188–189.
48. J. Buxton, *Religion and Healing in Mandari* (London: Oxford University Press, 1973), pp. 57–58, 175–176, 226, 254ff.

before and during cultivation.[49] *Bori* spirits of West Africa are associated with natural forces; they attack arbitrarily, cause most diseases and are used by witches as familiars, but somebody 'caught' by a *bori* is protected from other *bori*.[50]

Some spirits are associated with witchcraft. Shona believe witches are possessed by the spirit of the hyena which, like the witch, hunts by night and is necrophagous.[51] The Gabonese Fang believe the *evus* enters some people to enrich and protect them but, mostly unknown to them, also leaves their bodies at night and harms other people. Again, the *evus* is ambiguous, both a source of power and a curse, and Fang taboos are designed to control it.[52]

Human interaction with the spirit world

Human relationships with the spirit world take a limited number of forms.

Veneration

Most societies and individuals venerate spirits through ritual activity. Entire peoples or clans and families may have a habitual association with a divinity, and ancestor veneration has similar genealogical roots. In these cases relationships with the spirits are simply transmitted down the generations. However, families may develop an attachment to a spirit with which they had no traditional association, frequently following an initiatory incident of illness subsequently construed as spirit attack.

I. M. Lewis, ethnographer of Somali society, makes a socio-

---

49. L. Magesa, *African Religion: The Moral Traditions of Abundant Life* (Maryknoll: Orbis, 1997), pp. 207–208.
50. M. Onwuejeogwu, 'The Cult of the Bori Spirits among the Hausa', in M. Douglas and P. Kaberry (eds.), *Man in Africa* (London: Tavistock, 1969), pp. 279–280.
51. Lan, *Guns and Rain*, p. 36.
52. J. W. Fernandez, *Bwiti: An Ethnography of Religious Imagination in Africa* (Princeton: Princeton University Press, 1982), ch. 8.

logical distinction between central and peripheral spirit cults that is worth noting. Central cults are concerned with the ancestral spirits of the community, and are controlled by the 'establishment' whose morality and worldview they uphold. They are therefore conservative and non-ecstatic, as the inspired and unpredictable shaman constitutes a threat to established interests. By contrast, peripheral cults do not maintain the moral code, typically come from outside the society, and find their adepts among those peripheral to its politico-economic structures, mainly women and alienated men.[53] They compensate the excluded, giving leverage against social superiors where few other options are available. Such cults are often ecstatic as possession gives the marginalized an avenue of freedom, and perhaps a route to prestigious, even lucrative, new roles – as medium or shaman, for example.[54]

Attack

Generally, spirits initiate new relationships with humans through attack, but the initiative may come from the human side. Atuot believe that spirits 'seize' people through illness, but they also trade interests in spirits to manipulate them for private ends, as do Nuer.[55] Some societies seek the possession of one of their members by a tutelary spirit; when the priest of Soku in Kalabar dies, the diviner designates a substitute to be possessed by the spirit, Fenibaso.[56]

Nevertheless, generally spirits enter human experience through attack, which may be seen as initiating a new relationship to the

---

53. I. M. Lewis, *Ecstatic Religion* (London: Routledge, 1989), chs. 3–6.
54. This aspect of spirit possession has also been noted by Bill Musk in his study of folk Islam, ch. 10 in this volume.
55. J. W. Burton, 'The Village and the Cattle Camp', in I. Karp and S. Bird (eds.), *Explorations in African Systems of Thought* (Bloomington: Indiana University Press, 1980), p. 282; P. P. Howell, 'Some Observations on the Earthly Spirits among the Nuer', *Man* 53 (1953). pp. 86ff.
56. R. Horton, 'Types of Spirit Possession in Kalabari Religion', in J. H. M. Beattie and J. Middleton (eds.), *Spirit Mediumship and Society in Africa* (London: Routledge and Kegan Paul, 1969), p. 24.

advantage of both spirit and victim. Attacks involve physical affliction, particularly illness, although not all illness is necessarily understood as spirit-induced. The criteria that establish whether or not somebody is under spirit attack are culturally determined and may vary considerably. A basic distinction can be made between peoples for whom apparent mental derangement indicates spirit attack, perhaps accompanied by physical symptoms, and those for whom the symptoms are solely physical without any behavioural dimension: both types may be seen as possession.[57] Some societies believe spirits attack in different ways, the symptoms indicating the type of attack or spirit involved. Inducing spirit possession may itself be seen as the therapeutic *response* to an attack whose presence is manifested by physical symptoms alone. However, symptoms are often ambiguous and the diviner must choose among diagnoses culturally available.

Typically ancestors punish kin through physical attack, although other spirits may act similarly. 'Nature spirits sometimes cause affliction because they have been harmed in the earthly elements they inhabit. It is known, for example, that certain things and places are their habitat and reserved for their use.'[58] A range of symptoms, physical and psychological, including headaches, fever and anxiety, indicate *zar* attack.[59] The *shetani* spirits among the Segeju are seen as the usual cause of women's illnesses,[60] while Sidamo *shatana* spirits cause 'complaints of the head and nose, malfunctions of the gastro-intestinal tract, fever, and rheumatic conditions'.[61]

---

57. Cf. E. Bourguignon, 'World Distribution and Patterns of Possession States', in R. Prince (ed.), *Trance and Possession States* (Montreal: R. M. Bucke, 1968), pp. 9ff.
58. Magesa, *African Religion*, p. 176.
59. Cf. S. Messing, 'Group Therapy and Social Status in the Zar Cult of Ethiopia', *American Anthropologist* 60 (1958), p. 1120.
60. R. F. Gray, 'The Shetani Cult of the Segeju', in Beattie and Middleton (eds.), *Spirit Mediumship and Society in Africa*, p. 171.
61. J. and I. Hamer, 'Spirit Possession and Its Socio-Psychological Implications among the Sidamo of Southwest Ethiopia', *Ethnology* 5 (1966), pp. 394–395.

Cases of spirit possession manifested by behavioural symptoms are found throughout Africa. The symptomatology is remarkably uniform and bears close comparison with parallel phenomena encountered all over the world, and with descriptions of demonized persons in the synoptic gospels. The following account of *ukuthwasa* possession illness among the Nguni is representative:

> He or she may experience loss of appetite or develop unusual food preferences. There are complaints of aches and pains in different parts of the body; the affected becomes morose and may go about constantly weeping, and he is plagued by dreams . . . Agitated, unable to sleep or eat, the man or woman may disappear altogether. After a time the individual returns, looking totally mad and dishevelled after wandering about the land searching for roots and herbs seen in dreams. He may also have a snake draped about his neck . . . He becomes emaciated . . . The coming of convulsions, however, the use of snuff, the resulting sneezing and recurring yawning indicate that a spirit has entered the victim's body.[62]

In rural Ghana observed possession behaviour included flights into the bush or inhabiting a cemetery, nakedness, fits of frenzied motor activity – sometimes twelve a day – including leaping, dancing, shouting and extraordinary feats of strength or endurance, uncontrollability, and an unceasing tremor.[63] Sometimes spirit attacks have been contagious: there were epidemics of *amandiki* or *amandawa* possession among the Zulu in the early twentieth century.[64]

Response

Responses to spirit attack are culture-specific and depend on the

62. J. Gussler, 'Social Change, Ecology and Spirit Possession among the South African Nguni', in E. Bourguignon (ed.), *Religion, Altered States of Consciousness, and Social Change* (Columbus: Ohio State University Press, 1973), pp. 98–99.
63. M. J. Field, *Search for Security* (London: Faber and Faber, 1960), pp. 65 ff.
64. Gussler, 'Social Change, Ecology and Spirit Possession among the South African Nguni', p. 103.

identification of the spirit and its purpose. The phenomena resist easy classification but three principal strategies can be distinguished: appeasement, exorcism and accommodation.

Appeasement

Appeasement involves acknowledging and satisfying the attacking spirit's supposed grievances. In this category 'possessional' behaviour of the sort just described occurs in neither the illness nor the cure. The attack may be understood as possession, but it is possession characterized by physical symptoms alone. Typically appeasement is employed in propitiating ancestors when misfortune is attributed to them. The Mende sacrifice following a dream or series of misfortunes which show that the ancestors are angry, and sacrifices are accompanied by invocations on the offender's behalf:

> Ah, grandfathers, I have come to you: Momo is the one who is ill. The soothsayer informs me that you are angry with him because he has not 'fed' you for a long time. Do you, grandfathers, kindly pardon him. He is a small boy; he has no senses yet. I have come now to beg you. My heart is now clear.[65]

Among the Mandari, illness caused by a *jok* requires initial propitiatory sacrifice, the establishment of a shrine, and subsequent 'feeding' of the *jok*.[66] The victim and family are then deemed to have entered a new, but non-ecstatic, relationship with the spirit, which becomes their protector.

Exorcism

Exorcism means expelling an invasive spirit in order to sever all relationship with it. 'Spirits that are merely malevolent and unknown must be "expelled" or "driven away" so that they will not cause affliction . . . When such a spirit of affliction is diagnosed, it must be disowned and made to go "where it belongs," that is, to its

---

65. K. Little, 'The Mende in Sierra Leone', in D. Forde (ed.), *African Worlds* (London: Oxford University Press, 1954), p. 117.

66. Buxton, *Religion and Healing in Mandari*, pp. 69ff.

proper family or habitat.'[67] Exorcism may involve satisfying the spirit's demands, but the strategy differs from appeasement in that no lasting relationship is maintained or established.

Thonga use fumigation techniques and loud noise to expel *zulube* spirits, which enter victims to kill them.[68] Some peoples exorcise by transferring spirits to animals; a Shona victim of a *ngozi* inhales smoke which forces the spirit to identify itself, after which it is transferred to a hen.[69] Frequently exorcism involves a non-ecstatic, possibly sacrificial, rite of separation performed in the bush, thereby returning the spirit to what is considered its natural environment.

Accommodation

Accommodation embraces several strategies. As in appeasement a permanent relationship is established with the spirit, but possessional behaviour may be part of the original illness and is certainly part of the cure. The spirit is persuaded to possess its prey and state the terms under which affliction will cease. It may demand material objects and also future opportunities to repossess the victim. In return it becomes a benefactor, the illness ceases and, if this included bouts of uncontrolled behaviour, these are brought somewhat under control.

Accommodation may open up a new role for the erstwhile victim, perhaps as shaman (able to diagnose the afflictions of others and prescribe the appropriate remedies) or as medium (mouthpiece of the spirit and diviner for the community). Diviners' initiatory call-experiences are strikingly uniform: the original disease is followed by accommodation, leading to the commencement of 'professional practice'.

Others become members of spirit-possession cults, 'in which possession-trance is encouraged and in which women

67. Magesa, *African Religion*, p. 177.
68. E. Colson, 'Spirit Possession among the Tonga of Zambia', in Beattie and Middleton (eds.), *Spirit Mediumship and Society in Africa*, pp. 71–72.
69. M. Gelfand, 'Psychiatric Disorders as Recognised by the Shona', in A. Kiev (ed.), *Magic, Faith and Healing* (New York: Free Press, 1964), p. 171.

predominate, if not as members, then certainly as trancers'.[70] *Zar* cults are one example, found in north-eastern Africa and representative of similar cults elsewhere, such as the *migawo* cult among the Kimbu and Nyamwezi of Tanzania, or the Zulu *amandawe* cult.[71] Participation in *zar* begins with illness, when the patient is taken to the home of a *zar* doctor, a former patient who has become a shaman. The central stage of the healing process occurs at the dance held for the *zar* spirits, a regular occurrence for cult devotees; the new patient attends and becomes possessed when her *zar*'s tune is played. The shaman then asks the spirit what it wants so that it can be accommodated.[72]

Traditional divinity cults of the Nago-Yoruba occupy a more central position in society. Future 'horses' (possessed people) of the *orisa* are supposedly seized by them and become wild. The priest then teaches them to follow stereotyped behaviour patterns during possession to portray the character of their *orisa*.[73]

Finally, accommodation may involve no cult or new role at all, but a merely personal and familial relationship with the spirit. Douglas refers to situations in which

> the onlookers may make no attempt to control and try to use, nor to change the state, pacify or send away the invading influence. They assume that it is a channel of benign power for all. This is the positive cult of trance as such . . . the presence is sought for its own sake, for an unmediated form of communion between a god and his worshippers.[74]

---

70. Bourguignon, 'World Distribution and Patterns of Possession States', p. 20.
71. A. Shorter, 'The *migawo*: Peripheral Spirit Possession and Christian Prejudice', *Anthropos* 65 (1970), pp. 110–126; B. Sundkler, *Bantu Prophets in South Africa* (London: Oxford University Press, 1961), p. 23.
72. Cf. Messing, 'Group Therapy and Social Status in the Zar Cult of Ethiopia', p. 1120.
73. P. Verger, 'Trance and Convention in Nago-Yoruba Spirit Mediumship', in Beattie and Middleton (eds.), *Spirit Mediumship and Society in Africa*, pp. 50–51.
74. M. Douglas, *Natural Symbols* (Harmondsworth: Penguin, 1973), p. 105.

Conclusion

The African spirit world is complex, and the preceding discussion only hints at the huge variety of conception. It is a realm of moral ambiguity and danger, provoking anxiety among traditional religionists. Even ancestors are unreliable allies. Illness, drought, infertility, accident and death all mean that somewhere cosmic harmony has been disrupted, perhaps by a sorcerer, but just as likely by a spirit. Diviners then identify the cause and guide the afflicted towards appropriate remedies, perhaps including a costly renegotiation of their relationships with the spirit world. But the restored harmony is fragile, and subsequent ruptures are inevitable. There is no ultimate solution to the dilemmas of human existence in a world inhabited by potentially maleficent spirits, from which the Almighty is a distant and largely unknown absentee.

2 DEMONS AND DELIVERANCE IN AFRICAN PENTECOSTALISM

Allan Anderson

Demons and demonization in Africa

Estimates for Christian affiliation at the beginning of the twenty-first century reveal some amazing trends that any casual observer of African Christianity will not find so incredible, despite the difficulties with statistics. According to one statistic that included the predominantly Muslim north, 11% of Africa's population was 'charismatic' in 2000.[1] Even if this figure is only roughly approximate, Pentecostal and charismatic movements have undoubtedly become significant forms of Christianity in the sub-Sahara. Whatever our opinion or particular experience of Pentecostalism, it is a movement of such magnitude that Christianity itself will never be the same again. The mushrooming growth of Pentecostal and charismatic churches and the 'Pentecostalization' of older churches both Protestant and Catholic, especially in Africa and

---

1. P. Johnstone and J. Mandryk, *Operation World* (Carlisle: Paternoster, 2001), p. 21.

other parts of the Majority World, is a fact of our time.[2] Ghanaian Presbyterian theologian Cephas Omenyo suggests that the Pentecostal experience is becoming 'mainline' Christianity in Africa, 'not merely in numbers but more importantly in spirituality, theology and practice'.[3]

Pentecostalism is one of the most significant expressions of Christianity on the African continent today and probably the most rapidly expanding, not only in its thousands of denominational forms but also in its effects upon older churches. Pentecostals in general share a New Testament belief in the possibility of demonic influence in human behaviour. Some will call this 'demon possession', 'oppression', or 'demonization', but the net result is that the persons suffering from this form of affliction need 'deliverance' or 'exorcism'. This has always been a prominent part of Pentecostal and charismatic practice (especially in the Majority World), often conducted in the inner rooms and private counselling sessions of Pentecostal and charismatic churches and exhibiting a wide variety of procedures. Most Pentecostals and charismatics believe in the biblical position of a personal devil (Satan) and his messengers, known as demons or evil spirits. The corresponding experience of a foreboding spirit world for millions of people and the need for a Christian solution of liberation from it is particularly pertinent in those parts of the world where these unseen forces of evil are believed to be so prevalent. Exorcism, or, as it is better known in Pentecostalism, 'deliverance', is regarded as a continuation of the New Testament tradition and was a feature of the ministry of the healing evangelists (particularly of William Branham) and those regarded as having a special gift of 'deliverance ministry'. Although its incidence in Western Pentecostalism has probably declined, in some parts of the world it has become a very prominent activity. In West Africa, 'prayer camps' have been set up specifically for the

2. A. Anderson, *An Introduction to Pentecostalism* (Cambridge: Cambridge University Press, 2004), pp. 103–104.
3. C. N. Omenyo, *Pentecost Outside Pentecostalism: A Study of the Development of Charismatic Renewal in the Mainline Churches in Ghana* (Zoetermeer: Boekencentrum, 2002), p. 306.

purpose of providing places for exorcism for victims of witchcraft.[4] During two trips to Ghana in 2002–3, I visited three such camps, where the exorcism of 'patients' (usually women) who were considered to be possessed by demons was prayed for by a team of people (usually men) presided over by a prophet (or, in one case, by a prophetess) during deliverance services that might last a whole day.

Recognizing the holism of the African worldview is fundamental to understanding the role of the spirit world in Africa, where the fear of evil and the threat of evil spirits, gods or ancestors often overwhelms. When troubles arise, people need outside help to strengthen themselves against the uncertainties and unpredictability of life. The traditional healers, priests or diviners very often provide answers that people in trouble seek, or remedies for the restoration of lost power, directing the afflicted to the spirit world and often instructing them to give attention to the ancestors in order to resolve their problems. The ancestors are at the heart of the African spirit world. They may feel neglected, and their surviving families may not have fulfilled their responsibilities. Usually the ancestors are viewed as nearer to God than living relatives are, those nearer home, more easily related to, more easily understood, those whom people can argue with, plead their case with, and even scold. The ancestors are familiar people, and the strong community and family relationships are unaffected by death. But the ancestors can sometimes demand more than people are willing to give, or else do not always make their desires clearly known. Sometimes adversity will suddenly strike a family, and they will need to know which particular ancestor or other living person caused that adversity, and why. The answers to these perplexing questions are important, since without them the adversity will not go away. The family needs to know what it must do to appease the offended ancestor. This is when they will turn to the specialist diviners for solutions to these and other vexing

---

4. O. Onyinah, 'Akan Witchcraft and the Concept of Exorcism in the Church of Pentecost' (PhD thesis, University of Birmingham, 2002).

questions.[5] Pentecostalism has emphasized that these ancestors are spirits that have to be exorcized, and this too has provided a sense of release to people troubled by disturbing visitations and other occurrences.

Western scholars, particularly in the social sciences, have found the subject of evil spirits and demons in Africa fascinating. Their approach, however, has been largely reductionist and has not differed greatly from the Enlightenment paradigm that so greatly affected many of the nineteenth-century Protestant missionaries. They saw beliefs in witchcraft and evil spirits in Africa as 'superstitions' that would be removed with Western education. Some of the nineteenth-century pietistic missionaries in Africa, however, made the subject of demonism an important part of their preaching and practice, declaring African religions and their adherents to be satanic, although they did not usually offer deliverance from them, certainly not in tangible ways that Africans could relate to.[6] These missionaries thus contributed towards a rejection of the ambiguous and holistic nature of the African spirit world and promoted a dualistic understanding of religion in Africa in which the Christian God was set over against the 'pagan' world of the African religions and witchcraft, which were usually labelled with the term 'satanic'.

Anthropologists see the increase in demonic beliefs today as part of a reaction to modernity. Behrend and Luig write of the international proliferation of spirit possession cults and declare that 'the disappearance of spirits, as foretold by Westerners, has not taken place'. Instead, in Africa and throughout the world 'many spirits and their mediums are part of local as well as global or transglobal culture'.[7] They see this as a manifestation of

---

5. A. Anderson, *Zion and Pentecost: The Spirituality and Experience of African Pentecostal and Zionist/Apostolic Churches in South Africa* (Pretoria: University of South Africa Press, 2000), p. 176.
6. B. Meyer, *Translating the Devil: Religion and Modernity Among the Ewe in Ghana* (Edinburgh: Edinburgh University Press, 1999), pp. 83–84.
7. H. Behrend and U. Luig, 'Introduction', in H. Behrend and U. Luig (eds.), *Spirit Possession: Modernity and Power in Africa* (Oxford: James Currey, 1999), p. xiii.

modernity, and not as a return to a premodern or 'traditional' past. The missionaries, they say, created these 'enemies' against which this Christian God would be victorious and in effect made the African spirit world an essential part of understanding Christianity.[8] Birgit Meyer goes along with this interpretation and writes of the 'translation' of ancient gods and spirits in Ghana so that 'the image of Satan offers a discourse with which to approach these powers as "Christian" demons'.[9] She found that this discourse, which had translated many 'heathen' terms, appeared most frequently in Pentecostal churches. The spirits and gods of Africa have been reinterpreted from a Christian perspective into demons that can be exorcized.

Although pietistic Protestant missionaries demonized African religious practices and transferred them to the realm of Satan and his demons, they did not offer any real escape through exorcism or deliverance.[10] This was left to the charismatic 'prophets' that arose in the Protestant churches and in African independent churches,[11] and the Pentecostal missionaries of the early twentieth century who followed in the footsteps of their pietistic forebears but proclaimed freedom from and consequently a confrontational approach to the 'powers of darkness'. Pentecostal missionaries to Africa continued to demonize African religions as some of their predecessors had done. The first of these missionaries were ill-prepared for the rigours of intercultural and inter-religious communication. Everything happened at great speed, for the early missionaries believed that these were the last days before the imminent return of Christ, and there was no time for proper preparation through such things as language-learning and cultural and religious studies. Pentecostal workers from the white Anglo-Saxon Protestant world usually saw their mission in terms of from a civilized, Christian 'home' to a satanic and pagan 'foreign land',

---

8. H. Behrend, 'Power to Heal, Power to Kill: Spirit Possession and War in Northern Uganda 1986–1994', in Behrend and Luig, *Spirit Possession,* p. 22.
9. Meyer, *Translating the Devil,* p. xvii.
10. Meyer, *Translating the Devil,* pp. 103–104.
11. Onyinah, 'Akan Witchcraft', pp. 147–148.

where sometimes their own personal difficulties, prejudices and possible failures in adapting to a radically different culture, living conditions and religion were projected in their newsletters home.[12] Pentecostal missionaries saw Africa as the 'dark continent', the whole of the African spirit world as demonic, and all of African religions as 'demon worship' and 'pagan'.[13]

To give a typical example, British Pentecostal missionary Norman Burley gives graphic illustrations of his confrontations with 'the powers of darkness'. He wrote in 1921 of his encounter with 'three of Swaziland's greatest witch doctors, dressed in the most fearsome costume of their devilish trade'. He describes them 'chanting a weird lewd song' and says that 'a word from Heaven's Court assailed and broke down the arrayed power and splendour of Satan's assembly' so that they 'had to disband'.[14] Later, he describes a 'large heathen Kraal' with a family gathering for a traditional ritual killing, where 'all are called by the father to lay their hands on the sacrifice, while he calls upon Satan and his demons to behold their devotion, begging that sickness be kept from the Kraal'.[15] In yet another report, he describes 'all their demon and ancestral worship paraphernalia', which include a big drum, a 'demon designed and a demon-looking headgear', spears and axes, 'several bundles of "muti" (traditional medicines), dishes on which food was wont to be offered to demons and to Satan himself', baskets and clothes that were used 'at no other time and for no other purpose than in such devil worship, and by no other than a fully initiated medium'.[16] It is very unlikely that this Swazi ritual would have contained any reference whatever to 'Satan' or 'demons', but was a ceremony honouring the ancestors and using traditional medicines. The fact that so many

12. A. Anderson, 'Christian Missionaries and "Heathen Natives": The Cultural Ethics of Early Pentecostal Missionaries', *Journal of the European Pentecostal Theological Association* 22 (July 2002), pp. 4–29.

13. Onyinah, 'Akan Witchcraft', pp. 144–145.

14. N. Burley, *Things New and Old* 1/4 (October 1921), p. 32.

15. Burley, *Things New and Old* 2/3 (August 1922), p. 11.

16. Burley, *Things New and Old* 2/5 (December 1922), p. 7.

inaccurate, confrontational and tendentious comments were published in leading British Pentecostal periodicals not only displays the ignorance and prejudices of these missionaries, but also is in itself a reflection of the prevailing cultural and religious ethos of early Pentecostals. This is a far cry from the strategy of Paul, who used existing religious concepts to proclaim his message and was even commended for not blaspheming the goddess Artemis.[17]

The missionaries taught their converts well, and the demonizing of African religious concepts continues unabated today, particularly in Pentecostal circles. As we will see, it is quite normal for there to be a confrontational approach to traditional African religious practices, and people who have been involved in these are regarded as needing 'deliverance' from demons. 'Witchcraft' and 'demons' are interchangeable and synonymous terms in African Pentecostalism.[18] It is not the purpose of this chapter to enter into a description of all the traditional ideas of evil, but rather to depict how Pentecostals in Africa have appropriated some of these images of evil and invested them with biblical meaning. We will briefly look at West Africa and especially at Southern Africa for examples of the practice of exorcism. There are some similarities, but remembering that Ghana is geographically as far from South Africa as it is from Britain might help to give some perspective to the differences that certainly exist.

Deliverance ministry in West Africa

The 'deliverance ministry' has become a highly specialized and complex activity in West African Pentecostalism, and has been described in some detail by Paul Gifford,[19] and more recently by a Ghanaian scholar, Opoku Onyinah, who is a leader in the largest

---

17. Acts 19:37.
18. Onyinah, 'Akan Witchcraft', p. 236.
19. P. Gifford, *African Christianity: Its Public Role* (London: Hurst, 1998), pp. 97–109.

non-Catholic denomination in Ghana, the Church of Pentecost.[20] This practice has its origins in the African Christian 'prophets' and the 'spiritual churches' of the early twentieth century, classical Pentecostalism, and the new charismatic churches. The latter were stimulated especially by the ministry of Benson Idahosa of Benin City, whose training college was the centre out of which new charismatic churches and 'ministries' sprang up throughout West Africa. Idahosa had formal ties with other new Pentecostal and charismatic groups throughout Africa, especially in Ghana, where he held his first crusade in Accra in 1978. Through the influence of Idahosa and his protégés in Ghana, the subsequent visit (in 1987) of English charismatic and deliverance guru Derek Prince,[21] and the many booklets of Nigerian 'specialists' like Emmanuel Eni, the deliverance ministry has become a prominent, if controversial, part of West African Pentecostalism. Eni in particular wrote an elaborate account of his affair with a witch who could change her body into a snake, and his later intimate involvement with the 'Queen of the Coast', a mermaid-like water deity called Maami Wata, who would take him to a city under the sea and give him the power to change into an animal. He became a very powerful wizard until he was converted to Pentecostal Christianity in 1985.[22] Eni himself has travelled all over Africa with his story, coming twice to South Africa in 1992 and 1993 and preaching in the Praise Tabernacle Church in Soshanguve near Pretoria, on which occasions I was present. Not only did his testimony of intimate relations with evil spiritual powers as a priest of the water goddess fascinate African Pentecostals and this European African, but his high-powered preaching and exuberant dancing were welcome in a society where such religious enthusiasm was commonplace.

Not all African Pentecostals would identify with the extremities of Eni's account, but demonology is certainly an important

20. Onyinah, 'Akan Witchcraft', pp. 120–166, 231–293.

21. Ibid., pp. 220–223.

22. E. Eni, *Delivered from the Powers of Darkness* (Ibadan: Scripture Union, 1988).

feature of Pentecostalism in West Africa. There is widespread belief in the power of witchcraft throughout West Africa, including among educated people.[23] The many large charismatic churches there have teams of people who specialize in deliverance ministry and this has also become a feature in many of the older Protestant and Catholic churches.[24] In many ways the procedures used are similar to those employed by Western specialists in 'deliverance ministry' like Prince, but the cases treated are given a fundamentally African (often, traditional) orientation. West African religion has a complex pantheon of gods, ancestors and spirits often related to natural phenomena, and in Pentecostal Christian discourse these have been transferred or 'translated' to the realm of 'demons'. So when a person is prayed for deliverance, what is exorcized is a reconfigured African spirit. In research conducted in Ghana, Onyinah found that although some Church of Pentecost members had 'traditional [Western] Christian belief' that demons were 'fallen angels', many linked them with African deities and natural phenomena.[25] He also did extensive research among the 'prayer camps' of his denomination, and found that the method of giving counsel followed by prolonged prayer for 'deliverance' was 'just like' *abisa*, a Twi (Akan) word meaning a consultation with a diviner or traditional priest.[26] The relevance of the deliverance from 'demons' for the people suffering affliction is obvious, and those delivered will testify to their freedom from African psychic symptoms, ancestral curses and other similar disturbances. Of course, the identification of the work of demons is by no means limited to 'traditional' spirit beings, as modernity and globalization have resulted in a host of new threats to Christians living a holy life, including temptations in the modern market economy. These too are often ascribed to the work of demons.

---

23. Onyinah, 'Akan Witchcraft', pp. 234–235.
24. Gifford, *African Christianity*, pp. 106–107.
25. Onyinah, 'Akan Witchcraft', p. 238.
26. Ibid., p. 252.

Spirits and ancestors in Southern African Pentecostalism

Southern Africa is no exception to the continental trend of the growth of Pentecostalism. The latest statistics suggest that as many as 50% of the population of Southern Africa are linked in some way to Pentecostal, charismatic or African independent 'Spirit' churches.[27] Most of the latter practise some form of Pentecostal Christianity.[28] The different Pentecostal, Zionist and Apostolic groups influence and permeate one another and cannot be easily distinguished in theology and praxis. Daneel has shown through his extensive research in Zimbabwe the importance of identifying and removing witchcraft and exorcising evil spirits in Zionist and Apostolic churches, and he rejects any notion that such exorcism is the reappearing of traditional 'exorcism' in Christian guise.[29] The new Pentecostalism is relating to ever-widening circles of influence, not only from the Western world.

---

27. David Barrett et al. say that 21 million people in South Africa belong to these groups, out of a total population of some 40 million. Seventeen million of these are labelled 'neocharismatics', his label that includes African independent churches. D. B Barratt and T. M. Johnson, 'Global Statistics', in S. M. Burgess and E. van der Maas (eds.), *The New International Dictionary of Pentecostal and Charismatic Movements* (Grand Rapids: Zondervan, 2002), p. 227.
28. This chapter will refer to 'South African Pentecostalism' as constituting three main groups: (1) classical Pentecostals, with origins in North American and Western Europe at the beginning of the twentieth century and established in South Africa from 1908 onwards; (2) independent charismatics , who have arisen since the 1980s and are also influenced by Western Pentecostalism and the charismatic movement; and (3) the majority of African independent 'Spirit' churches, mostly known in Southern Africa as 'Zionist' and 'Apostolic' churches, of which the largest is the Zion Christian Church, also with origins in the early twentieth-century healing and Pentecostal movements. Anderson, *Zion and Pentecost*, p. 27.
29. M. L. Daneel, *Old and New in Southern Shona Independent Churches*, 2 (The Hague: Mouton, 1974), pp. 239–254, 341–343.

Nigerian evangelist Emmanuel Eni with his elaborate West African demonology was one of the first outside African visitors to minister exclusively in black charismatic churches in South Africa in the early 1990s. His ideas resonated with traditional ideas of evil spirit powers and with the experiences of young people caught up in the violent conflict in South African schools, especially in the urban metropolises.[30]

Evil spirits have reappeared in Southern African Pentecostalism in abundance. The encounters described in this chapter are based on traditional ideas of evil spirits that have been appropriated in a Christian context. Exorcism of evil spirits is a regular part of pastoral ministry in Pentecostal churches. Sometimes evil spirits are associated with bad dreams, and Pentecostals will seek help from a pastor, a prophet or another church leader. One member was told that the nightmare he had experienced was the result of a visitation by an evil spirit called Tokoloshe, the best-known evil spirit in urban areas. Other spirit creatures exist, but it seems that Tokoloshe is the only one who has survived to be universally known today. Countless stories are told about this troublesome ogre, *Uthokoloshe* (of Nguni origin), better known in the northern provinces simply as *Tokoloshe*, an infamous spirit to South Africans. It is probably unlikely that he can be accurately described as a 'spirit' after the idea of 'ghost' – for an ethereal, phantom-like creature does not seem to exist in African mythology. Tokoloshe is a capricious, anthropomorphous, dwarf-like male animal (usually described as about a metre high) with obscene sexual connotations and witchcraft associations. For this reason Tokoloshe can be conjured up by specialists and used by people seeking to harm others. People usually experience Tokoloshe as a nuisance, making noises inside or outside a house (especially on or in the roof), throwing

30. This research considers Pentecostal responses to and encounters with the African spirit world, drawing upon fieldwork conducted in Soshanguve in the 1990s, in what is now north of Gauteng, the most populous province in the country. Representatives of all three Pentecostal groups were interviewed during this research. More detail on this research is given in Anderson, *Zion and Pentecost*, pp. 175–198.

things around, and troubling people while they sleep. He is believed to sprinkle witchcraft concoctions around the house and on its inhabitants. Tokoloshe causes dogs to bark and cats to fight, and he makes strange noises, but people have seldom seen him. He makes people uncomfortable at night, making them feel either extremely hot or extremely cold. After his visit to a house, the inhabitants sometimes find it difficult to sleep properly. He gets into the kitchen and eats food, usually spilling it all over the ground. Sometimes the problem is more sinister, as Tokoloshe is also believed to beat children, to have intercourse with girls at night and to strangle people while they sleep. Some people still raise their beds from the ground in order to make it more difficult for the short Tokoloshe to climb on to them.

When Tokoloshe troubled people in the past, a visit was made to the traditional healer who would diagnose the cause of the affliction and prescribe a remedy. Perhaps a sorcerer or a malicious neighbour had sent the Tokoloshe. Some Pentecostals felt that becoming a Christian solved the problems of Tokoloshe. A woman related how her family had been troubled by Tokoloshe – 'before I was born again', she added. She said that her neighbour had turned her son into Tokoloshe at night. It would sit on top of a tree in their yard and cause them not to sleep properly and to have nightmares. They consulted a healer, who was unable to get rid of the spirit; the trouble only got worse. The problem was solved only when they moved house. When troubled by the Tokoloshe, Pentecostals and Zionists usually turn for help not to traditional healers but to church leaders, who sometimes offer remedies that are adaptations from traditional practices. The largest of all South African churches, the Zion Christian Church (ZCC) has various methods of dealing with Tokoloshe, including cracking a whip to destroy his power, and many methods that a ZCC minister said were secrets of his church that could not be divulged. One ZCC member went to her minister, who burnt brown paper in the house and sprinkled water and salt around the property. The Tokoloshe did not return. An Apostolic member said that when her family were being troubled at night they called for the prophets, who came to the house and fasted and prayed. They told her that they had seen the Tokoloshe and had chased it away, although she said that the family had seen nothing at all. Water was sprinkled around the house and green and white ropes (the colours of her church) were fastened around the property and on the doorposts of the house. This seemed to have had the desired effect, as the creature did not trouble the family after that. Another respondent heard noises on the roof of her house at night, and when she and her husband went outside they could see nothing. They reported the disturbances to an Apostolic prophet, who identified it as Tokoloshe, came to the house, prayed for water and sprinkled it around the house and on the roof. The Tokoloshe did not return and the respondent joined the church. In this and many other stories told, a prophetic exorcism resulted in conversion to the church. Perceived felt needs were being met, resulting in a more meaningful experience of Christian faith. The interminable uncertainty, fear, and the threatening spirits like the Tokoloshe inherent in African popular religion result in bewildering questions with seemingly no secure answers. Pentecostal and Zionist/Apostolic churches, with their emphasis on the omnipotent Holy Spirit who fills people's being, have provided relevant answers to at least some of these perplexing problems, by providing hope of deliverance from the troublesome Tokoloshe and other evil spirits.[31]

The cult associated with ancestor commemoration is still the most prominent feature of Southern African religion. Ancestors reveal themselves to their relatives mostly through vivid dreams, but also less frequently through (day) visions and through diviners. Ancestors usually identify themselves in some way, either by stating their name or by showing some characteristic that enables someone who remembers them to identify them. One woman said that she had a dream in which she was pregnant. Someone took her to a gravestone on which was written the name 'Isaac'. The following day she enquired from an older family member who said that Isaac was a grandfather who had died many years previously. A month later the woman fell pregnant and the baby boy was called Isaac. She thereafter prayed and thanked the ancestors for

31. Anderson, *Zion and Pentecost,* pp. 176–179.

their gift of the child. The child thereby, following traditional custom, received the 'ancestor spirit' of the deceased ancestor Isaac. Many Pentecostals reject this practice, which is regarded as demonic.

When ancestors appear, it is usually a sign that something has gone wrong. Ancestors can be angered and thereby can bring calamity to their descendants, especially when their instructions are not carried out. Because they are 'parents', they have the responsibility to discipline their 'children' when they are disobedient. One man told us that when a car knocked down his cousin, the family visited a diviner to discover the reason for this disaster. They were told that the cousin had not carried out the 'rules' of the ancestors as revealed in a dream, and that this was why the accident had occurred. Similarly, a ZCC member said that a diviner had told his brother that the ancestors wanted to kill him for failing to carry out their instructions. He was thereafter knocked down by a car and killed. This man believed that the ancestors had the power to kill people, their children or their livestock when they were not obeyed.[32]

Members of classical Pentecostal and independent charismatic churches were generally unqualified in rejecting ancestor commemoration and were the most confrontational of church members with regard to key traditional beliefs. The ancestors are believed to exist, but Christians do not need to do anything about them, because they have no power over Christians. Nearly all of the 140 Pentecostals and charismatics interviewed said that they did not commemorate the ancestors or consult diviners. They rejected these customs and showed a radical break with what are regarded as 'pagan' practices. Pentecostals were quite sure that a person who is 'saved' does not do these things. They represent the 'old life' out of which everything has become new. Pentecostals were more forthright in their rejection of those practices they see as incompatible with Christianity than the members of other churches were. Many Pentecostals demonized ancestor manifestations as the work of 'evil spirits'. 'The devil is able to disguise

---

32. Ibid., pp. 180–182.

himself in the form of a person who died long ago,' one explained. 'He pretends as if he has come to help and protect you, while all the time the ancestor is the devil himself.' Another said: 'Ancestors are evil spirits. Satan is able to change these spirits so that they resemble your parents who have died. He will tell you, "These are your parents", and you will believe that.' Another Pentecostal member said: 'Ancestors are evil spirits that come in the form of our grandparents. This is the devil's trick so that we can worship them instead of worshipping God. They help some, and make many others suffer.' The general reaction of Pentecostal people was that ancestors were powerless in Christians' lives, and that they were evil spirits that should be rejected and exorcized if necessary.[33]

Exorcism plays a major role in the activities of Pentecostal and independent churches, even though the 'theory' behind exorcism is unknown to many members and only a few were able to say much about it.[34] Nevertheless, exorcism is 'considered to be of importance to the pastoral ministry in the African context'.[35] In this regard, in spite of personal misgivings about methods used, in what follows I identify with those who emphasize the 'liberating value' of a ministry of exorcism, 'which appears to confront the existential needs and fears of people in a ritually understandable and therefore psychologically and religiously satisfying manner'.[36] At least overtly, there seemed to be a relatively greater emphasis upon exorcism in Pentecostal churches than in Zionist and Apostolic ones.

Soshanguve church members gave several descriptions of exorcisms. One Zionist member said that a woman with a demon was

33. Ibid., pp. 184–186.

34. The following discussion is based on ibid., pp. 266–271.

35. G. C. Oosthuizen, 'The interpretation of and reaction to demonic powers in indigenous churches', in P. G. R. de Villiers (ed.), *Like a Roaring Lion: Essays on the Bible, the Church and Demonic Powers* (Pretoria: University of South Africa Press, 1987), p. 77.

36. M. L. Daneel, 'Exorcism as a Means of Combating Wizardry: Liberation or Enslavement?', in *Missionalia* 18/1 (April 1990), p. 220.

'possessed by the ancestral spirit' and was a fellow member of the church choir. During a choir item, this woman began behaving strangely, running away from the rest of the choir members. Some of them gave chase and eventually caught and subdued her after a struggle. They gathered around her shouting at the demon, singing and clapping their hands. A prophet then gave her ashes that had been prayed for (this is a traditional healing method), which she ate, resulting in her being 'delivered'. Another Zionist related how a demented man came into the church and could not be controlled by ten men. He was tearing his clothes, screaming terribly. Eventually he was forced to drink 'blessed water' and was tied with ropes around his wrists, ankles and waist. For three days, church members prayed for him day and night until he was set free. Some Zionist and Apostolic members said that demon possession meant that a person was mentally deranged or retarded. One ZCC respondent told of his brother, who spent a lot of time 'talking alone to himself'. He took him to the 'Apostolics', where he was delivered.

Exorcism is practised among Pentecostals to varying degrees. In some churches it is seldom seen, while in others it is a fairly common occurrence. A person may be demonized in various ways. Usually the manifestations occur when prayer is being offered. These manifestations include shouting and screaming, unkempt or unwashed appearance, restlessness, violent contortions of the body (often accompanied by extraordinary strength), jumping, falling to the ground, and running around the room. Pastors and people specializing in a 'ministry of deliverance' will sometimes pray for demonized people for a long time until the demons are subdued and exorcized. Pentecostal churches often have members whose special ministry it is to cast out demons. Not only must they deal with the problem in the church services, but they must also follow up the people for some time until they are established. One of the new independent Pentecostal churches in Soshanguve now makes exorcism one of the most important and prominent features of its Sunday prayer time, with many 'deliverances' taking place every week. Exorcism becomes a very important feature in pastoral therapy. As Daneel points out in relation to Zionists and Apostles in Zimbabwe, 'many church leaders use exorcism as a pastoral instrument to combat wizardry beliefs, the accompanying fears and the antisocial forces thought to be at work'.[37]

A woman told us something she had seen at a Pentecostal tent campaign. A deranged woman was brought into the tent and tied down with chains. After prayer was made she began to shriek, jump and fall on the ground, until she became still. Many people in that tent heard her later 'testify' about what had happened and that she had been set free. Another Pentecostal told of another case of a demonized man in a house meeting in Soshanguve. The Christians had been fasting and praying the previous day for this specific meeting, which was in an outsider's home. When an 'altar call' was given at the end of the service for those who wanted to 'receive Christ', a man stood up, sat down, and stood up again. When the pastor started to pray for him, he began to jump up and down and scream. The member said that when she looked into his eyes they had changed colour and had become 'fiery green'. The Christians prayed and tried to hold the man down, but he pulled them around the room. Eventually he lay flat on the floor, still screaming and coughing. After some time, while the Christians continued to pray, the demon left and the man was quiet.

A woman from a charismatic church related how a young woman had attended one of the regular Wednesday night 'home cell' meetings in her house. While her husband was 'sharing the Word of God' this woman began to behave strangely, laughing uncontrollably. The member said she was annoyed and began to rebuke what she perceived as an evil spirit, 'in the name of Jesus Christ'. The woman jumped up, continually laughing and lifting up her dress, running around the house and becoming violent. The Christians prayed for her, rebuking the demon in the name of the Lord for about four hours, until eventually the woman spoke: 'You don't like me. I will go away.' During all this time she was in a type of trance. She finally became quiet and was delivered. A week later another incident occurred, in the same house, that was also perceived as demon activity. A neighbour visited the meeting and at the end started screaming while people were praying. The Christians began

---

37. Ibid., p. 220.

to rebuke the demon. The evil spirit began to speak through the woman, saying that she was supposed to have gone to Giyani in the Limpopo Province, as her father, a Tsonga diviner, had wanted her to be trained in his trade. The woman had refused and her father had bewitched her. On this occasion, which also was a four-hour session of deliverance, the woman vomited and shook violently and her legs swelled. She too was delivered; she no longer had these problems and became a member of the church.

One cannot reflect on the descriptions of these 'deliverances' without honestly acknowledging the reality of the help that was received. To suggest that the exorcisms reinforced the sufferer's preoccupation with the African spirit world and the fear of evil spirits, as some have done, ignores the fact that for many Africans exorcism provides certain relief from psychological stress.[38] Daneel, with a case study of Bishop Nyasha's ministry of exorcism in Zimbabwe, proposed that the correct Christian response should be to 'confront those beliefs [in wizardry] with the message of the one Scapegoat, Christ, and exorcise the invading spirits as part of the solution to a tradition-based problem, despite the risk of misinterpretation in certain quarters'. He concluded that the exorcisms of Nyasha and his assistants had a relevance that applies equally to the exorcisms described here:

> In this enacted theology of ritual and symbol they have made and are making a more original, more effective contribution to wizardry-related pastoral care than many a mission church which misunderstood, rejected and ultimately negated the wizardry beliefs and the concomitant needs of African people.[39]

It is also apparent that for most Pentecostals, demon possession and 'ancestor possession' were the same thing, and a few were bold enough to spell this out in unambiguous terms. It was clear for many members that the 'ancestor' was in fact a demon impersonating

---

38. A. Shorter, *Jesus and the Witchdoctor: An Approach to Healing and Wholeness* (Maryknoll: Orbis, 1985), p. 197.
39. Daneel, 'Exorcism', pp. 227, 246–247.

departed relatives. It needed to be exorcized in the name of Jesus Christ and by the power of the Holy Spirit. The exorcisms therefore pointed to a confrontation between the Holy Spirit and the so-called 'ancestors'. A member of an Apostolic church said that a person who believed in ancestors could be possessed by demons. The 'ancestor' who purported to speak out of this person was not an ancestor at all, but a demon. She felt that diviners who said that the ancestors wanted things done were deceiving people. People tried to please the 'ancestors', but nothing good came from all their efforts. She said: 'I absolutely do not believe in ancestors. We need to pray hard so that we can be strong enough to stand against them.' Two different Apostolic church members who were clearly opposed to prophets said that prophets were possessed by demons, and this was why they were able to predict the future. Another member suggested that a prophet who did not speak the truth was demon-possessed. Another said that diviners were possessed by demons. Likewise, a member of a Swazi Zionist church defined a demon-possessed person as one who had the spirit of the ancestors who would speak through that person, in other words a diviner. This curious anomaly between 'ancestors' and demons was well demonstrated by an interview we had with a ZCC minister in October 1991. His response to the question, 'Have you ever seen someone possessed by demons?' was significant:

> As a pastor and a member of the ZCC I have seen a lot of people being 'possessed' by what you call 'demons'. But we do not believe that people are 'demon-possessed' – people have got the ancestral spirit. When white missionaries came to our countries they looked at us as people who needed deliverance. They did not bother themselves to try to understand our culture, our ancestors and our background . . . The Bible might call it 'demon possession', but we in our culture, in our context in Africa do not call it that. We know this is the spirit of the ancestors, and we respect a person with such a spirit because that person is able to communicate on our behalf with the ancestors.

Similarly, a member of St Paul Spiritual Church of God said the following in response to the question, 'Have you ever seen someone possessed by demons?'

> Yes, I have seen someone possessed by 'spirits' – we don't call them 'demons', we call them 'spirits'. This person will jump around and fall to the ground. We call this spirit in a person the spirit of the prophet, because when one sees something one is able to speak a message to the people after one has recovered.

It seems that for many members of the independent churches, to be 'demon-possessed' is not necessarily a bad thing – and the term is certainly stripped of its Western negative theological connotations. These members obviously thought that the expression, although foreign to African culture, described a certain condition of traditional ancestor possession that was regarded with respect. This fact may explain why some members of the ZCC and other Zionist and Apostolic churches thought that a prophet had a 'demon' spirit. They did not say, however, that the 'demon' needed to be exorcized. Part of the reason for this may have been a reluctance to reveal, in a patently Western intrusion into African religion, any opposition to the ancestors that might display a disregard for African cultural values. Others may have said this to deliberately criticize the prophets for their own reasons. In the Zionist and Apostolic churches, few patients are likely to seek out therapy prophets who are known to have 'demon' spirits. The ambivalence possibly exists more in the theoretical reflection asked for in our interviews than in actual practice. This would be more accurately measured by further empirical observation of exorcisms.

Conclusion

The African spirit world infiltrates the whole of life. The same essential experience permeates everywhere and is not easily verbalized. All things are saturated with religious meaning. Any religion that caters only for one portion of African experience – which portion in isolation does not have any real meaning or even existence – will often appear inadequate. African religious phenomena such as these encounters with the spirit world and the practices of exorcism should be evaluated in the light of similar manifestations in Pentecostal and charismatic churches worldwide. When a

Christian transformation takes place in African Pentecostalism, it often meets needs more substantially than does either its traditional 'counterpart' or the theology imported to Africa in Western philosophical garb. The old types of spirit possession, divination as practised by traditional healers, the ancestors, and traditional medicines and charms are rejected and replaced by an African Christian transformation. Generalizations about beliefs and attitudes of Pentecostals and Zionists with regard to ancestors and evil spirits must not give the impression of finality, especially when dealing with such dynamic and constantly changing movements.[40]

The introduction of the terms 'Satan' and 'demon' or 'devil' into religious terminology in Africa marks the strict boundary between Christianity and 'paganism' in the minds of the users.[41] Far from being a resurgence of ancestor possession, once we have separated the forms of the Spirit phenomena from their meanings, the revelations of the Spirit in African Pentecostalism throughout the sub-Sahara point to both a dialogue and a confrontation between the new, 'powerful' Christian faith and the old beliefs in spirits and ancestors. The encounters with spirits and ancestors sketched in this chapter are evidence of problems that face people in daily life, for which religious solutions are coveted. Pentecostal Christianity responds to these particularly African problems, and thereby attains an African character eluding many older, Western forms of Christianity by realistically penetrating the old and creating the new. In the process, African religion is reintegrated into Christianity through the confrontation with 'Satan'. It is this synthesizing character of Pentecostalism that makes it an attractive alternative to older forms of Christianity and pre-Christian African religions.

---

40. Anderson, *Zion and Pentecost,* p. 196.

41. Meyer, *Translating the Devil,* p. 149.

3 PENTECOSTALS AND ANGELS

William K. Kay

Introduction

Angels made their way into European culture through the Bible. There are angels with fiery swords in Genesis 3 and they appear intermittently throughout the text of Scripture, most famously in relation to the birth of Christ, but also in Acts, the epistles, and the unfolding drama of the Apocalypse of St John. From this textual beginning, angels are to be found in iconography and statuary, particularly in the Orthodox Church, in Christian art, and in the theology of the greatest theologians. For Augustine, angels illustrate issues concerned with the origin of evil, since, if some angels fell and others remained blessed within the uncontaminated regions of heaven, evil must eventuate in the will rather than in the environment. Moreover, as his discussion in book 11 of the *City of God* shows, evil comes after the original creation; in other words it is not born out of an eternal principle, and the angels themselves illustrate distinctive orders within the created universe. There are different modes of being, ranked according to a divine purpose and differentiated in terms of rationality and sentience, and this scale arranged in a purposeful order manifests divine power and wisdom.

Aquinas also considered theological implications to be adduced from the presence of angels by reflecting on the relationship between form and matter, and the cognition available to pure intelligences that need only to gain knowledge by an instantaneous appreciation of the rational consequences of propositions and without impressions gained through bodily senses.[1] Moreover, in addition to knowledge, both love and will may be manifested by angels, who were, probably, created in a graced state – a state consonant with the formalized Roman theology of grace. Even during the Renaissance angels adorn and theologically support the art of the period in the work of Michelangelo or Raphael, and, after the Reformation, within the poetry of Shakespeare ('Good night, sweet prince, and flights of angels sing thee to thy rest'[2]), Donne ('Aire and Angels') and Milton ('Then with expanded wings he steers his flight aloft, incumbent on the dusky air'[3]).

Pentecostal history till 1965

The twentieth-century Pentecostal moment can be traced back phenomenologically to the largely North American holiness revivalism of the late nineteenth century and theologically to the second-blessing experiential theology of Wesley. There are disputes among Pentecostal scholars as to whether the Pentecostal revival should be seen as spontaneously emerging in a number of different centres in different countries of the world (Mukti in India, the United States, Asia)[4] or whether it is best understood as springing out of the theological understanding of Charles Fox

1. Thomas Aquinas, *Summa Theologiae*, 58:1–4, referring to the translation by Timothy McDermott (Allen: Christian Classics, 1989), pp. 98–99.
2. *Hamlet*, V.ii.360.
3. *Paradise Lost*, I.i.225f.
4. See A. Anderson, *An Introduction to Pentecostalism* (Cambridge: Cambridge University Press, 2004), pp. 128ff.

Parham in Topeka, Kansas, and the revival led by W. J. Seymour in Azusa Street, Los Angeles, from 1906 to 1913, but by 1920 Pentecostalism had been firmly established. The paradigmatic Azusa Street revival was not, however, attended by reports of angels. Nor was the analogous event within the United Kingdom, the outpouring at Sunderland in 1907 and the subsequent annual international Sunderland conventions (1908–14) that helped to shape the Pentecostal movement within Britain and, to an extent, in other parts of Europe.

While there were no obvious angels at these key events, there were spiritual phenomena apart from speaking with tongues. Parham reported that 'a glory fell on her [Agnes Ozman], a halo seemed to surround her head and face' when Ms Ozman began to speak in tongues in 1901.[5] Alexander Boddy reported on a prayer meeting at All Saints Vicarage in 1907 when mysterious light portended special visitations:

> I was opposite the window and so looked out at the church. A wonderful light suddenly filled the room and lingered over the church roof. One brother fell to the floor very suddenly, crying with tremendous vehemence, 'It is the Lord, there is no deception, brothers, it is the Lord Himself.' This continued on and on, the light lingering over the roof of the church, an emblem it seemed of blessing that was to be connected with this place.[6]

In 1948 the Latter Rain Revival, a renewal movement within Pentecostalism, began in Canada, and George Hawtin described the day when the first prophecies broke out. 'My description of it would be that a great awe possessed us all . . . that sort of godly fear and reverence one would experience if suddenly he found himself in the presence of an angel.'[7] So perhaps there was an angel there, though nobody saw one.

---

5. W. K. Kay and A. E. Dyer (eds.), *Pentecostal and Charismatic Studies: A Reader* (London: SCM, 2004), p. 11.
6. *Latter Rain Evangel* (February 1909).
7. Kay and Dyer, *Reader*, p. 2.

If angels did not attend the birth of Pentecostalism, they only rarely made an appearance during its youth. Alexander Boddy testified in *Confidence* that he had been saved as a child by angelic intervention: 'On the sloping roof of the Manchester Royal Exchange as a youth, whilst watching a Sunday School procession, I slipped on soot-covered glass, and rolled to the edge, but His angels prevented me going eighty feet down into the crowd below.'[8] *Confidence* did carry accounts of the Angels of Mons: 'Another time when in the trenches we heard a voice sounding through the air, about 9 o'clock at night, and the moon was clear, and I saw an angel flying with a trumpet in his mouth!'[9]

This hardly constitutes a specifically Pentecostal emphasis, though, since angels in the First World War were reported in contemporary books as well as in the *Church Times* and the *Evening News*.[10]

Between 1924 and 1939, in the British Assemblies of God denominational magazine *Redemption Tidings*, there were seventy references to angels; sixty-three are to biblical passages from the nativity story explaining the theology of angels,[11] very occasionally with a warning[12] not to get too involved; there are also ten references to personal testimonies of angels.[13] Most of these appear to

8. A. Boddy, *Confidence* (February 1914), p. 23. *Confidence* was a magazine of the early British Pentecostal movement.

9. There are fifteen references in this issue of *Confidence* alone: e.g. J. Easy, 'The Mons Angels' and 'Angels at the Front', *Confidence* (January 1916) pp. 5–6, 1ff.

10. H. Price, *Angels: True Stories of How They Touch Our Lives* (Basingstoke: Macmillan, 1995), p. 94.

11. E.g. S. Wigglesworth, 'Nativity Story', *RT* 2/2 (February 1926), p. 4; C. L. Parker, *RT* 10/8 (August 1934), p. 6; T. Myerscough, *RT* 2/2 (February 1926), p. 19.

12. E.g. D. Gee, 'Trying the Spirits', *RT* 2/4 (April 1926); W. Luff, 'Angels of Light', *RT* 3/19 (September 1927), p. 5.

13. S. May, 'Protection in Tibet', *RT* 5/1 (January 1929), p. 12; 'Again in China', *RT* 7/6 (June 1931), p. 9; 'Spencer May's Daughter Healed in India', *RT* 14/19 (September 1938); most were accounted for outside of Britain on the mission field.

be missionary testimonies of protection. What appears to have happened is that, once Pentecostal denominations were set up, there was a regularization of Pentecostal doctrine and practice. Since the early Pentecostals had largely come out of other Christian groups, in the first years they simply carried over from these groups many of their expectations about church life and supernatural phenomena. They did make room for the charismatic gifts of 1 Corinthians 12 – 14, but this was a different matter from regulation over the less obviously biblical phenomenon of strange lights and, in any case, as we shall see, a theology of angels stood in some ways in contrast to a theology of the Holy Spirit.

If the denominational officials policed the teaching of Pentecostal preachers, the independent healing evangelists were not subject to such constraints. Among the most dramatic, William Marrion Branham (1909–65) began conducting healing crusades from 1933. Coming from a dirt-poor and uneducated background in the hills of Kentucky, Branham believed himself to have been guided by angels from childhood. He either belonged to or was associated with Oneness Pentecostal churches, but largely played down the distinctiveness of their beliefs when his crusades began to attract national attention.[14] In 1946 he reported that he had a meeting with an angel in a cave and was given power to discern the thoughts and illnesses of those he met. His website tells us:

> It was about the eleventh hour that he saw a soft Light appearing before him. He looked up and rose to move toward this Light and there hung that Great Star again . . . Then he heard footsteps, and a man of great stature approached him. According to Brother Branham, the man appeared to be about two hundred pounds in weight, had a dark complexion, no beard, with shoulder-length hair . . .
>
> 'Fear not! I am a Messenger sent to you, from the Presence of Almighty God. I want you to know that your strange life has been for a

14. D. J. Wilson, 'William Marrion Branham', in S. Burgess and E. Van der Maas (eds.), *New International Dictionary of Pentecostal and Charismatic Movements*, 2nd edn (Grand Rapids: Zondervan, 2002), pp. 440–444.

> purpose in preparing you to do a job that God has for you to do. You have been ordained, even from birth, to do this job. If you will be sincere and get the people to believe you, nothing shall stand before your prayers, not even cancer!'[15]

Several photographs exist of Branham with either a halo or a pillar of fire or, in one instance, with a fiery altar, and, once he acquired a manager in Gordon Lindsay in 1947, and the later support of the Full Gospel Businessmen's Fellowship International, his ministry and reputation rose. However, his support was eroded by his insistence that believers baptized by a Trinitarian formula must be rebaptized in the name of 'Jesus only', and by his declarations that he was the prophet Elijah preparing the way for the second coming of Christ. His doctrine that Eve's sin involved sexual relations with the serpent and that their descendants are destined for hell further undermined his credibility. When he proclaimed himself to be the angel of Revelation 3:14 and prophesied that by 1977 all denominations would be incorporated within the World Council of Churches under Roman control, his angelic revelations, however accurate they appeared to be in relation to diagnosis and healing, were called into question.[16] Such was the power of his reputation, though, that, after his accidental death in 1965, he was expected to rise from the dead, and his burial was postponed until Easter 1966.

Pentecostal theology

Characterizations of Pentecostal theology have drawn attention to a variety of features. First, it is broadly conservative, biblical and evangelical, and stands within or alongside this tradition, with the result that the major Pentecostal churches are members of the Evangelical Alliance in Britain or the National Association of

---

15. See <www.biblebelievers.org/giftplus.htm>, accessed 21 March 2006, and cf. W. J. Hollenweger, *The Pentecostals* (London: SCM, 1972), p. 354.
16. Hollenweger, *Pentecostals,* p. 355.

Evangelicals in North America. Moreover, both Pentecostals and evangelicals essentially seek a correlation between their doctrine and specified religious experiences. Evangelicals associate regeneration with the understanding of the personal work of the Holy Spirit, while Pentecostals go further than this by looking for a baptism with the Holy Spirit subsequent to conversion and, almost inevitably, distinct from it. This emphasis on experience within the Pentecostal movement is also perpetuated by an expectation that the Spirit will continue to operate within congregational life by the manifestation of charismata, which may be more or less tightly defined and enumerated.[17]

Second, Pentecostal theology is partially developed by an oral tradition of personal testimony. Whether this is a testimony of salvation on evangelical lines or a broader testimony of God's dealings with the individual through prayer, visions, miracles and other spiritual occurrences, its narrative form and dramatic content can become normative. Such testimony may be, and often is, shared within loosely structured Pentecostal meetings, but it may also be sung or in some way incorporated into open prayer. The result of this is that Pentecostals learn from each other: experience is not private, secret and guarded but rather paraded before the public eye in extrovert fashion; testimonies create plausibility structures and theological shelters under which congregations can find protection from the prevailing climate of secularism.

Third, as a corrective against openness to experience and the wilder fringes of personal testimony, Pentecostals have developed criteria, usually based upon Scripture, by which judgments can be made. In Pentecostal denominations, there are normally tenets, fundamental truths or statements of belief against which church

---

17. Whereas classical Pentecostal writers like Harold Horton believed that there were only nine gifts of the Spirit and that these were listed in 1 Cor. 12:8–10 (H. Horton, *The Gifts of the Spirit* [Luton: Redemption Tidings Book Room, 1934]), others, like Peter Wagner (C. P. Wagner, *Discover Your Spiritual Gifts: A Self-Guided Quiz – Includes Explanation of all the Spiritual Gifts* [Ventura: Regal, 2002]), consider that a far greater number exist.

life is measured.[18] These statements or tenets are normally constructed by deduction from biblical texts and fall into alignment with standard evangelical documents that perform the same function. The only difference between Pentecostal and evangelical statements of this kind is that the Pentecostal ones will include reference to charismatic gifts and, possibly, to apostolic or prophetic ministries. Within the life of congregations, however, pastoral leaders become adept at 'judging' prophecy or other utterances by reference to rules of thumb that tend to be unspoken and un-debated and yet, in the main, ensure that no-one is led into obviously controversial areas of doctrine or given outrageous advice.[19] Additionally and importantly, emphasis on the charisma of divine healing implies an automatic feedback loop that functions as a critical and pragmatic check on reality. If the charisma of divine healing is operated and the person who is ill remains ill, and does not recover, it is obvious that the charisma has not done its work. Thus, in the most balanced Pentecostal churches, the text 'Do not put out the Spirit's fire' is as valued as the one two verses later, 'Test everything. Hold on to the good' (1 Thess. 5:19, 21).

In respect of demonology, however, the feedback loop is much less easy to recognize. If an attempt has been made at exorcism and the person exorcized improves and then deteriorates, it is possible to argue that the demons have been expelled but then returned (Matt. 12:45). If, on the other hand, the person exorcized does not improve, then it is possible to argue that the demons are still present. What is not tested, unfortunately, is the initial diagnosis that the problem was one that required exorcism. In other words, once the presumption is made that exorcism is necessary, attempts to carry this out cannot be tested against the condition of the exorcised person unless he or she dramatically and per-

18. W. K. Kay, *Pentecostals in Britain* (Carlisle: Paternoster, 2000).

19. W. K. Kay, *Prophecy* (Mattersey: LifeStream Publications/Mattersey Hall, 1991); M. Bickle with M. Sullivant, *Growing in the Prophetic* (Florida: Strang Communications, 1996), pp. 178–181; S. E. Parker, *Led by the Spirit: Towards a Practical Theology of Pentecostal Discernment and Decision Making* (Sheffield: Sheffield Academic Press, 1996).

manently improves. As we shall see, a rather similar situation occurs in relation to angels: the person who claims to have received angelic help *may* have received it. There is no way of verifying the claims.

Fourth, concentration upon charismata has helped to create a functional trinitarianism in the vast majority of Pentecostal churches. There are Oneness Pentecostal churches that espouse a form of modalism, that is, a belief that God is manifested as Father or Son or Spirit but does not exist as a co-eternal Trinity. Statistical data about the prevalence of Oneness Pentecostalism suggests that only about 1% overall follow this doctrine, though in the United States the percentage is higher.[20] Branham's testimony to angelic visitation and help may stem from his theological predispositions, since one effect of the Oneness position is to generate a dialectic between the immanence and transcendence of God and to confine the 'personhood' of God to the incarnate Christ and to leave the Spirit as indicative of the otherness of God. Thus angels personalize spiritual experience because the experience is of a person rather than of a faceless divine force.

In respect to the trinitarian orthodoxy of the vast majority of Pentecostals, it is clear that where spiritual experience is attributed to the Holy Spirit, it becomes much more important to work from a biblical basis to define what it is the Holy Spirit does and how the Holy Spirit relates both to the Christ and to the Father. But passages in John 14 – 16 (e.g. 'I will ask the Father, and he will give you another Counsellor to be with you for ever – the Spirit of Truth', 14:16) and in Acts 2:33 ('Exalted to the right hand of God, he [Christ] has received from the Father the promised Holy Spirit and has poured out what you now see and hear') differentiate the persons of the Trinity and partially delineate their relationship. Exegetical focus on these and similar loci has produced an ethos in Pentecostal churches that allows the attribution of spiritual phenomena with greater precision than might be expected (or, perhaps, merited). It is not just a case of saying that an experience or an event is attributable to God. Rather, there is the potential for

20. Kay and Dyer, *Reader*, p. xxvii.

specification about whether an event took place through the Holy Spirit or as a result of the power of Christ, or the Father, or all Persons of the Trinity working jointly. Although it would be foolish to claim too much on this point because there is, within Pentecostal circles, considerable differentiation between non-academic theology and academic theology (to use a distinction made by Barth and accepted by Macchia[21]), there may be hesitation among Pentecostals about attributing to angelic beings actions that ought to be attributed to God. In effect, a Pentecostal understanding of divine agency reduces the space left for angelic agency. Or, to put this another way, if the Holy Spirit indwells the church so that the church may glorify Christ and bring honour to the Father, it becomes clear that the normal manifestation of spiritual life – the *phanerōsis* of 1 Corinthians 12:7 – is due to the Holy Spirit and not to angelic mediation. Indeed, angelic mediation is expressly warned against in an early Pauline epistle, Colossians, written to combat incipient Gnosticism.

This said, the distinction between the work of the Holy Spirit and that of angels within the book of Acts has not been subjected to extensive scholarly scrutiny. Nevertheless, even a cursory reading demonstrates that, in the most dramatic and central case within Acts, the role of angels is a physical one, that of rescuing Peter from prison, and that this contrasts with the work of the Holy Spirit in empowerment for preaching, healing and guidance. It is in the area of guidance that there is, as it were, a divine option. In Acts 8 Philip is guided by an angel (verse 26) and also by the Spirit (verse 29). Similarly, in Acts 10 an angel appears to Cornelius (verse 3), while Peter is guided by the Spirit (10:19) on hearing Cornelius' request for help. If a distinction can be drawn between the two kinds of guidance, it is that the more certain and important guidance comes from angels – as if the visual presence of another being is more necessary than the promptings of the Spirit to override the dictates of common sense or ingrained prejudice. Philip needed an angel to tell him to leave the revival in Samaria. In

21. F. D. Macchia, 'Pentecostal Theology', in Burgess and Van der Maas (eds.), *New International Dictionary*, pp. 1120–1141.

the case of Cornelius, however, there is at the stage of the angelic visitation no possibility that he might be guided by the Spirit, since he has not yet been welcomed into the community of the church where the Spirit dwells. One further case where guidance might have been given either by the Spirit or by an angel occurs during Paul's tempestuous voyage to Rome. He sees an angel promising the safety of the crew just before shipwreck on Malta (Acts 27:23), but the life-threatening circumstances justify this special assurance.

Fifth, there has been speculation about the nature of glossolalia. Early Pentecostals in some instances undoubtedly thought that the tongues were knowable foreign languages and that those who spoke through the inspiration of the Spirit could go straight on to the mission field and preach, and their glossolalia (or, strictly, xenolalia) would be immediately understood by the indigenous people.[22] Others have speculated that glossolalia may be the 'tongues of angels' on the basis of 1 Corinthians 13:1. The suggestion here is that human beings can be endowed with angelic speech which may be particularly useful in spiritual warfare, but such a suggestion is hardly probable, since, in Acts 2, the diverse pilgrims within the city of Jerusalem who heard the apostles speaking in tongues recognize them as praising God. When Cornelius and his household spoke in tongues in Acts 10:46, Peter recognized the phenomenon as being similar to what had occurred on the Day of Pentecost: this was how he deduced that the Holy Spirit had been poured out on the Gentiles (Acts 11:15). Yet in the house of Cornelius no-one said they could understand the tongues-speaking of the Gentiles. Thus the reference to 'tongues of angels' is likely to be poetic and simply indicative of eloquence.

Sixth, much Pentecostal theology has been built around the ministry of Christ. The Elim Pentecostal Church in Britain, following Aimee Semple McPherson, spoke of the fourfold gospel and of Christ as Saviour, Healer, Baptizer and King.[23] This fourfold theme created an ethos of devotion to Jesus as well as an

---

22. E.g. Charles F. Parham. See <www.fwselijah.com/Parham.htm>.

23. Macchia, 'Pentecostal Theology', p. 1123.

opportunity to model Pentecostal ministry on his example. Christ as the Spirit-endowed sinless man, a theme taken up from Edward Irving, demonstrated how Christians might overcome evil, preach the gospel and heal the sick. There was little room within this theological configuration for angels and, where angels did act, they functioned to support Christ after periods of temptation or stress (Matt. 4:11; Luke 22:43). There is no evidence of Christ ever praying to or for angels, even if angels were at his command and might have rescued him from the clutches of Pilate (Matt. 26:53). The Holy Spirit, by contrast, not only rests upon Christ but is also made available by Christ to his followers, and it is through the Spirit that his followers perform miracles both before and after Pentecost. And, as far as spiritual warfare is concerned, Christ engages in it during his temptation in the wilderness and he wins his battles not by shouting at the skies or binding the spirits but by quoting Scripture appropriately when he is tested.

Pentecostal history diversifies

William Branham was only one of a series of healing evangelists who appeared in the United States in the 1940s. Their ministries were amplified by burgeoning radio broadcasting and began to become influential enough in the popular mind to eclipse the church groupings from which they had sprung.[24] The 1948 Latter Rain revival, which emphasized the restoration of spiritual gifts and at the same time criticized the rigidity of denominational officialdom, partially reflects the ethos of these healing evangelists and demonstrates the attraction of Pentecostal phenomena outside the framework of denominational structures.[25] Branham was certainly involved in the early stages of the Latter Rain

24. D. E. Harrell Jr, 'Healers and Televangelists after World War II', in V. Synan (ed.), *The Century of the Holy Spirit* (Nashville: Thomas Nelson, 2001), pp. 325–347.

25. E. L. Blumhofer, *Restoring the Faith: The Assemblies of God, Pentecostalism and American Culture* (Chicago: University of Illinois Press, 1993).

movement,[26] and, although angels were not specifically associated with most healing evangelists, other relevant cultural currents were already beginning to flow in the United States.

After 1945, the era of the Cold War was marked both by a stark realization of the self-destructive capacities of the human race, which possessed nuclear weapons, and by ideological hostility between the great geopolitical blocks of capitalism and communism. In the summer of 1947 the so-called 'Roswell incident' involving a crashed flying saucer occurred just two weeks after reports of unidentified flying objects (UFOs) had first been reported. In the same year an astrophysicist from Yale had speculated on a radio programme that Earth might already have been visited by Martians. A Gallup poll conducted in August 1947 asked North Americans about the flying-saucer sightings; 16% thought they were either Russian or American secret weapons, but no-one attributed them to extraterrestrials.[27]

Ten years later, changes were clearly afoot. Gordon Cove, a one-time healing evangelist, had woven the hypothesis of extraterrestrials into his biblical eschatology and, in a booklet entitled *Who Pilots the Flying Saucers?* (c. 1955) suggested that angels were the obvious answer. Only angels could cope with the stunning velocity of these craft and only angels could cope with aerial manoeuvres generating huge gravitational forces.[28] But if Cove is seen as a maverick, Billy Graham certainly belongs to mainstream American religious culture; his 1975 book *Angels: God's Secret Agents* discusses the possibility that angels and UFOs (which might be the 'wheels within wheels' of Ezekiel) belong together, before concluding that all such discussion is 'at best, speculation'.[29] Gallup surveys of

26. R. M. Riss, 'Latter Rain Movement', in Burgess and Van der Maas (eds.), *New International Dictionary*, pp. 830–833.
27. B. Appleyard, *Aliens: Why They Are Here* (London: Scribner, 2005), pp. 13–19.
28. The other view, of course, is that flying saucers are piloted by demons (Appleyard, *Aliens*, p. 141).
29. B. Graham, *Angels: God's Secret Agents* (London: Hodder and Stoughton, 1975), p. 35.

North Americans between 1978[30] and 1992 show that belief in angels rose from 64% to 76%, while belief in extraterrestrials rose from 34% in 1966 to 51% in 1978 and then fell back to 30% in 1996.[31] Stephen Spielberg's atmospheric film *Close Encounters of the Third Kind* was first shown in 1977 and may have contributed to the peak in these figures. His smash hit *ET: The Extra-Terrestrial* followed in 1982 and moved into a different key by domesticating space travellers while continuing to befriend them. By the mid-1980s, then, we have, in North America at least, evidence of a variegated culture containing both great technological sophistication and a swathe of beliefs involving the paranormal, the supernatural and the downright peculiar.[32]

In the churches on both sides of the Atlantic many other factors were at work generating change in the post-war decades. There are numerous interpretations of the causes and effects of the charismatic movement that broke out in the mid-1960s.[33] For the purposes of this discussion, the charismatic movement can be understood as a force for change not only within the denominational and traditionally non-Pentecostal churches but also within

---

30. Angels were firmly embedded in North American culture. Frank Capra's delightful *It's a Wonderful Life*, made in 1946, has a friendly angel called Clarence as one of the main characters.
31. G. Gallup Jr and D. M. Lindsay, *Surveying the Religious Landscape* (Harrisburg: Morehouse Publishing, 1999), p. 158, 39.
32. The mass suicide of thirty-nine members of Heaven's Gate in March 1997 in order to ascend to a higher level of evolutional consciousness, connected with the arrival of the Hale-Bopp comet, is an example from A. Grünschloss 'Ufology and UFO-Related Movements', in C. Partridge and J. Gordon Melton (eds.), *Encyclopedia of New Religions* (Oxford: Lion, 2004), p. 372; E. Von Daniken, *God from Outer Space* (New York: Bantam Books, 1972) popularized the notion that aliens were mistaken for divine beings and are therefore the source of world religions, and P. Apolito, *The Internet and the Madonna: Religious Visionary Experiences on the Web* (Chicago: Chicago University Press, 2005), provides information about communications from the Virgin Mary enhanced by the internet.
33. E.g. P. D. Hocken, *Streams of Renewal* (Carlisle: Paternoster, 1997).

the Pentecostal churches themselves. The Pentecostal doctrine and practice that had been established from the 1920s to the 1960s now began to be challenged and reviewed. In many instances, where Pentecostals had slipped into a form of legalism, this challenge was entirely beneficial.[34] In other instances, when the Pentecostals had made charismata routine, fresh expressions of prophecy or new styles of healing also served to loosen up practice and to revive Pentecostal distinctives.

Among the challenges to traditional Pentecostal practice were those in the area of demonology. It is difficult to trace exactly how these teachings were first formulated and disseminated, but one line of influence would appear to come from Derek Prince, an imposing and charismatic figure with impressive scholarly credentials and a command of several languages including the biblical ones. In a series of tapes and books Prince began to teach about spiritual warfare, using texts from Daniel.[35] He distinguished between angels that he recognized as existing in different ranks (the 'principalities' and 'powers' of Ephesians 6:12 being seen not as synonymous but as different categories of angel) and demons that existed at a lower level but also within the hierarchy of the infernal kingdom. In his view angels never sought embodiment within the material world, since they had spiritual bodies of their own. Demons, as bodiless spirits, constantly sought to live within the material world and to utilize animate beings to express themselves.

---

34. M. M. Poloma, *Assemblies of God at the Crossroads* (Knoxville: University of Tennessee Press, 1989).

35. D. Prince, *War in Heaven* (Baldock: Derek Prince Ministries, 2003); *Spiritual Warfare* Whitaker House, 1992); *Expelling Demons* (Baldock: Derek Prince Ministries, unknown date). Prince's tapes were issued largely unrevised as books, and the books went through successive reprints. It is difficult to place a chronology on his teachings, but the essence of them was in place in the 1970s. I can recall hearing them on reel-to-reel tape recorders probably in 1970. Prince points out that an angel sent to Daniel is delayed by the prince of Persia before the deadlock is broken by Michael. The 'prince of Persia' is understood as the spiritual power in control of Persia, and Michael is the archangel.

Within the satanic kingdom angels controlled demons, but demons could be expelled by exorcism through the authority of Christ, whereas evil angels had to be overcome by spiritual warfare. In what he admitted to be a speculative suggestion, demons were thought to be the spirits of pre-Adamic races[36] (which explained their lust for embodiment), whereas evil angels were those who were hurled out of heaven during the satanic revolt against God described in the apocalypse (Rev. 12:7, 8).

It is arguable that Prince's teaching diversified in two directions. In one direction it led to a complicated set of criteria for distinguishing whether human beings were oppressed or possessed by demons and how these demons might be removed. This led to a classification of different kinds of demons, speculation about where in the body the demon might live, theological debate about whether demons might inhabit born-again Christians and attempts to distinguish between illnesses caused by demons and illnesses with purely physical causes.[37] As indicated above, these debates were most successful where they paid closest attention to the biblical text. Where there were attempts to argue entirely from experience, most Western Pentecostals found themselves on the verge of scepticism, and there is some evidence that a worldview in which spiritual warfare is central is linked with particular personality dispositions.[38]

In another direction Prince's teaching may be said to have led to the belief that particular geographical locations were under the power and influence of nameable malevolent angelic forces. It was the task of the church to identify the spiritual force in control of a

---

36. An alternative suggestion is that demons were the offspring of wicked angels who procreated with humans in the period before the flood and who are mentioned in Genesis 6:1–4 and 1 Enoch 6:3; 8:3; Ma, J., *When the Spirit Meets the Spirits* (Berlin: Peter Lang, 2000), p. 146.
37. F. Hammond and I. M. Hammond, *Pigs in the Parlour* (London: Impact Books, 1976); B. Subritzky, *Demons Defeated* (Chichester: Sovereign World, 1986).
38. W. K. Kay, 'A Demonised Worldview: Dangers, Benefits and Explanations', *Journal of Empirical Theology* 11/1 (1998), pp. 17–29.

city or defined geographical area and to defeat it by prayer and proclamation so that subsequently the gospel might be preached with greater ease and more success. Peter Wagner's writings[39] on spiritual warfare, which largely elaborated and simplified Prince's teachings, were thought to be persuasive and became influential. As a further popularization of this teaching about spiritual warfare, Frank Peretti's novels imagined an entire world preyed on by spiritual powers that acted either in obedience to satanic dictates or in response to the prayers of faithful Christians.[40] In these bestselling stories, God's troops, angels, are largely dependent on believers' prayers, because, without them, they cannot act effectively against the sinister networks of spiritual agents ravaging civil society.[41] Whatever their dramatic force, these novels had little place for the Holy Spirit. There was no obvious connection between the prayer of believers and the work of the Spirit, nor was the Spirit's sanctifying and empowering role within the Christian life given much emphasis; rather, Christian prayer helps angels to do their work. As a result Christians were situated a long way from God and separated from direct divine help by countless spiritual intermediaries.

A vision of human beings engaged in a great cosmic drama involving hosts of invisible angels, some good and some evil, is brought into existence by this theology. In the hands of Third Wavers (those who had embraced the baptism of the Spirit but either left or never joined Pentecostal or charismatic groups), such a theology made ample room for angelic ministry. It is a theology that is coherent and can be used to explain obdurate resistance to

---

39. Cf. C. P. Wagner, *Wrestling with Dark Angels* (Ventura: Regal Books, 1990); C. P. Wagner, *Engaging the Enemy* (Ventura: Regal Books, 1991) and *Territorial Spirits* (Chichester: Sovereign World, 1991). See also <www.wagnerleadership.org/browse_all_courses.html>, accessed 21 March 2006.

40. F. Peretti, *Piercing the Darkness* (Ongar: Monarch, 1990).

41. Ibid. The web page <http://bblmedia.com/frank_peretti_biography.html> says that Peretti's first two books, *Piercing the Darkness* and *This Present Darkness*, have sold 3.5 million copies between them.

the gospel as well as periods of revival and collective blessing. Normal explanations of crowd psychology or cultural traditions are almost entirely replaced by reference to exchanges within the spiritual realm, so that, for example, Subritzky[42] can say that the wild behaviour of young people at a rock concert is brought about by spiritual activity rather than by adolescent psychology. Similarly, Terry Law, at a British Assemblies of God conference in the 1980s, preached that Lucifer was in charge of the worship in heaven before he fell and that, as a consequence, one of the main mechanisms for satanic deception and entrapment is the secular music that drives youth culture.

The presumption is that angelic forces of a wicked kind inflame the behaviour of young people so that the only way to rectify the situation is to address the spiritual forces themselves and to 'bind' them, and that this is more effective than addressing the young people directly. In any event, the interplay between the visible and the invisible is part of this understanding of the universe. A variant of this kind of thinking occurs during the Marches for Jesus,[43] where the public proclamation of Christ on the streets of big cities is partially to register Christ's victory before the watching angelic hosts. Of course, public marches with music and banners may make an impact upon the mass media and the residents of an area, but these are often not the real targets of the activity. Again, the presumption is that, once the strongholds of satanic power are dislodged within the spiritual realm, there will be beneficial consequences on the earth among the unenlightened and unconverted masses who have no idea of the tremendous battle being raged around them.

It is reasonable to treat this theology and these phenomena within the broad compass of Pentecostalism, although, as the term 'Third Wave' suggests, a division between different types of Pentecostalism is desirable. In the sense that Pentecostals, charismatics and Third Wavers share a basic appreciation of the active function of the Holy Spirit within the contemporary

---

42. Subritzky, *Demons Defeated*, p. 34.

43. E.g. G. Coates, *An Intelligent Fire* (Eastbourne: Kingsway, 1991), p. 116.

church, they are similar; yet there are differences between them in ecclesiology and in crucial areas of theology. In respect of the practices of spiritual warfare that involve fallen angels, the absence of a denominational tradition within the Third Wave category is likely to lead to less standardized approaches. Or, putting this another way, Third Wavers who belong to apostolic networks, and who hark back to the independent Pentecostals of the 1940s, will tend to be more mobile, flexible and pragmatic than Pentecostals, whose roots almost always go back to doctrinal statements similar to those drawn up by evangelicals for purposes of interdenominational co-operation. In relation to the present discussion, what matters is that the criteria for judging angelic manifestations may be less obvious within the milieu of the Third Wave. Moreover, and importantly, there is no way of empirically testing the effectiveness of spiritual warfare, since if, after engaging in spiritual warfare, there are spiritual breakthroughs in a particular geographical area, these can be attributed to the effectiveness of the warfare. On the other hand, if there are no breakthroughs, spiritual warfare can be assumed to have been conducted with insufficient fervour or accuracy. Or, conversely, if there are successes that take place, as, for example, within Billy Graham crusades, where no spiritual warfare has been conducted in advance, the advocates of spiritual warfare can still claim that in some previous battle the forces of darkness were bound and it is this, rather than anything else, that led to the success of the Graham crusades.

Concluding reflections

Billy Graham's book of 1975 can be seen as an attempt to answer the increasing fascination by Westerners with the weird phenomena of spiritualism, clairvoyants, poltergeists, alien abduction, UFOs and the like. Arguably, he wanted to demonstrate that there is, within biblical Christianity, a much bigger and wider view of life than is normally contained within the modernist/rationalist account of our world. He wanted to show that Christianity has much to say to those who feel intellectually boxed in by consumerist culture and materialistic conceptions of the universe. Angels are indicative of the spiritual world and of God's constant activity outside the confines of religious buildings.

From a theological perspective, angels sharpen every systematic account of our relationship with God. For Augustine, they help to explain the origin of the evil; for Aquinas, they throw light on the nature of knowledge. This is why a consideration here of the Oneness theology of Branham and his angelic messenger is relevant. The indication is that a non-trinitarian theology prevents any proper personalization of our experience of God. We may say that Branham needed to experience an angel because he had no way of appreciating the personal presence of Christ through the action of the Holy Spirit. Trinitarians, and trinitarian Pentecostals particularly, would want to note that angels function as messengers and agents of God in the material realm, but in almost every case they operate in a self-effacing way, and in the New Testament they always draw attention to God rather than themselves. They announce the coming of Christ to Mary and to the shepherds, and at the resurrection they ask the visitors, 'Why do you look for the living among the dead?' (Luke 24:5). At the ascension they again speak about Christ. In this respect angels, like the Holy Spirit, draw attention away from themselves to the God whom they worship and whose majesty they fully recognize. At the same time, and in contrast to angelic ministry, it is the Holy Spirit who is central to the charisma of healing (1 Cor. 12:9) and who makes Christ real to the church. It is because of the Spirit that Christ can say, 'I am with you always' (Matt. 28:20); he does not say, 'My angels will be with you always.'

While Pentecostals of all kinds may be particularly open to angelic accounts because of the experiential component of their theology, the particular gift of Pentecostals to the whole church ought to derive from their capacity to operate in the realm of discernment. Not only are Pentecostals accustomed to making distinctions between manifestations of the Holy Spirit through the charismata listed in 1 Corinthians 12 – 14, but also, because their meetings are less structured and less ordered than in many other sections of the church, their pastors and leaders develop an ability to sift out all kinds of congregational contributions, from those that are spiritual, insightful and sincere to those that are self-aggrandizing and even deceptive. It is not only the judgment of prophecy (1 Cor. 14:29) but also the discerning of spirits (1 Cor. 12:10) that is part of the Pentecostal heritage. Yet, more even than this, Pentecostals with their non-liturgical services and their free-ranging music ought to be able to learn and to teach others how to emulate the adoration given by the innumerable angels of heaven to the Lamb upon the throne.[44]

---

44. My thanks are due to Mrs Anne Dyer for further research provided and comments on an earlier draft of this chapter.

4 THE CHARISMATIC DEVIL: DEMONOLOGY IN CHARISMATIC CHRISTIANITY

Nigel Scotland

Charismatic Christianity first emerged in the 1960s as an identifiable phenomenon in both the United Kingdom and North America. In England it was prompted by Evangelical Anglicans,[1] most notably Michael Harper who was curate of All Souls, Langham Place, from 1959 to 1965, together with a number of independently minded Christian Brethren, including Arthur Wallis and David Lillie.[2] In the United States the first real signs of charismatic teaching and worship appeared among Roman Catholics and High Church Anglicans in the Episcopal Church of America. Prominent individuals were Dennis Bennett, followed a little later by Graham Pulkingham from the Church of the Redeemer in Houston[3] and Terry Fullam, Rector of St Paul's Episcopal Church

1. P. Hocken, *Streams of Renewal* (Carlise: Paternoster Press, 1997), p. 86.
2. N. A. D. Scotland, *Charismatics and the New Millennium* (Guildford: Eagle, 2000), p. 298.
3. See M. Harper, *A New Way of Living* (London: Hodder and Stoughton, 1973).

in Darien. Most scholars take charismatic Christianity to be one of a piece with the earlier expressions of Pentecostalism. Andrew Walker, for instance, referred to the charismatic movement as 'the gentrification of Pentecostalism'.[4]

Since the 1960s, charismatic Christianity has become a dominant force in Evangelical Christianity. The two largest churches in England, Kingsway International Centre and Kensington Temple, are both charismatic churches. The Alpha Course in basic Christianity, which has impacted every continent in the world, is based at Holy Trinity, Brompton, which is the focus of the largest network of Anglican churches in the UK. Alongside the denominational expressions of charismatic Christianity, several very prominent and expanding independent denominations emerged, among them Covenant Ministries, led by Bryn Jones, Ichthus, led by Roger and Faith Forster, Salt and Light, which looked to Barney Coombs for apostolic oversight, New Frontiers International, headed by Terry Virgo, and the Vineyard movement, which emanated from John Wimber. These strands represent the most resilient expressions of charismatic Christianity in England. Charismatics have also been major players in organizing Bible conferences such as New Wine, Stoneleigh, Grapevine and most notably Spring Harvest, which has attracted upwards of 60,000 participants each Easter.[5]

Clearly, therefore, charismatic Christianity is a broad church in terms of its ecclesiology; but it nevertheless has a number of distinctive features which are shared by all its different strands. They include a strong and sometimes overwhelming experience of the Holy Spirit usually referred to as a 'baptism' and often accompanied by speaking in tongues; lively, vibrant, participatory worship; fellowship marked by love; sharing and caring; the practice of the spiritual gifts of speaking, healing and service; an emphasis on the kingdom of God as both present and future rather than on the church; and evangelism and an emphasis on the

---

4. Scotland, *Charismatics*, p. 16.

5. Information from Spring Harvest, 25 February 2002.

spiritual battle. It is this latter aspect of charismatic Christianity that forms the focus of this chapter.

Charismatic demonology

Charismatic Christians have found that the experience of baptism in the Holy Spirit has given them a new awareness of unseen spiritual realities. In general terms they have a strong sense of evil and an increased perception of a personal devil and the powers of darkness. They are conscious that life is a struggle against what they perceive as Satan and his demon hosts and they frequently engage in what they term 'spiritual warfare', intercessory prayer and deliverance and exorcisms.

There are a number of reasons why charismatic Christianity came to have what is clearly a heightened focus on demonology. Perhaps most obviously it emerged at a time when the occult was burgeoning on both sides of the Atlantic. The year 1959 witnessed the repeal of the Witchcraft Act; 45,000 witches were reported to have been active in the UK at the time. Pop groups like Black Sabbath and Electric Lucifer were suddenly all the rage. Films such as *Rosemary's Baby* and *The Exorcist* were a sell-out. Newspapers in the late 1960s blatantly proclaimed that it was 'the Age of Aquarius'. In 1962 the New Age Christ was said to have been born.[6] Indeed, in this very same year, the celebrated New Age Community was set up at Findhorn in Scotland by Peter and Eileen Caddy. In the United States on 30 April 1966 Anton Szandon LaVey (1930–1997), the self-styled 'black pope' and founder of the Church of Satan in San Francisco, declared the arrival of 'the Age of Satan' and three years later published *The Satanic Bible*.

---

6. New Agers believe Lord Maitreya, channelled by Benjamin Crème, to be 'the Master of Masters', 'the Christ of the New Age'. He is said to have been born in February 1962 and to have made a number of appearances in various parts of the world. See for example, B. Crème, *Maitreya's Mission*, 1, and an interview with Crème, *New York Times*, 20 July 1996.

On account of their experience of the Holy Spirit, charismatics have come to approach Scripture in new ways. The Word of God is the sword which the Holy Spirit takes and implants in people's minds with poignancy and relevance. Charismatics take the Bible seriously and often literally. They are therefore acutely aware that the Son of God came into the world to destroy the works of the devil and to set people free from the influence of principalities and powers. They are clear that Jesus was an exorcist and the ministry of deliverance was part of the commission given to the church. Charismatics along with others are familiar with the temptation narratives and recognize that Jesus believed in the reality of the devil and indeed had an acute sense of conflict with him. This encounter with evil is a marked theme in the New Testament documents, which cannot easily be ignored.

In addition to these influences, there is the fact that the experience of baptism in the Holy Spirit has given many charismatics a sense of empowerment. This has often led to aggressive and even triumphalist expressions of Christianity, with marches for Jesus commanding the forces of evil to 'bow down' or get packing altogether. As will be apparent shortly, this led to the composition of warfare songs and to what has become known as strategic level spiritual warfare (SLSW).[7] As charismatic Christians become imbued with a strong, sometimes overwhelming sense of the presence of God through the Holy Spirit, so they have also developed a stronger perception and awareness of the presence and activity of evil in the world.

In reality, of course, there is no one charismatic demonology. On the ground, charismatics are probably as diverse a bunch as, say, the clergy of the Church of England or the members of the Liberal Democrat Party. For this reason, I want to suggest that there are certainly two, and probably three, distinct charismatic understandings of demonology. I was tempted to follow Andrew Walker and call them D1, D2 and D3. However, I categorize them as follows: the 'expansives', who are probably the majority, 'the

---

7. F. and I. M. Hammond, *Pigs in the Parlour* (London: Impact Books, 1973).

moderates', and, for want of a better term, the 'progressive charismatics'. The way in which I attempt to analyse these three categories is by their understanding of the devil; the nature, extent and role of evil spirits; their teaching on territorial spirits, principalities and powers; and their approach to the question of demon possession and exorcism. Not all charismatics fit neatly into one of these groupings but nevertheless I think this distinction proves helpful.

The expansives

Expansive charismatics trace their influence back to William Branham, a high-profile American Independent Baptist, who enjoyed considerable notoriety in the 1930s and '40s. He exercised a flamboyant signs-and-wonders ministry but was later dismissed for preaching Arianism. Branham, who was 'bonded for life' to Paul Cain, one of the Kansas City Prophets, impacted Frank and Ida Hammond, who in turn handed on their demonology to Derek Prince, Bill Subritzky and Peter Horrobin of Ellel Ministries in England. Other prominent figures among the expansives include Don Basham, Graham and Shirley Powell, and John Wimber, at least in his earlier writings.

In general terms, the expansives live in a world which is ruled by an exceptionally big and powerful devil, who at times appears almost as an evil opposite equivalent to Jesus. The nations are believed to be ruled over by the prince of demons, and the skies and just about every human activity and relationship are infested with Satan's evil minions. There are demons of practically everything, including eating Polo mints,[8] chocolate addiction and the fear of lumpy custard.[9] Demons not only have unbelievers in their clutches, but cling to Christians and in many instances dwell within them. In some expansive circles there is almost paranoia as believers have a strong foreboding that Satan is constantly attacking them and their

---

8. See *News of the World*, 22 February 1998.
9. See Scotland, *Charismatics*, p. 147.

situations. In order to protect themselves, therefore, such Christian people must constantly be on their guard and engage in 'spiritual warfare' by covering themselves with the blood, donning the whole armour of God and utilizing a whole range of binding, rebuking and casting-out strategies.

For the expansives the devil is a gargantuan figure much in the style of Voldemort in the Harry Potter books. For the Hammonds, the devil is 'the god of this world', whose minions are the rulers of darkness of this age.[10] For Peter Horrobin, also, 'Satan is real!' and 'reigns as the ruler of this world'. He is not felt to be omnipresent but his reign is extended 'through a hierarchy of demonic power'.[11] Satan is particularly concerned to attack 'wherever believers are seeking to be obedient to the will of God and move forward under the anointing of the Holy Spirit'.[12] In these endeavours he is supported by 'a very, very large number of fallen angels carefully organised into a hierarchy of Satanic power around the world'.[13] Satan's attacks 'may include sickness, accidents, financial problems and relationship breakdowns'.[14] For the Hammonds, Horrobin, Subritzky and their friends, this is a paranoid universe dominated by the devil, who is a skilful, scheming individual supported by his hugely well-organized legions of fiendish allies all bent on destruction.

Martin Percy takes the view that in the writings of John Wimber, 'Satan has virtually become incarnate, as tangible a person as Jesus was'.[15] In fact, Percy contends that Wimber needs Satan because when there is a power failure in the ministry it can be accounted for in a concrete way; namely, there is a powerful

---

10. P. Horrobin, *Healing Through Deliverance* (Chichester: Sovereign World, 1991), p. 61.
11. P. Horrobin, 'Angels and Demons are Real', *Renewal* 181 (June 1991), p. 22.
12. Horrobin, *Healing*, pp. 76–77.
13. Horrobin, 'Angels', p. 22.
14. M. Percy, *Words, Wonders and Power* (London: SPCK, 1996), p. 95.
15. J. F. MacArthur, *Charismatic Chaos* (Grand Rapids: Zondervan, 1992), p. 142.

adversary who has cut the power by causing a break in the circuit. Thus, for example, when the late Canon David Watson, the Church of England evangelist, contracted cancer of the liver and prayer was unanswered, 'Satan murdered him.'[16] Whatever people may feel about Wimber's explanation for David Watson's death, the fact is that many charismatics take the view that if there is opposition to the work, or things go wrong or there is dissension in the camp, it is the enemy who has done it![17]

The major means by which the enemy of souls operates, as has been noted, is through his demonic hierarchy. It is at this point that the expansive elements in the charismatic world are at their most visible. For instance, John and Ida Hammond identified fifty-three clusters or demon groupings. Cluster 11, for example, is 'escape', and 48 is 'sexual impurity'. Number 11 includes 'spirits of stoicism, sleepiness, alcohol and drugs', and 48 includes 'spirits of fantasy, lust, masturbation, exposure and frigidity'.[18] These clusters, say the Hammonds, 'are much the same in organisation as the army of the United States which has the President as Commander-in-Chief followed by generals, colonels, captains, lieutenants on down to the lowest rank of private'.[19] Horrobin endorses the Hammonds' view that Satan's hosts are well organized, with ruling spirits over the nations and hierarchies over different regions, cities, towns and districts.

Representatives of the expansive group are precise in their understanding of the demons. Subritzky, for example, tells us on the basis of Daniel 9:21 and Matthew 12:43 that 'demons can be clearly distinguished from angels because angels usually have wings' and demons do not.[20] One demon he encountered was 'eight feet high and clothed in a black garment'.[21] Demons can also

16. See N. A. D. Scotland, 'Don't Blame the Devil for Everything which Goes Wrong', *Skepsis*, in *Anglicans for Renewal* 85, pp. 27–34.

17. Hammond, *Pigs*, p. 22.

18. Ibid., p. 6.

19. Horrobin, *Healing*, p. 94.

20. B. Subritzky, *Demons Defeated* (Chichester: Sovereign World, 1992), p. 65.

21. Ibid., p. 60.

transfer from one person to another. Subritzky explains, 'When sexual intercourse takes place outside of marriage . . . demons of lust and perverted sex can pass from one body to another.'[22] When this teaching was expounded at a charismatic conference in Sheffield it caused one participant to call out, 'Wear a condom!'[23] Both Derek Prince and Peter Horrobin offer similar teaching on this point, Horrobin asserting that spirits can travel down a family line, 'causing the same symptoms in generation after generation'.[24] Horrobin believes that spirits can also reproduce. The question is often asked, he writes, 'Can demons multiply and can they breed?' Referring to Genesis 6:1–4 he writes, 'Clearly the capacity for "breeding", of a sort, is implied in this passage.' Wimber was less emphatic at this point and simply stated that Christians can be 'demonized' by 'inherited demons that are passed from parents to children'.[25]

Expansive charismatics are adamant that particular demons have particular functions. Horrobin notes that the work of some is to bring sickness generally, and others are 'highly specific to particular conditions, only causing, for example, arthritis, cancer, paralysis or some other condition'.[26] Peter Lawrence recalled having cast out two demons, called Gregory and his companion Harold, who confessed to causing 'tiredness'. [27] Other spirits encourage homosexuality, pornography and violence.[28] There are also spirits which operate through other religions such as Sikhism, spirits of Freemasonry,[29] and spirits which operate in the red-light

22. Ibid., p. 8.
23. A. Walker, 'The Devil You Think You Know: Demonology and the Charismatic Movement', in T. Smail, A. Walker and N. Wright, *Charismatic Renewal: The Search for a Theology* (London: SPCK, 1993), p. 94.
24. Horrobin, *Healing*, p. 89.
25. J. Wimber, *Power Healing* (London: Hodder and Stoughton, 1986), p. 130.
26. Ibid., p. 89.
27. P. H. Lawrence, *The Hot Line* (Eastbourne: Kingsway Publications, 1990), p. 146.
28. Ibid., p. 94.
29. Ibid., p. 99.

districts of cities like London.[30] John Wimber, in much the same vein, observed that demons have special tasks to perform. They can, for instance, cause storms,[31] influence cultural trends and 'cause a spirit of apathy to reign over a city'.[32]

There is general agreement among the Hammonds, Subritzky, Horrobin and Wimber that when people fall into temptation they make themselves vulnerable to attack and at that point they can become demonized.[33] This, according to them, is a demon's one great objective. In the words of the Hammonds, their aim is to 'invade and indwell human bodies'.[34] John Wimber put it more starkly:

> There are many demons that don't have a body. Having a body [for a demon] is like having a car. They want to have a car so they can get around. If they don't have a body, they're a second-class demon. They're not first class. I'm not kidding you, that's the way it works. And so [to them] having a body is a big deal. That's why they won't give it up.[35]

This conviction that demons enter into human beings is linked to the teaching of 'entry points'. The evil spirits are believed to enter people through particular points in the body, such as the eyes, the mouth, the ears and even the genitals. Release, according to some exorcists, can come only as the entry point is prayed over, signed with the cross or anointed with oil. Roland Howard in his book *Charismania* charted the tragic case of the former leader of the London Healing Mission, Revd Andy Arbuthnot, and his wife, who ministered to a congregant known as Mary in 1994 at their Notting Hill Centre. In a chapter entitled 'The Notting Hill Sexorcist' Howard chronicled over a two-year period a number of

---

30. Ibid., p. 94.
31. J. Wimber, Spring Harvest address, Easter Day 1992.
32. J. Wimber, conference notes, from *Teach us to Pray* (1986) cited by Percy, *Words*, p. 183.
33. Horrobin, *Healing*, p. 111.
34. Hammond, *Pigs*, p. 1.
35. Healing seminar, 1981, tape 1. See also Subritzky, *Demons*, p. 12.

marathon-length sessions in which Mary's private parts were anointed with consecrated Dubonnet. The whole case ended in tragedy with police intervention and a court case for abuse.[36] The Arbuthnots are by no means the only ones to have taught 'entry points'. Peter Horrobin's Ellel Ministries gave instruction on 'demonic entry points' in their 'Healing: The Jesus Model' course at Glyndley Manor[37] in 1994 and 1995. Roland Howard, writing in 1997, reported similar instances of ritual anointing and commented that 'listening to Horrobin speak it is clear that there is virtually nothing that cannot lead to picking up demons'.[38]

Not only do evil spirits invade the lives of believers and unbelievers alike; according to this section of charismatic Christianity, they rule the world by means of a carefully ordered hierarchy of wickedness. In Subritzky's words, 'Satan places unseen princes and powers of the air over every nation and city with descending orders of authority all the way down to demons which walk on the ground and seek a home.'[39] He continues, 'These spirit beings seek to rule over countries, over cities, and even over churches by bringing with them hordes of demonic powers such as envy, jealousy, unbelief, pride, lust and ambition. All of these descending orders of authority are under the control of Satan himself.'[40] Another instance of this took place at the Dales Bible Week in 1977, at Yorkshire's Harrogate Showground, when Ern Baxter from Fort Lauderdale expounded the nature of the demonic kingdom along similar lines. Having completed his homily, he then invited all those present 'intelligently and purposefully' to bind a powerful, national evil spirit called 'The Prince of Great Britain' and to 'paralyse the power of that dark-winged spirit that hovers over

36. R. Howard, *Charismania* (London: Mowbray, 1997). See also *Sunday Telegraph*, 1 October 1995.

37. See Ellel Ministries Training Courses Programme, 1994, with calendar for 1995, p. 10 and back cover.

38. Howard, *Charismania*, p. 95. See also *Sunday Telegraph*, 15 January 1995.

39. Subritzky, *Demons*, p. 12.

40. Ibid., p. 13.

London'.[41] Both the Hammonds[42] and Horrobin[43] make similar assertions about the land being in the grip of similar local and national fiends.

It is contended that, in order to gain the victory, Christians must actively fight and wrestle against these principalities and powers. Peter Wagner of Fuller Seminary in Los Angeles, with whom John Wimber was closely associated for a time, was at the forefront of this thinking and developed the concept of 'strategic level spiritual warfare'. He set out a threefold strategy. First, discern the territorial spirits assigned to a city. Second, deal with the corporate sin in a city or area. Third, engage in aggressive 'warfare prayer' against territorial spirits. Wagner holds it to be crucial to identify the names and nature of the assignments of demonic princes who rule over a given local area.[44] At this point, mention should be made of the concept of 'spiritual mapping', developed by George Otis Jr. His contention is that malevolent spirits lie behind the rulers and powers of this age and also influence the religious beliefs, social life and culture of a nation or region. By plotting these on a map of the area it becomes possible to identify the character of these territorial agents of Satan and even to identify their names. Once this has been done, the way is open to engage in aggressive warfare prayer. This is where individuals such as Cindy Jacobs, President of Generals of Intercession, come to the fore. Basing her teaching on Jesus' authoritative rebuking of the devil during his temptations, Jacobs has developed a series of powerful 'Away with you, Satan' prayer strategies. Once these have been completed and the opposing forces driven out, the way will have been cleared for an effective advance of the gospel and the

41. Cited in N. Wright, *A Theology of the Dark Side* (Carlisle: Paternoster, 2003), p. 147.

42. Hammond, *Pigs*, p. 6.

43. Horrobin, *Healing*, p. 94.

44. C. P. Wagner, *Confronting the Powers: How the New Testament Church Experienced the Power of Strategic Level Spiritual Warfare* (Ventura: Regal, 1996), cited by C. Arnold, *Three Crucial Questions about Spiritual Warfare* (Grand Rapids: Baker Academic, 1997), p. 165.

kingdom of God. Other battle strategies include the use of the high praises of God with marching songs and warfare choruses. More recently, in 2002, John Paul Jackson, a former Kansas City Prophet, has been teaching the doctrine of 'heavenly portals'.[45] These are spherical openings, located across the globe, through which additional hosts of good angels can descend from the third heaven through the second heaven to the earth. Believers need to locate these heavenly portals (one of which is in Jerusalem, and another, significantly, on Jackson's own land in New Hampshire, USA) and then come together in those places in united intercessory prayer. This will release legions of good angels, who will then anoint and empower believers to perform even greater works than Jesus did.

One final and controversial aspect of expansive charismatic demonology remains to be considered, and that is the issue of demon possession and exorcism. Here the particular hot potato is whether or not a Christian can be possessed by the devil. At this point expansive charismatics appear to be agreed that if by the term 'possession' 'complete ownership' is meant, no Christian can be possessed, since they are owned by Christ.[46] That said, both the Hammonds and Wimber come close to the idea of total possession. The Hammonds assert that Christians can be indwelt by demons, but that the demons are confined to the body and the soul, not indwelling the spirit.[47] Wimber suggests that 'believers can be sifted by Satan, tempted and then finally attacked, resulting in the believer becoming possessed to a greater or lesser degree by an agent of Satan (demon)'.[48] All the expansives share the conviction that Christians can, however, be 'demonized', by which they mean that evil spirits can influence, take hold of or attach themselves to believers. The Hammonds, who assert that demons take

---

45. J. P. Jackson, *Heavenly Portals* (2002), <www.streamsministries.com/PI-HeavenlyPortals.html>.

46. See G. Otis, *Informed Intercession* (Ventura: Regal Books, 1999).

47. See Hammond, *Pigs*, p. 136, and Horrobin, *Healing*, p. 290.

48. J. Wimber, *Signs, Wonders and Church Growth*, ch. 11, section 7, cited by Percy, *Words*, p. 92.

up residence in the lower abdomen,[49] believe that everyone is demonized to some extent at least.[50] Horrobin is also clear not only that 'Christians [can] have demons after their conversion, they were there before conversion'. They can also 'receive further demons through the practice of sin'.[51] The need, then, is to develop deliverance ministries, and charismatic expansives therefore devote much time and energy to engaging, binding, rebuking and casting out demons. The great danger in all of this, as Nigel Wright observed, is that such individuals become like a golfer who only ever uses one club regardless of the particular situation. In short, such enthusiasts are suffering from 'demonophilia'.[52]

The moderates

I have given a little more time and space to the views of what I have termed 'expansive charismatics' because their views tend to dominate the charismatic world. I now want to consider more briefly the views of what I have termed the 'moderates' and the 'progressive charismatics'. It has to be said that, as with all attempts at categorizations, nothing is a perfect fit and inevitably there is overlap at some points.

The 'moderates' as I perceive them are represented by individuals such as Clinton Arnold, Michael Green, Graham Dow, Clive Calver, John Wimber [53] in some of his later writings, and a host of others. In general their concept of the devil is still personal and powerful but there is less emphasis on his organizational skills. They are less impressed with the influence and impact of demons and the authority of principalities and powers. For them the capacity of evil spirits to damage and take hold of believers is less,

49. Hammond, *Pigs*, p. 108.

50. Ibid., p 12.

51. Horrobin, *Healing*, p. 46.

52. Wright, *Dark Side*, p. 125.

53. It should be noted that in the later 1990s Arnold's writings were endorsed as standard for the Vineyard.

and deliverance ministry has a smaller place in their scheme of things. Clive Calver and Michael Mitton both represent the moderates well in the following comments. Calver wrote in *Prophecy Today*: 'The great number of Christian books about Satan and all his works speak volumes for the unhealthy fascination which the subject can be made to hold, by the devil, for the people of God.'[54] Michael Mitton in similar vein commented, 'There is . . . a very articulate fringe which will still deliver anything that moves and which talks about vast hierarchies of demons. It will name demons, demons of Lucozade and goodness knows what, which I don't have much sympathy with.'[55]

In considering the devil, the moderates, while acknowledging his 'destructive influence and evil activity on the earth',[56] nevertheless stress that Satan is a defeated foe. In fact, the point was well made by the title of Michael Green's book *I Believe in Satan's Downfall*. Clinton Arnold echoes it in the following lines: 'Christ did win a decisive victory over the powers through the cross . . . thereby enabling him to rescue people from Satan's domain and install them as members of the Kingdom.'[57] Michael Green allows that the devil is 'a menacing reality',[58] a 'great counterfeiter',[59] 'more powerful than man' and 'possessing an empire'.[60] Yet, for all that, he is a fallen creature who can be designated as personal only in a limited sense.[61] He is 'a defeated foe, who received his death-blow at Calvary'[62] and hence no longer has any rightful authority over people.[63] In short, writes Green, 'the power of

---

54. *Prophecy Today* 3/1 (Jan.–Feb. 1987).
55. Interview with Michael Mitton, 7 June 1994.
56. Arnold, *Spiritual Warfare*, p. 93.
57. Ibid., p. 122.
58. E. M. B. Green, *I Believe in Satan's Downfall* (London: Hodder and Stoughton, 1984), p. 33.
59. Ibid., p. 20.
60. Ibid., p. 46.
61. Ibid., p. 30.
62. Ibid., p. 16.
63. Ibid., p. 49.

Satan was shattered on the cross, shattered by the invincible power of love'.[64]

When it comes to the matter of demons, moderate charismatics are fully prepared to acknowledge their existence. Graham Dow, Bishop of Carlisle, asserts that 'wherever there's a besetting sin that people are not getting the victory over there's a real possibility, I would say, that there's a spirit holding them in it'.[65] Green points out that these demons have functions, but not with the same specificity that the expansives would have us believe. We see this, for instance, in the realm of illness, though not all illness can be attributed to satanic activity.[66] Quoting 1 Timothy 4:1, Green reminds us that 'Christians are certainly not exempt from the principalities and powers'.[67] Their impact is also seen in the gods of other world faiths, but more particularly in cults such as Transcendental Meditation, where 'the Satanic handiwork is obvious'.[68] Yet, for all this, Green does not settle for the demon-infested universe of the far left of the charismatic firmament. The New Testament writers, he emphatically reminds us, 'had no interest in building up demonologies'.[69] There is no need, as the Apocalypse put it, to search out 'the deep things of Satan' (Rev. 2:24, RSV).[70]

In speaking of 'principalities, powers and thrones', Green counsels that the New Testament writers used these terms both of human rulers and of the spiritual forces which lie behind them.[71] He does incidentally underline how important it is to keep the powers separate and distinct from the structures and the institutions they seek to influence. If the two are totally conflated, we

---

64. Ibid., p. 95.
65. G. Dow, *Anchoring the Healing and Deliverance Ministries in the Life of the Local Church*, audio tape.
66. Green, *Satan's Downfall*, p. 86.
67. Ibid., p. 88.
68. Ibid., p. 177.
69. Ibid., p. 82.
70. Ibid.
71. Ibid., p. 84.

restrict Satan's activity and become overly negative towards society.[72]

On the matter of demonic possession and exorcism, Green notes that the devil entered Judas Iscariot and that Satan 'filled the heart of Ananias' in Acts 5, but he goes on to endorse Michael Scanlan's differentiation between exorcism and deliverance. 'Solemn exorcism' is appropriate only in cases of complete 'possession', where Satan has so taken over the personality that the patient's free will is rendered inoperative.[73] Such instances are rare and extreme, and may be handled only by priests specially authorized by the local bishop.[74] In contrast, 'deliverance', or what the Roman church calls 'simple exorcism', is a ministry for the relief of all believing Christians and can be performed by clergy and lay people alike.[75] For this kind of ministry, Green advises, it may be prudent to have 'a cross, material for an informal Holy Communion, holy oil for anointing as the Scripture indicates and holy water'.[76] In the matter of deliverance, however, Green cannot stress too strongly the need to go lightly, since it can so easily become all-absorbing.[77] Indeed, the danger, as Leanne Payne so wisely highlights, is that such people begin to practise the devil's presence rather than God's.[78]

On the issue of spiritual warfare the moderates counsel that the Bible nowhere lays down or instructs us how or whether we are to engage high-ranking territorial spirits. Wimber wrote in 1990 that 'Christians are now becoming aware of territorial spirits. Territorial spirits are powerful fallen angels – principalities, powers, dominions, thrones, rulers – who exercise influence over cities, regions, even nations. They influence every aspect of

---

72. Ibid., p. 85.
73. Ibid., p. 132.
74. Ibid.
75. Ibid.
76. Ibid. p. 138.
77. Ibid., p. 139.
78. L. Payne, *The Real Presence* (Grand Rapids: Baker Books, 1997), p. 147.

culture much as soil types determine which crops can be grown in different regions.'[79] Clinton Arnold nevertheless gave the following counsel: 'I can find no Scriptural evidence suggesting that we have the right or authority to "serve notice", "evict" or "bind" spirits over cities, regions or nations.'[80] This view was in fact endorsed by Wimber in 1993–4 when all leaders at the Anaheim Vineyard were instructed to follow Arnold's teaching on this issue. Leanne Payne emphasizes that Christian people are not sent to battle for God, but to be used by God in his battlings.[81] 'Too many Christians' prayers', she counsels, 'are filled with speaking to demons – mostly non-existent ones.'[82] The focus should always be on 'ministering to God'. 'As we practice the presence of God', she writes, 'the demons, principalities or powers are discerned directly in our path and can be commanded to go.'[83]

Progressive charismatics

Finally, I turn to my third suggested category, which I have termed the progressive charismatics. Following Dave Tomlin's *The Post-Evangelical*, I was tempted to use the term 'post-charismatic'. However, these individuals certainly have not rejected their charismatic experience of the Holy Spirit or the practice of spiritual gifts, nor do they renounce belief in the devil or the demonic; yet their emphasis and practice represent a progression from the views that have so far been considered. Among others in this group, I include Wayne Grudem, Thomas Smail, Max Turner, Andrew Walker and Nigel Wright. Their general contention is that the biblical record has very little to say about the devil. Indeed, Andrew Walker underlines the fact that the word 'devil', meaning 'destroyer' is not used

79. J. Wimber, *The Dynamics of Spiritual Growth* (London: Hodder and Stoughton, 1991), p. 186.
80. Arnold, *Spiritual Warfare*, p. 183.
81. Payne, *Presence*, p. 183.
82. Ibid., p. 207.
83. Ibid., p. 209.

in the Old Testament'[84] and that in the New Testament there is 'no explanation of his origins'.[85] When it comes to the ministry of Jesus, it is clear that he believed in demons, but 'he certainly did not see all sickness and evil under devilish control' and 'he showed no interest whatever in the minutiae and mechanisms of the demonic realm'.[86] Nigel Wright commented similarly in his *Theology of the Dark Side* that 'the New Testament says very little about the internal workings of the kingdom of darkness'.[87]

In a more detailed consideration of the devil, Wright is quick to emphasize that 'there is a tendency for people to use "devil language" to project their own inner struggles', and therefore 'all that is called devil is not therefore devil'.[88] Wright, although regarding the devil as a spirit being, also prefers to refer to the devil as 'it', because the devil is less than a person.[89] Indeed, along with Andrew Walker he asserts that the devil as revealed in Scripture 'cannot be said to exhibit the traits of personhood'.[90] Although the devil must have some form of objective existence, Wright is loath to credit him with carefully planned hierarchies and organized schemes. The devil's nature, he suggests, is 'not reason but unreason, not organisation but chaos'.[91] We should note at this point Wayne Grudem's counsel 'that not all sin is caused by Satan or demons, nor is the major influence or cause of sin demonic activity'.[92]

On the issue of demons Walker is clear that there is enough evidence 'to support a proper Christian dualism', but urges that only modest claims can be made about 'the origins of devils, the workings of the demonic world and the methodology of exorcisms when

84. Walker, 'Devil', p. 96.
85. Ibid., p. 97.
86. Ibid., p. 98.
87. Wright, *Dark Side*, p. 111.
88. Ibid., p. 24.
89. Ibid., p. 29.
90. Ibid., p. 29.
91. Ibid., p. 112.
92. W. Grudem, *Systematic Theology* (Leicester: IVP, 1994), p. 422.

the Bible remains virtually silent about these matters'.[93] Grudem likewise is clear that 'demons are limited by God's control and have limited power'.[94] He also underlines the fact that very little space in the New Testament is given to discussing demonic activity'.[95] His views are very far from the Hammonds' clusters and Horrobin's travelling minions. Commenting on 1 Corinthians Grudem writes:

> In 1 Corinthians, when there is a problem of dissensions, Paul does not tell the church to rebuke a spirit of dissensions, but simply urges them to 'agree' and 'be united' in the same mind and in the same judgement' (1 Cor. 1:10). When there is a problem of incest, he does not tell the Corinthians to rebuke the spirit of incest, but tells them they ought to be outraged and they should exercise church discipline until the offender repents (1 Cor. 5:1–5) These examples could be duplicated many times in other New Testament epistles.[96]

Progressive charismatics recognize that the devil and demons have some role to play in inflicting sickness and disease, but, as Professor J. C. Thomas has pointed out in *The Devil, Disease and Deliverance*, 'neither James nor John gives any hint that the devil or demons have a role to play in the infliction of infirmity'.[97]

Some progressive charismatics are also guarded in their understanding of 'territorial spirits'. Wright, for example, is clear that conservative biblical scholarship does not subscribe to the views put forward by Subritzky. While he does not deny the reality of the demonic, for Andrew Walker the dark powers must be seen primarily as 'interpenetrating the power structures of society, so that we fight evil not in the realm of fantasy or the heavenlies, but in the public world of economics'.[98] For Professor Max Turner, the

---

93. Walker, 'Devil', p. 99.
94. Grudem, *Systematic Theology*, p. 415.
95. Ibid., p. 420.
96. Ibid.
97. J. C. Thomas, *The Devil, Disease and Deliverance* (Sheffield: Sheffield Academic Press, 1998), p. 301.
98. Walker, 'Devil', p. 99.

battle is 'not with individual petty-pillaging demons, nor with territorial powers, but with the whole confederacy of worldwide powers of darkness'.[99]

When it comes to spiritual warfare, there is a strong cautionary emphasis. Walker wrote: 'I find myself reeling from much of the literature, tape ministries and theologies that some modern-day charismatics promote under the broad rubric of "spiritual warfare".'[100] Grudem agrees. He writes:

> In marked contrast to the practice of those who today emphasise 'strategic level spiritual warfare', in no instance does anyone in the New Testament (1) summon 'territorial spirits' upon entering an area to preach the gospel, (2) demand information from demons about a local hierarchy, (3) say that we should believe or teach information derived from demons, or (4) teach by word or example that certain 'demonic strongholds' over a city have to be broken before the gospel can be proclaimed with effectiveness. Rather, Christians just preach the gospel, and it comes with power to change their lives.[101]

For Grudem, as for Max Turner, who points out that Jesus had no programme of strategic level spiritual warfare, the spiritual battle does not have to be highly dramatic. There is no suggestion in the New Testament, he says, that demons are hard of hearing and need to be shouted at or confronted in long-drawn-out battles.[102] For Turner the spiritual battle is mainly a 'defensive one'.

On the issue of demon possession, Walker, Wright and Grudem are guarded and are of the view that possession is an inappropriate term. Grudem points out that it is not used in the New Testament.[103] Wright underlines the fact that simply to tell someone he or she is possessed can cause what appear to be

---

99. M. Turner, 'The Christian "Band of Brothers"', *LBC Review* (Spring 2002), p. 5.
100. Walker, 'Devil', p. 87.
101. Grudem, *Systematic Theology*, p. 421.
102. Ibid., p. 430.
103. Ibid.

demonic manifestations. He cites Dr Monty Barker's study of a group of twenty individuals for whom he was responsible. A high proportion had had charismatic ministry but in his view none of them was demonized. Human beings, Wright maintains, are socially and psychically more complex than we imagine.[104] We must therefore, at the very least, be open to the possibility that phenomena which are often perceived to be of demonic origin may simply have their origin in the psychic reservoirs that some people develop the ability to tap.[105] 'The realm of the psychic', according to Wright, 'may be regarded as neither holy or demonic in itself but when orientated towards God it becomes integrated with the total life in communion with God. When orientated towards the devil it becomes the realm of unwholesome demonic activity.'[106] Wright concludes that it is therefore wise to be reluctant to conclude that a person is demonized. All alternatives need to be explored before reaching this conviction.

Conclusion

Of these three broad charismatic understandings of the devil and demonology, it seems clear that the expansive viewpoint is that which prevails. Certainly it is the one which has been, and is, presented in the majority of popular magazines such as *Prophecy Today*, *Charisma* and *Christianity and Renewal.* It is also what is proclaimed at healing centres, warfare seminars and summer conferences. At this expansive end of the charismatic spectrum, the Hammonds, Horrobin, Prince and others are clearly constructing a universe in which almost every problem is scrutinized through a demonic grid. Indeed, as one issue of *The Church of England Newspaper* complained,[107] we are fast reaching a situation where there are more deliverers than demons. Clearly there is an unwillingness to

104. Wright, *Dark Side*, p. 115.

105. Ibid.

106. Ibid., pp. 116–117.

107. *Church of England Newspaper*, 26 May 1995.

recognize that there are other sources of temptation and evil apart from Satan and his unsavoury scheming hosts. References to the fact that the New Testament warns against three great enemies, the world, the flesh and the devil, in that order, are very limited. A further danger with impassioned demonologies is that they can create a sense of fatalism and remove human responsibility for evil. The explanation that 'the devil made me do it' thus becomes a cover for every piece of unacceptable behaviour.

Incidentally, perhaps nowhere is it more apparent that charismatic Christianity is driven by consumerism than in its more extreme views on demonology. It is here that we see constant hype and an ever-flowing stream of new techniques and teachings each designed to gun down Satan's hosts and deliver the afflicted from their clutches. These new spiritual-warfare weapons include naming the demons, confronting the powers, street marches, battle songs, entry-point teachings, ritual anointings, spiritual mapping, warfare prayer, stamping on the devil and opening up the heavenly portals, to name but a few.

By contrast, at the other end of the spectrum, it is clear that the writing and teachings of the moderate and progressive charismatics are beginning to influence the more thoughtful among the denominational clergy. Here we are witnessing the beginnings of a more temperate understanding of the nature and impact of evil both in people's lives and in the structures of the society in which we live. It is here also in the reactions of the more moderate and progressive charismatics that the beginnings of what might be termed 'post-charismatics' are observable. These are those who have not rejected their experience of the Holy Spirit and his gracious gifts, but they are and have been turning away from those who proclaim what is an in-your-face and overheated demonology. In their favour it can be said that the number of recorded exorcisms in the New Testament appears to have been relatively few. Furthermore, Jesus did not believe in a demon-infested universe, nor did he engage with principalities and powers or bind and rebuke territorial spirits.

5 BINDING THE STRONG MAN: THE FLAW OF THE EXCLUDED MIDDLE

Martin Parsons

Introduction

In 1982 Paul Hiebert wrote a seminal paper entitled 'The Flaw of the Excluded Middle',[1] in which he argued that while Christians in the West have tended to believe in God, who is up above in heaven, unlike many non-Western cultures they have had little real belief in the middle layer of angels and demons as impacting events on earth. Essentially, Hiebert was challenging the assumption of many 'Bible-believing' Christians in the West that the worldview they functioned with really equated to a biblical worldview.

Since Hiebert's paper there has been the beginnings of a sea change in the West, at least among evangelicals. A significant number of books by mainstream evangelicals, such as Neil Anderson's *Bondage Breaker* series, have drawn attention to the need for Christians to not only receive forgiveness of sins but also be

1. P. G. Hiebert, 'The Flaw of the Excluded Middle', *Missiology* 10/1 (1982), pp. 35–47.

set free from various degrees of demonic bondage that may have been inherited, or acquired in other ways, such as through curses.[2]

However, when it comes to the 'powers and principalities' described in Ephesians 6, most Christians in the West still functionally operate with a worldview that has an 'excluded middle'. While many 'Bible-believing' Christians are ready to accept from Scripture the existence of such higher spiritual powers, this view is frequently held in uneasy tension with an assumption that such powers have little impact on human life and can therefore be ignored by Christians.

However, such a view is open to challenge both from exegetical considerations and from practical experience of pastoral ministry. This chapter will seek to demonstrate on exegetical grounds that Scripture provides a significantly greater level of detail concerning powers and principalities than most Western Christians have assumed, and that it speaks of specific ways in which the church is called to stand against these powers. It will then relate this to practical experience of Christian ministry.

Hermeneutics

It is necessary to develop a hermeneutic that allows an understanding of this subject both to be based on the final form of Scripture as whole[3] and yet also to take account of practical ministry experience. This hermeneutic needs to combine the following elements:

(a) A willingness to allow ministry experience to raise questions that Western theology has traditionally not addressed. The issues raised may sometimes challenge the adequacy of some

---

2. N. T. Anderson, *The Bondage Breaker* (London: Monarch, 1993).
3. This does not negate the importance of historical verification of the text. However, an attempt to relate Scripture theologically to the outworking of faith in practical Christian ministry must begin from the final form of Scripture.

traditional theological answers. However, biblical exegesis must always be the primary determinant of the interpretation of ministry experience in order to provide a system of checks and balances in deliverance ministry.

(b) An allowance for contemporary prophetic insight to raise issues that Western theology has traditionally left unaddressed. However, again prophetic insight must always be checked for its compatibility with Scripture. This primarily involves checking that the prophecy is consistent with the story of salvation history set out in Scripture and is in no sense incompatible with biblical teaching on specific issues.

(c) A commitment to take seriously the purpose and context of Scripture. One of the exegetical fallacies that 'Bible-believing' Christians have frequently fallen into during discussions of spiritual warfare is that of refusing to believe anything about Satan's kingdom for which they cannot find specific chapter and verse. Although in many respects this displays a commendably high view of Scripture, it is actually asking the Bible to do something that it never sets out to do. Put simply, the Bible does not set out to be an encyclopaedia of Satan's kingdom. Indeed it would be a very dark book if it did this. Rather, it describes God's plan of salvation history, and, in doing so, almost incidentally touches on the fact that there is a kingdom hostile to God that includes Satan, powers and principalities, demons and so forth.

(d) A firm grounding in biblical theology, rather than the studies of individual biblical authors' theology, such as Lukan studies, Pauline studies, etc., which have dominated Western biblical studies. This does of course need to start from the individual biblical books, so that the specific terms used by individual biblical authors can be determined from their own context. However, a biblical theology needs to move beyond the study of individual books and take greater account of intertextuality than has been the case in much biblical scholarship.[4] For

---

4. Cf. F. Watson, *Text and Truth* (Edinburgh: T. and T. Clark, 1997), pp. 1–29, especially pp. 5–6, which criticizes the neglect of intertextuality in biblical studies.

example, an understanding of Pauline theology requires an interpretative framework that starts from the fact that his churches were taught an oral tradition of Jesus' life and teaching which equates in at least some measure with the synoptic Gospels, after which Paul wrote his epistles in order to correct certain misunderstandings.[5]

(e) An approach which takes the worldwide church rather than the academy as its hermeneutical community.[6] This will involve a reworking of much Western theology to determine the extent to which its conclusions are influenced by assumptions incompatible with a biblical worldview, either of the authors themselves or more indirectly through dominant opinions within the predominantly Western academy of biblical scholars.

The New Testament teaching on binding the strong men: the example of Jesus

All three synoptic gospels present Jesus' reference to 'binding the strong man'[7] as an apologetic for his deliverance ministry in the face of claims by the Pharisees that he cast out evil spirits by Beelzebul, the prince of demons. Jesus' response may be summarized as follows: 'Far from operating by the power of the prince

---

5. This is surprisingly neglected by many New Testament scholars, e.g. J. D. G. Dunn, *The Theology of Paul the Apostle* (Edinburgh: T. and T. Clark, 1998), while admitting the probability that 'Paul himself had a much richer theology than he ever actually put on paper', nonetheless contends that 'a theology of Paul cannot be more than the sum of the theology of each of the individual letters' (p. 14). Consequently, his discussion of Paul's view of the heavenly powers (pp. 104–110) makes no reference at all to the teaching of Jesus.
6. R. J. Bauckham, *Mission as a Hermeneutic for Scriptural Interpretation*, CWC position paper 106 (Cambridge: Cambridge University Faculty of Divinity, 1999), pp. 3–4; P. Hiebert, *Anthropological Perspectives on Missiological Issues* (Grand Rapids: Baker, 1994), pp. 30–31, 103.
7. Matt. 12:22–29; Mark 3:27–30; Luke 11:21–26.

of demons, I have actually had to bind "the strong man" in order to be able to plunder his possessions – as you now see me doing by delivering people of evil spirits through the power of the Holy Spirit.'

Jesus' teaching raises the question of exactly when he had bound the strong man. The context of Jesus' apologetic for his deliverance ministry indicates that this is a past event, which makes a reference to the cross inherently improbable.[8] The most probable occasion appears to be Jesus' forty days' prayer and fasting in the wilderness.[9] This possibility is given added weight by the implication in Matthew 4:2–3 that the specific temptations of Satan recorded by Matthew came at the very end of Jesus' forty days' fasting. Such a scenario also resolves the problem of why the Spirit drove Jesus into the wilderness, an event not easily explained simply in terms of Jesus' temptation.[10]

The exact identity of the 'strong man' is not clear in the synoptics. However, the context of Jesus' apologetic implies a reference to Beelzebul, which was probably originally a polemical Israelite epithet given either to the local Canaanite god Baal[11] or possibly the Philistine god Ekron,[12] and more specifically to the demon understood to be behind these pagan gods.[13] Jesus' statement, recorded in Matthew (12:25–26) and Mark (3:23–26) about Satan driving out Satan is probably best understood as referring to demons being cast out on behalf of Satan's kingdom, which is how Luke appears to interpret it (Luke 11:17–18).

---

8. S. H. T. Page, *Powers of Evil* (Leicester: Apollos, 1995), p. 106.
9. G. R. Beasley-Murray, *Jesus and the Kingdom of God* (Exeter: Paternoster, 1986), pp. 108–111; E. Best, *The Temptation and the Passion* (Cambridge: Cambridge University Press, 1990), pp. 12–15; J. S. Stewart, 'On a Neglected Emphasis in New Testament Theology', *SJT* 4 (1951), pp. 292–301, esp. pp. 297–298; N. T. Wright, *Jesus and the Victory of God* (London: SPCK, 1996), pp. 453–454.
10. Beasley-Murray, *Kingdom*, pp. 109–110.
11. F. F. Bruce, 'Baal-Zebub, Beelzebul', *NBD2*, p. 110.
12. H. Bietenhard, '*Diabolos*', *NIDNTT* 3, pp. 468–472.
13. Cf. Deut. 32:17; Ps. 106:37.

Matthew's account could conceivably mean that Beelzebul and Satan are understood as the same figure. However, Mark (3:22, 30) appears to rule out this possibility by stating that the Pharisees identified Beelzebul as an evil spirit (*pneuma akathartos*),[14] a term Mark, in common with all the New Testament writers, only ever applies to beings subordinate to Satan. Jews at the time appear to have understood the 'binding' of evil spirits to refer either to their eschatological imprisonment[15] or to their being restrained from all activity at least temporarily.[16] It is therefore noteworthy that the ensuing narratives in the synoptic gospels do not in any sense suggest that the gospel writers understood Satan to be bound.[17] The strong man Jesus bound must therefore be presumed to refer to a powerful spiritual being other than Satan himself.

According to Luke, Jesus immediately followed his comments on binding the strong man and plundering his possessions with the parable of the evil spirit returning to the empty house it had left (Luke 11:24–26). This juxtaposition implies that the house guarded by the strong man is the 'house of Israel', or possibly its central institution, the Jerusalem Temple.[18] Either way, failure to respond to Jesus' teaching will result in its coming under greater demonic influence than before. This may help explain why Matthew emphasizes that Jesus' deliverance ministry was essentially restricted to Israel;[19] that is, Jesus has bound the strong man over Israel and can therefore plunder his possessions by evicting demonic influence from people's lives.

---

14. *Contra* Best, *Temptation*, p. 11, who ignores the significance of Mark 3:30 despite his assertion that the verses in 3:24, 26 are a corporate reference to 'the whole assemblage of devils'.
15. Cf. 1 Enoch 10:4–6, 11–12; 18:13–16; 21:6; 54:5–6.
16. Tobit 8:3.
17. Cf. Matt.13:24–39; 16:23; Mark 4:15; 8:33; Luke 8:12; 22:3.
18. Wright, *Victory*, pp. 456–461, links this with the saying of Matt. 23:38 = Luke 13:35, 'your house is left to you desolate'.
19. Matt. 10:6–8; 15:24.

The early church

The detailed reference to Jesus' teaching on binding the strong man in all three synoptic Gospels suggests that the evangelists regarded it as of ongoing importance in the life of the church. The most likely reason for its significance is that it formed a core part of Jesus' teaching on deliverance from evil spirits, a ministry that he had specifically commissioned them to continue.[20]

Three further pieces of evidence also point to this conclusion. First, the synoptics portray Jesus' assault against the strong man's possessions as done by the power of the Holy Spirit.[21] This is particularly significant as the synoptic Gospels present a theology that indicates that whatever Jesus does by the power of the Holy Spirit, the church is expected to continue in the power of the same Spirit.[22] Secondly, Luke10:19 records Jesus' teaching that he has given his disciples authority to 'overcome *all* the power of the enemy' (*epi pasan tēn dynamin tou echthrou*). Thirdly, significant intertextual links exist between the synoptic 'strong man' passages and the discussion of powers and principalities in Ephesians 6:10–20. These include references to a demonic prince (Matt. 12:24 = Mark 3:22 = Luke 11:15; Eph. 6:12), to overcoming the enemy by the power of the Spirit (Matt. 12:28[23] = Eph. 6:17), and the use of similar language such as 'strength' (Matt.12:29 = Mark 3:27; Luke 11:21; Eph. 6:10) and 'armour' (Luke 11:22; Eph. 6:11, 13) to contrast the two kingdoms. The word armour (*ho panoplia*) is a particularly significant intertextual link as it occurs only in Luke's strong-man passage and Ephesians 6. This suggests that the

20. Matt. 10:5–8; Mark 3:14–15; Luke 9:1.

21. See Matt. 12:28–32; Mark 3:29, while the designation 'finger of God' in Luke 11:20 appears to equate with this.

22. Conversely, the church is clearly not intended to continue those acts clearly done by Jesus' own innate authority, such as sending the Spirit and delegating authority to others over sickness and evil spirits in his own name.

23. Also implied in Mark 3:29, while Luke 11:20's 'finger of God' equates to this.

armour on which the strong man relies (Luke 11:22) is being contrasted with the armour of God (Eph. 6:11–17).

Interestingly, Ephesians 6:17 exhorts the Ephesian church to fight with 'the sword of the Spirit, which is the word of God'. This teaching almost certainly reflects Jesus' use of Scripture as a weapon in the wilderness.[24] It therefore appears probable that Ephesians 6:10–20 is alluding both to Jesus' teaching on binding the strong man and to Jesus' time in the wilderness, which, we earlier observed, was the most likely occasion on which Jesus himself bound the strong man.

It therefore appears likely that, in both the churches for which the synoptic Gospels were written and in the Ephesian church, Jesus' teaching about binding the strong man was regarded as extremely important and of practical significance.

Limits to authority

It is significant that Jesus only bound 'the strong man'; the Gospels give no suggestion that he tried to evict him. Luke 11:21–22, in fact, implies that the strong man relies for his security on armour, presumably meaning lesser evil spirits and the hold they have over people. Jesus' teaching that this armour is taken away when people are set free from demonic influence in their lives points to a gradual undermining of the influence of the strong man rather than a direct attempt to evict him. Moreover, the purpose of binding the strong man is to divide up his spoil; that is, rescue people from demonic influence, rather than actually to try to evict the strong man himself.

If we are correct in seeing Jesus' forty days in the wilderness as the occasion on which he bound the strong man over Israel, then the synoptic Gospels caution against undertaking such encounters

24. F. F. Bruce, *The Epistles to the Colossians, to Philemon, and to the Ephesians*, *NICOT* (Grand Rapids: Eerdmans, 1984), p. 409; H. W. Hoehner, *Ephesians: An Exegetical Commentary* (Grand Rapids: Baker, 2002), pp. 852–853.

lightly. All three evangelists speak of Jesus being specifically sent by the Spirit into the wilderness, and record Jesus' lengthy fast. Luke also presents a theology in which, in the power of the Holy Spirit, the church continued to do 'all that Jesus began to do and teach' (Acts 1:1). However, this implies that Jesus' delegation of authority over the enemy (Luke 10:19) has been given to the church as a body, rather than for individuals to exercise on their own initiative. Ephesians 3:10 presents a similar theology, stating that it is through the church that the manifold wisdom of God is made known to the powers and authorities in the heavenly realms. This suggests that Ephesians 6 calls the whole church, rather than isolated individuals, to put on the armour of God and to struggle against the powers and principalities.

Personal ministry experience

The discussion which follows includes observations based on personal ministry experience and, as such, contains a subjective element. However, this does not negate its importance, as the New Testament provides ample precedent for interpreting the significance of spiritual experience in the light of Scripture. This chapter represents such a biblical theological reflection on pastoral practice.

Before we understood the need to 'bind the strong man', we might expect to struggle to evict a single demon for one to two hours before it finally left its victim, often manifesting significantly as it did so.[25] When we started to 'bind the strong man' we found that not only did demons leave much more quickly and with less struggle, but also that many more demons would leave the person. Moreover, some of these demons were powerful spirits, such as 'Leviathan' and 'Jezebel', that we had not previously realized were present.

---

25. I am indebted to John Webster of New Covenant Ministries for first drawing my attention to the importance of this subject in deliverance ministry.

Deliverance ministry normally begins by binding the strong man. Sometimes it is sufficient in general terms to bind all the strong men and cut off their influence from the person in the name of Jesus; at other times we have sensed the Lord giving us the names of specific strong men that need to be bound, such as 'Leviathan' or 'Antichrist'.

Sometimes, during times of worship, we have sensed God opening our eyes so that we can physically see some of the main spirits that are afflicting particular individuals present. At other times we have sensed God giving us discernment in the form of prophetic visions showing, for example, how particular spirits are working with other spirits to maintain their hold on a person. In both types of discernment we have subsequently discovered that some of the forms in which spirits such as Leviathan have been seen bear significant similarities to the biblical images used to describe them.

Specific strong men

Although Jesus speaks of, and appears to assume that his hearers were familiar with, the concept of demonic 'strong men', none of the New Testament writers claim to give a comprehensive exposition of them. What we do find, however, is specific local application of this concept. For example, Ephesians 6:12 starts by referring to these powers in general terms as 'rulers' and 'authorities',[26] but goes on to give a very specific local colour by the use of the term *ho kosmokrator*, meaning 'cosmic ruler'. This term was so widely understood in the Ephesus region as the principal accolade of Artemis that Paul appears to be deliberately referring to the demonic strong man behind Artemis-worship.[27] For Paul to use this term in Ephesus would have been the first-century equivalent of speaking about 'the White House' while standing in Pennsylvania Avenue, Washington; that is, everyone would know exactly what was being referred to unless one clearly defined one's terms otherwise.

---

26. RSV, 'principalities and powers'.
27. Cf. C. E. Arnold, *Ephesians: Power and Magic* (Cambridge: Cambridge University Press, 1989), pp. 67–68.

Paul's local application of Jesus' teaching on the strong man is instructive, as it indicates that Paul at least understood Jesus' teaching to mean that there were potentially a whole variety of different strong men that would be evident wherever the kingdom of Satan was active in opposing the kingdom of God.

The following list attempts to describe some of the 'strong men' (powers and principalities) that the Bible describes. It does not, however, in any sense claim to be comprehensive. Indeed, it is our experience of deliverance ministry that whenever any person or object is unduly given the sort of devotion or worship that rightfully belongs only to God, there is the real possibility, and indeed probability, of a demonic stronghold being established behind it.

In the following list the biblical exegesis is given first, followed by comments relating to how this particular strong man has been encountered in ministry situations.

Leviathan

The Old Testament refers on a number of occasions to Leviathan (*livyātān*). Job 41 describes Leviathan as a crocodile-like figure, but uses imagery, such as breathing fire (41:18–21), that implies that something more than a mere crocodile is being described.[28] Isaiah 27:1 similarly refers to YHWH eschatologically using his fierce, great and powerful sword to punish Leviathan the coiling serpent, the monster (*tannîn*) of the sea. Clearly, at least in Isaiah, a powerful spiritual being hostile to God is being described.[29] Psalm 74:13–14 refers to YHWH's having crushed the heads of Leviathan (*livyātān*) and broken the heads of the monster (*tannîn*) at the exodus when he divided the sea. The depiction therefore appears to be of a multi-headed monster, which was a spiritual power defeated by YHWH at the exodus.

28. J. E. Hartley, *The Book of Job*, *NICOT* (Grand Rapids: Eerdmans, 1988), pp. 521–522, who argues that the context demands that Behemoth and Leviathan are both terrestrial creatures and cosmic forces.

29. J. A. Motyer, *The Prophecy of Isaiah* (Leicester: IVP, 1993), p. 221, who links it with Isaiah 24:21's punishment of the heavenly powers.

Archaeological discoveries appear to indicate that a serpent-like spiritual being known by various names similar to Leviathan was widely known and feared by many people in the ancient Near East (ANE). The closest ANE parallel to the Old Testament depiction of Leviathan appears to be the Ugaritic Baal myth, in which Baal destroys Leviathan, the sea serpent.[30] Although some Old Testament scholars have claimed that the Old Testament has borrowed from the Baal myth,[31] this is inherently improbable, given the Old Testament's strong and incessant polemic against other ANE religions.[32] In fact, the Old Testament characterization of Leviathan is best understood as a polemical 'contextualization' against the Baal myth.[33] It is important to understand that this contextualization does not in any sense reject the existence of Leviathan as a hostile spiritual being, but in fact affirms its existence by asserting that it is YHWH, rather than Baal, who has defeated Leviathan. The occasion on which he did this was the exodus and crossing of the Red Sea; that is, Leviathan is implicitly identified as a spiritual power over Egypt at the time of the exodus.

The book of Job gives the most detailed description of Leviathan. Job 3:8 appears to refer to those in Job's day who were skilled in seeking to arouse Leviathan, implicitly by casting a spell that placed a curse sending Leviathan to afflict people.[34] Job 40 – 41 gives a detailed description of 'Behemoth', a beast from the

---

30. J. Day, *God's Conflict with the Dragon and the Sea* (Cambridge: Cambridge University Press, 1985), *passim*.

31. E.g. J. Van Henten, 'Dragon', in K. van der Toorn, B. Becking and P. W. van der Horst (eds.), *Dictionary of Deities and Demons in the Bible*, 2nd rev. edn (Leiden: Brill, 1999), pp. 265–267.

32. E.g. Exod. 20:1–6; Num. 25:1–5; this is a principal theme of Isa. 40 – 55.

33. A. H. W. Curtis, 'The "Subjugation of the Waters" Motif in the Psalms; Imagery or Polemic?', *JSS* 23 (1978), pp. 245–256; Day, *Dragon*, p. 27, also recognizes a polemical element against Baalism in Ps. 89:10–15 and other comparable passages.

34. Hartley, *Job*, p. 94; H. H. Rowley, *Job*, *NCB* (London: Oliphants, 1976), p. 41, cites archaeological evidence of such curses.

land. and 'Leviathan', a beast from the sea. Leviathan is described as causing dismay to go before him (41:22) and as being king over all that are proud (41:34).

The depiction of the beast from the land accompanied by a beast from the sea occurs again in Revelation 13. Revelation 13:1–18 clearly distinguishes both of these beasts from the dragon of 12:1 – 13:1, which has earlier been explicitly identified as Satan (12:9). Nonetheless, both the beast from the sea and the beast from the land are clearly depicted as evil spiritual powers that influence the whole world (13:3–4, 7–8). Revelation 13:1ff. describes the beast from the sea as having seven heads and ten horns and characterizes him as uttering 'proud' words, a characteristic similar to that which we earlier noted in Job's description of Leviathan. He is also described as having a worldwide dominion over every tribe, people, language and nation; blaspheming and slandering not only God but also those who live in heaven; making war on the saints; and receiving worship from all those who do not worship Christ. Revelation 16:13 additionally depicts other evil spirits described as being like frogs coming out of the mouths of the Dragon (presumably Satan, cf. Rev. 12:9), the beast from the sea and the false prophet respectively, suggesting that each of these three has lesser demonic beings under its control.

In ministry situations we have encountered two forms of Leviathan; one, related to pride, is often seen as a snake or dragon, while the other, related to dismay, is often seen as a large slug. We have consistently found Leviathan spirits to have lesser spirits, normally seven, closely associated with them, that have to be evicted in order to expel Leviathan.[35] We have also encountered situations similar to those described by Job, where people have become afflicted by a Leviathan spirit as a result of a curse.

---

35. R. Ing, *Spiritual Warfare* (New Kensington: Whitaker House, 1996), gives detailed accounts of similar ministry experiences in dealing with Leviathan (pp. 200–214) as well as accounts relating to Babylon/Jezebel (pp. 30–71), Antichrist (pp. 215–226) and Death and Hades (pp. 251–261), although his accompanying biblical exegesis is not consistently reliable.

Antichrist

The Johannine letters refer on a number of occasions to spirits called 'antichrist'.[36] 1 John 2:18 refers to the eschatological appearance of a specific antichrist (*antichristos*), but also speaks of the present existence of many, implicitly lesser, spirits of antichrist (*antichristoi polloi*). The 'antichrist' and the 'many antichrists' are spoken of in terms of being spirits (*pneuma*) (1 John 4:3) and also referred to as people through whom the spirits are operating (1 John 2:18–19). 1 John 4:3 characterizes the work of spirits of antichrist in general terms as seeking to prevent people 'confessing Jesus', while 1 John 2:22 and 2 John 1:7 more specifically refer to their promotion of denial that Jesus is the Messiah and that he has come in the flesh.

These latter statements need to be understood in the context of the way Christology is expressed in the Johannine literature. John's Gospel describes Jesus as 'the Word of God', the visible form in which God, who dwells in unapproachable light, relates to his creation as creator (1:1–3, 18), judge (5:22, 27) and so forth. The designation of Jesus as 'the Word of God' in the Gospel's prologue serves to define the title 'Son of God', which replaces it subsequently. Therefore, the characterization of spirits of antichrist – as denying Jesus coming in the flesh – appears primarily to refer to these spirits attempting to cause people to deny the biblical teaching of who God is; that is, that God is not merely Father, but also Son who became incarnate. This explains why 1 John 2:22 refers to the spirit of antichrist causing people to deny 'the Father and the Son'.

Revelation 13 appears to depict a further reference to the antichrist. As we observed above, this parallels Job 40:15 – 41:34 in depicting both a beast from the land and a beast from the sea. In Job these are identified by the names 'Behemoth' and 'Leviathan', although in Job it is unclear exactly what Behemoth denotes. However, in Revelation 13:11–18 this beast from the land is described in terms that parody Revelation's depiction of Christ:

---

36. 1 John 4:3; cf. also 2:18, 22; 2 John 1:7.

(a) He has two horns like a lamb, but speaks like a dragon (13:11). Christ was depicted as a Lamb earlier (5:6–13).
(b) Just as Christ exercises the Father's authority over all things (2:27; 12:10; 17:14), so the beast from the land exercises 'all the authority of the first beast on his behalf' (13:12).[37]
(c) The beast from the land causes the earth and its inhabitants to worship the beast from the sea (Rev. 13:11–17), who in turn causes people to worship the dragon (13:4). Revelation specifically contrasts this worship with worship of the Father and Christ inspired by the Spirit (5:6–14; 19:10; cf. 13:8, 12–15; 14:7, 11).[38]

Revelation 13 describes this second beast as performing signs and wonders that deceive men and women into worshipping the first beast, a worship that this second beast both instigates and enforces by intimidation. From Revelation 16:13 onwards the second beast is referred to as the false prophet (16:13; 19:20; 20:10), as his role is essentially that of being the spokesman for the first beast and misleading people with his message.[39]

In ministry situations we have encountered spirits of antichrist in relation to family or personal involvement in non-Christian religions. Ministry experience suggests that the spirit of antichrist is not normally the main spirit in these religions, but appears to work alongside it like an additional root that strengthens and supports the tree.

Babylon/Jezebel

Revelation uses two feminine images to denote the people of God (the woman giving birth to the Messiah and the Bride of Christ), and two to denote opposition to God (Jezebel and Babylon). This imagery ultimately derives from the Old Testament depiction of God as the husband of his sometimes unfaithful people.

---

37. Interestingly, the first beast's own authority has been given to him by the dragon (Rev. 13:2).
38. However, attempts to find here a parody of the Trinity ill fit the text.
39. R. G. Bratcher, *A Translator's Guide to the Revelation to John* (London: United Bible Societies, 1984), p. 132.

In Revelation, Christ's bride is characterized by dependence on God her husband (12:6, 14; 19:8); she is beautifully dressed for him (19:7–8; 21:2) and united with him (21:2–3), and reflects her husband's glory (21:9–11, 23). However, Babylon/Jezebel is characterized by defiance of God (2:20–21; 17:5; 18:7–8), she dresses for her own splendour (17:4–5; 18:14–17), engages in adultery rather than faithful union (2:20–22; 17:2, 5) and is concerned only for herself (2:21; 18:3–7, 14).[40]

These antithetical feminine images form a symmetrical literary framework in the structure of Revelation. The woman who gives birth to the Messiah (12:1–17) and Babylon (17:1 – 18:24) stand either side of the centre of the book, while Jezebel (2:20–25) and the Bride of Christ (21:1 – 22:6)[41] form an *inclusio*, framing almost the entire book of Revelation. The use of similar images, words, phrases and ideas within these four passages further strengthens the links between them.[42]

Although Revelation contrasts Babylon with the Bride of Christ, the depiction of Babylon suggests that it refers to somewhat more than just human beings who are opposed to God. In fact, a number of descriptive elements in Revelation 17 actually distinguish Babylon from humans. She is described as the great prostitute who 'sits on' (*kathēmenēs epi*) many waters (17:1), these waters subsequently being identified as the 'peoples, multitudes, nations and languages' of the earth (17:15); the kings of the earth are said to commit adultery *with* her (*meth hes eporneusan*) (17:2); while the inhabitants of the earth are similarly intoxicated *with* the wine of *her* adulteries (17:2). It therefore appears that in Revelation, 'Babylon' refers both to a spiritual power of evil and to the human beings through whom that spirit operates. This parallels our earlier observation that John uses 'antichrist' to refer both to the 'spirit of antichrist' and to those through whom that particular spirit operates.

---

40. Cf. P. B. Duff, *Who Rides the Beast* (Oxford: Oxford University Press, 2001), pp. 90–93.
41. The anticipation of this in Rev. 19:6–9 does not negate this, but simply gives it a 'forward momentum'.
42. Duff, *Beast*, pp. 83–84.

Four aspects stand out in Revelation's description of Babylon: sexual immorality, witchcraft, domination and murder.

First, the descriptive title 'mother of prostitutes and of the abominations of the earth' (17:5) implies that she is in some way the spiritual source of sexual immorality, although the word abominations (*bdelygma*) probably widens this to include religious practices described in the Old Testament as detestable to YHWH.[43]

Secondly, 18:23 speaks of her having led the nations astray by her 'magic spell', the word *pharmakeia* suggesting the image of a magical potion, which echoes the earlier statement of 17:2 that Babylon has 'intoxicated' the earth's inhabitants with her adulteries; that is, Babylon is characterized as a source of magic enchantment.

Thirdly, 17:18 speaks of Babylon as 'the great city that rules over the kings of the earth'. However, 18:6–7 indicates that her rule is not a just rule, but a wrongful domination that has brought torture and grief to the innocent while she has grown rich from excessive luxuries (18:3, 9).

Fourthly, Babylon is also characterized as the spiritual source of the persecution of God's saints, prophets and apostles (18:20) as well as of *all* killing that has taken place on earth (*pantōn tōn esphagmenōn epi tēs gēs*) (18:24).

The latter is one of a number of factors that point to Babylon as a global power. While first-century Rome clearly is particularly in view (17:9–10), Revelation also refers figuratively to Babylon as 'Sodom' and 'Egypt', speaks of it as the place where Christ was crucified (11:8; 16:19), and applies to her language originally applied to Old Testament Babylon (18:2). She is also depicted as sitting on the Leviathan beast, which, we earlier saw, had worldwide dominion (13:3–4, 7–8) and herself described as having spiritual influence over all of the world's nations (17:1, 5; 18:3). Revelation therefore appears to depict Babylon as a global spiritual power opposed to God.

---

43. Cf. the use of *bdelygma* in the Septuagint of Isa. 66:3; Dan. 9:27; 11:31; 12:11 and in Matt. 24:15 = Mark 13:14.

However, when addressing a local situation in Thyatira, Revelation uses remarkably similar descriptions to refer to a person to whom it gives the polemical epithet of 'Jezebel'.[44] This designation suggests that she bears similar characteristics to the aggressive Old Testament queen who effectively usurped her husband's headship and led God's people into idolatry and its incumbent sexual immorality.[45]

Revelation describes Babylon and Jezebel using a cluster of similar images and descriptions. There are only four feminine images in Revelation and, as we earlier noted, the literary structure of Revelation sets Jezebel as the antithesis to the Bride of Christ in a manner similar to the contrast between Babylon and the woman who gave birth to the Christ child in Revelation 12. This suggests that there is a degree of equivalence between Babylon and Jezebel.[46]

Both are also characterized by the use of (perverted) maternal imagery as being the source of sexual immorality (2:20–23; 17:5). Moreover, several aspects of the description of Babylon in Revelation 17 – 18 appear deliberately to echo the Old Testament Jezebel: for example, her designation of herself as a queen (18:7) who spilt the blood of prophets (17:6; 18:24), and whose flesh was devoured by beasts (17:16). It therefore appears that Revelation deliberately portrays Jezebel as being on the local scale what Babylon is on a global scale.

Moreover, both Jezebel's equivalence to Babylon and the description of her as a source of immorality and leading astray suggests that, in a way similar to Babylon, Jezebel denotes both a spiritual power and the human beings in opposition to God in whom this spirit operates. The identification of Jezebel as a spiritual power

---

44. G. Campbell, 'Antithetical Feminine-Urban Imagery and a Tale of Two Women Cities in the Book of Revelation', *TB* 55/1 (2004), pp. 81–108; cf. esp. pp. 84–85.

45. Sexual immorality is strongly implied by Jezebel's promotion of the fertility cult of Asherah (1 Kgs 18:19).

46. Duff, *Beast*, who devotes ch. 5 (pp. 83–96) of his work to a detailed study of the equivalence between Jezebel and Babylon in Revelation.

hostile to God is further confirmed both by the description of Jezebel as seeking to lead God's people astray (*planaō*, a verb that elsewhere in Revelation is used only for spirits hostile to God),[47] and by God's people being told to come out from the influence of Jezebel/Babylon so that *they* do not share in *her* sins (2:22; 18:4).

In ministry situations we have encountered three main forms of the Jezebel spirit, related to domination, sexual immorality and witchcraft. We have found Jezebel to be one of the most difficult spirits to evict, often hiding its presence behind other spirits. We have also frequently discovered Jezebel holding on to Leviathan as means of maintaining her position, a situation that parallels the portrait of Babylon in Revelation 17:3. Jezebel/Babylon appears to be one of the most aggressive spirits, and a person afflicted by such a spirit (whether he or she knows it or not) is particularly likely to attack church leaders and those with prophetic gifting. Where the person afflicted is a married woman, it is also extremely common to find her exercising an unhealthy degree of marital domination. All of these characteristics closely parallel the biblical depiction of Jezebel/Babylon.

Other strong men

We observed above that Ephesians 6 appears to take the principle of the existence of strong men who need to be bound from the teaching of Jesus and applies it to the local situation at Ephesus. In a similar manner the biblical material outlined above points to the potential existence of other demonic strong men. Those we have encountered in ministry situations include strong men of death,[48] mind control, witchcraft and rebellion, murder and violence, religion, rejection, accusation, and deceit and deception, as well as strong men related to non-Christian belief systems such as Freemasonry.

---

47. Satan (Rev. 12:9; 20:3, 8, 10); the beast from the earth/false prophet/antichrist (13:14; 19:20); Babylon (18:23).

48. Limitations of space prevent discussion of 'Death' here, but cf. the depiction of the four horsemen including 'death' in Rev. 6:1–8 as the antithesis of the spirits of heaven in Zech. 1:8–11; 6:1–9.

Conclusions

The biblical material discussed above suggests that, far from the Bible saying almost nothing about 'powers and principalities', it both acknowledges their existence and gives specific examples of them. The repetition by all three synoptic Gospels of Jesus' teaching on binding the strong man, and the echoes of this elsewhere in the New Testament, suggest that this was an important theme in the early church, probably because it was understood to form a core part of Jesus' teaching on deliverance from evil spirits.

6 THE SURA–ASURA THEME IN HINDUISM

Theodore Gabriel

This chapter centres on the hypothesis that, contrary to popular views, the sura–asura dichotomy in Hinduism does not represent a stark distinction between good and evil, but rather embodies contrasts in the nature of beings in the pre-creation and post-creation worlds. This hypothesis will be tested against Vedic mythology, Samkhya philosophy, Advaitic philosophy and sociological concepts.

The idea of angels and demons is clearly a Judeo-Christian-Islamic concept that does not find a true equivalent in Hinduism. This is probably due to contrasts in creation accounts in the two faiths. Angels and demons are not totally opposed categories in Hinduism as in the Christian sense. Angels as pure, good heavenly beings and devils as unmitigated evil personified and opposing everything good are not to be found in the Hindu pantheon. However, a close parallel can be found in the concepts of sura and asura. In spite of its apparent polytheism, most Hindus would aver that God is one – 'Bhagwan ek hai' is a common saying among them. This would indicate that, at least in contemporary times, there is the general consciousness that Hinduism is monotheistic or rather monistic in the ultimate analysis. Other than the supreme beings of Brahma (a personification of the ultimate reality, the impersonal Brahman) and Vishnu and Shiva, who are comparable to God or Yahweh in the Semitic sense, the great number of other deities and spiritual beings form a corpus roughly equivalent to what is termed angels in the Judeo-Christian-Islamic tradition. Apparently there is a great host of these beings in Hindu belief. In addition to pan-Indian deities such as Vishnu, Shiva and Krishna, there are also regional gods such as the Ayyappan and Muttappan of Kerala. The 33 million gods (gods with a small g), demigods (including sons of gods such as Arjuna and Bhima), various celestial beings like Gandharvas, Kinnaras (celestial musicians), apsaras (celestial nymphs), and theriomorphic deities such as Airavata the elephant, Nandi the bull, Garuda the eagle, and Sesha the serpent, can perhaps be equated with angels as beings on the side of the gods and good, while asuras, rakshasas, yakshas, yakshis (usually known for drinking human blood like vampires of Western legends), and bhutas (horrible-looking spirits guarding the abode of Shiva and some other gods) can perhaps be looked upon as demons, evil and malevolent beings opposed to the gods.

However, the categorization of suras as virtuous and asuras as evil is neither precise nor valid. For among the asuras there are virtuous figures such as Bali, or Prahlada, and there are many a rakshasa, like Sukeshin, who have meditated upon and worshipped gods such as Shiva and acquired great boons and powers. On the other hand, there are gods who have committed actions which are less than perfect, gods who have been amoral, gods who have resorted to devious stratagems and in many ways compromised the notion of gods being holy. Moreover, there are hints in Hindu myths and beliefs which may even suggest that the asuras, who pre-existed the suras, actually denote stability and virtue in the world, while suras stand for dynamism and disruption. Varuna, a great asura who later joined the suras, is said to be the guardian of the moral order, being the conserver of Rta (cosmic law and truth). In the Vishnu Purana the gods tell Brahma, 'Even though we and the demons are both born of portions of you, nevertheless we see the universe as divided, a distinction caused by ignorance (*avidya*).

Varuna

The demons are virtuous.'[1] This clearly shows that the suras and asuras are both creations of Brahma or rather emanations from the Brahman, and, while the asuras are not under the grip of *avidya* (ignorance), the suras are, since they fall short of the monistic understanding of creation. That the early suras were almost personifications of natural powers shows that they are closely related to the phenomenal world. The asuras are thus virtuous or in *moksha* (liberation), and the suras have not attained this state.

There are hints in the Rg Veda that Varuna is the same as Vishnu. Vishnu at rest is lord of the primeval waters as Varuna is. Zaehner states: 'Varuna is not only guardian of the moral order but also of Maya' (the world of appearances).[2] And Brahman is the creator of the world of *maya*. In a sense the primordial world is the reality and the world of duality the illusion. Salvation thus might be the return to the undifferentiated world of unity that pre-existed the present world of appearances and differentiation. In that sense the role of asuras, while confrontational with gods in

1. W. D. O'Flaherty, *The Origins of Evil in Hindu Mythology* (London: University of California Press, 1980), p. 60.
2. R. C. Zaehner, *Hinduism* (Oxford: Oxford University Press, 1966), p. 29.

the sense of belonging to an entirely different world order, need not be evil and demonic, as they appear to be categorized in later texts of Hinduism.

Mircea Eliade writes:

> The Vedic mythology and religions presents us with a situation which is at first sight paradoxical. On the one hand there is a distinction, opposition and conflict between the Devas and Asuras, the gods and demons, the powers of Light and Darkness. But on the other hand, numerous myths bring out the consubstantiality or brotherhood of the Devas and Asuras. One has the impression that Vedic doctrine is at pains to establish a double perspective: although as an immediate reality, and as the world appears to our eyes, the Devas and the Asuras are irreconcilably different by nature and condemned to fight each other, before the creation or before the world took its present form they were consubstantial. What is true of eternity is not necessarily true in time.[3]

Thus the asuras may be children of eternity and the suras temporal. Moreover, it may not be precise to state that the asuras represent darkness. Because the categories of light and darkness came at the beginning of the present creation and the emergence of duality, asuras must represent a state when such a duality of light and darkness was non-existent, rather than darkness itself.

The word 'asura' in later Hinduism certainly has the connotation of being demonic and evil, though many great gods of Hinduism have, in the earliest scriptures, such as the Rg Veda, been termed asuras. These include Indra, Varuna, Agni, Soma and Mithra. Indeed, the cognate word 'Ahura' in the Zoroastrian religion implies the Supreme Being, while Deiva (sura or Deva in Hinduism) stands for forces of evil. This is a complete reversal of the terminology of Hinduism as it is understood today.

The asuras seem to be deities of the pre-creation period who dwelt in the primeval waters (perhaps comparable to the pre-creation waters in Genesis over which the spirit of God hovered). This state of stability and undifferentiated unity comes to an end

---

3. Quoted in O'Flaherty, *Origins of Evil*, p. 59.

when the god Indra calls forth, from the waters heaven and earth, light and darkness, *sat–asat* (being and non-being) and many other dualities. It is apparent that the primeval waters had contained the germs of life, for a small clod of earth came to the surface, floated about and became a mountain which was the repository of life forces. The god Indra is the agent of the creation of the world of reality from this world of potentiality by fighting against Vrtra (lit. resistance), often portrayed as a dragon, whom he slays, releasing four rivers which flow down the slope of the hills, and fire, which becomes the sun. The origins of Indra himself are unknown. Since the term 'asura' is applied to him, it is possible that he was a more adventurous member of the asuras who wanted to venture forth from the stability of the primordial world. Zaehner terms Indra's actions a takeover bid.[4] Zaehner states: 'Indra is an upstart king. Varuna on the other hand, the great asura, guardian of the cosmic law, was universal monarch from the beginning.'[5] This shows the supremacy and precedence of asuras in Hindu mythology. All creativity is in a sense disturbing the status quo.

Now, along with the many dualities of the new world, a new class of beings known as the suras or Devas arose, led by Indra (a name which merely means 'a king'), and the asuras remain confined to the nether world of the primordial waters, upon which the new world is believed to rest. It is interesting that the Supreme Being, Vishnu (termed Saguna Brahman or Brahman with qualities by Ramanuja), is portrayed as sleeping in this cosmic sea. The act of sleeping is evocative of a state of peace, stability and rest, denoting the primordial stability before the emergence of the new world of dualities.

Some of the asuras later became Devas and are classed as Devah asura and the others as Adevah asura. Though the primeval war has been won by the suras, the potential of danger remains, and the asuras remain as a threat to the new world of the cosmos. The asuras remain in the nether waters as a potential source of reversion to the undifferentiated world. Vishnu's Varaha (boar)

---

4. Zaehner, *Hinduism*, p. 27.
5. Ibid., p. 26.

avatar happens when the asura Hiranyaksha drags the world to the bottom of the cosmic ocean, testifying to the fact that the asuras can restore the world to its former status. In this particular incident Vishnu fights Hiranyaksha, kills him and lifts the world up out of the cosmic waters. Vishnu and Hiranyaksha here symbolize the opposing forces of the two world orders. Thus, like Indra, Vishnu here takes the world back to its present dualistic form after it had been restored temporarily to its pre-creation undifferentiated status. In Hinduism the cosmos is cyclical, and the end of the world in *pralaya* (flood) also perhaps denotes a reversion of the universe to its pre-creation status. The metaphor of water is a common link between the destruction of the phenomenal world and its return to its pre-creation status. Creation then will commence anew (probably someone like Indra will come along to initiate the process), and thus the cycle will go on.

The most notable asura who goes over to the side of the gods is Varuna, who is considered as a powerful god, the guardian of morality and lord of the waters, the latter term implying that he still has something to do with the nether world of the asuras. Indeed, in the Mahabharatha there is mention of Varuna being attended by asuras. An attempt has been made to resolve this anomaly by considering Varuna to be the gaoler of the asuras.[6] Varuna thus remains a liminal figure, mediating between the sura and asura worlds. The god of death, Yama, is another such figure. Zaehner suggests that Varuna is the same as Vrtra (both names come from a root meaning 'to envelop'), indicting that Varuna is a force that resists the creation of the world of dualities and therefore a force associated more with the primordial undifferentiated world of stability than with the world of appearances, to which he has later been appropriated.[7] It is possible that the suras are merely asuras who have been called by Indra to be gods, beings of supremacy in the new world of activity and duality from the primordial state of stability and undifferentiation of the universe.

---

6. Mentioned in F. B. J. Kuiper, 'Basic Concept of Vedic Religion', *History of Religions* 15/2 (1975), p. 115.
7. Zaehner, *Hinduism*, p. 29.

The close causal link between the two is reflected in the Rg Vedic verse, which states that *sat* was born of *asat*.[8]

The asuras are certainly not unmitigated personifications of evil, such as the fallen angels of Christendom. Kuiper calls them potential gods.[9] And the relationship of sura and asura is not always one of confrontation. A great act of co-operation between them is the churning of the primordial waters, another creation story in Hindu mythology but one of lesser cosmic significance than the story of Indra and the slaying of Vrtra.

The churning of the primordial ocean is necessitated by the need for gods to acquire immortality. Ambrosia and nectar are required to preserve their life. It is significant that immortality is conferred by the primordial waters, indicating clearly that the pre-creation state is the state of *moksha* and eternal life. Immortality rises out of these waters in the form of ambrosia and nectar (*amrt*). Creation takes place by the churning of the waters or disturbing the tranquillity of the primeval ocean. The gods and demons come together in this great act, the gods holding to the tail, and the asuras to the head, of the great serpent Vasuki and using Mount Mandara as a churning stick. Many objects come out of it: the celestial elephant Airavata, the goddess Lakshmi, Uchisravas the celestial horse, Chandra the moon. It is significant that one of the products of the churning is Kalakuta, the deadly poison which could have destroyed the universe but for the timely act of Shiva, who swallowed this and became *Nilakanta* (the Blue-throated) when the poison stuck in his gullet. Thus creative activity is shown to be a productive as well as a dangerous act, giving rise not only to life but also to grave danger and death. Life and death are thus one of the pair of dualities that this act of creation generates. The pot of nectar which comes up is said to represent the *Brahmanda Kataha* (the cauldron of the egg of Brahma or the universe) in which Brahman lies in *amrt* (nectar) form. It is said that when the ambrosia comes the asuras get hold of it, again signifying their predominance on the question of eternity and

---

8. Rg Veda 10.72.2, quoted in Kuiper, *Vedic Religion*, p. 116.

9. Kuiper, *Vedic Religion*, p. 114.

immortality. But the god Vishnu is said to have tricked the ambrosia out of their hands by assuming a beautiful female form, the Mohini, clearly a symbol for *maya* (illusion), which is the characteristic of the new universe. According to O'Flaherty, the theme of suras stealing from asuras extends also to Agni and Soma, the sacrifices and the entire universe denoting asura superiority over the sura.[10]

Samkhya philosophy

The Samkhya school, founded by Kapila (sixth century BC) admits two basic metaphysical principles, *purusha* (soul) and *prakriti* (materiality). *Prakriti* consists of three *gunas* or qualities: *sattva* (light or goodness), *rajas* (activity or passion), and *tamas* (darkness or inertia). When these constituents are in equilibrium, *prakriti* is static. However, disturbance of the equilibrium initiates a process of evolution that ultimately produces both the material world and individual faculties of action, thought, and sense. The *purusha* appears to be bound to *prakriti* and its modifications, and may become free only through the realization that it is distinct from *prakriti*.

It is clear that the pre-creation state of the universe (described as a primeval ocean) corresponds to the *sattva guna*. Kesarcodi-Watson associates *sattva* with Brahman, the ultimate reality.[11] Indra as denoting the dynamic active principle generating the world of dualities belongs clearly to *rajas* (as his name Indra, 'king', also reveals). Indra is evidently an apotheosis of the Kshatriya, the warrior-king. An assessment by Samkhya philosophy would therefore deem the asuras to be associated with *sattva*, rather than with *tamas* (darkness and dissolution), as later Vedic texts seem to imply. Of course, the metamorphosis of the asuras Indra, Varuna and Agni etc. to suras would indicate that they have moved from the *sattva* to the *rajas guna* mode.

10. O'Flaherty, *Origins of Evil*, p. 121.

11. I. Kesarcodi-Watson, 'Devas', *Religious Studies* 12/D (1976), p. 470.

Advaitic (non-dualistic or monistic) philosophy

The Advaitic philosophy sometimes known as Vedanta refers to the ultimate reality in which the entire cosmos is subsumed. Self-awareness is the key to achieving union with the ultimate. The aphorisms *aham brahmasmi*, *tat tvam asi* and *Brahma satyam Jagat mithya*[12] indicate turning towards one's real self.

Brahman is the ultimate reality, while the suras and perhaps the asuras, especially in the dualistic sense, are imperfect manifestations of the Brahman. They are closer to the Brahman than ordinary mortals, except for the great sages and others who have attained enlightenment and are far ahead of the two. The asuras of the pre-creation period, existing in the primal waters and beyond time, are closer to the Brahman than are the suras, since they precede the world of delusion, of differentiation, of temporality and dualities. Of course, this is not the view that is taken in later Vedic texts, which portray the demons as much lower than men and far from the state of self-awareness and enlightenment. But this is only a crystallization of human perspectives into mythology in a Levi-Straussian sense, and goes against the general view taken by the Rg Veda.

Kesarcodi-Watson opines that the Devas symbolize particular aspects of the ultimate but are still in the realm of *maya* and in the ultimate analysis do not exist, even as human souls, while seeming to be individual centres of consciousness, in reality do not exist in differentiation from the Brahman.[13]

Good demons and bad gods

That the suras and asuras represent irrevocably good and evil in later Hinduism is compromised by certain anomalous figures in the pantheon. Though later Vedic Hinduism represents asuras as

---

12. 'I am the Brahman'; 'You are that'; 'Brahma is the truth, the world is illusion.'
13. Kesarcodi-Watson, *Devas*, p. 468.

mortal, disruptive and prone to evil actions, there are quite a few who are virtuous, peaceful and compassionate. One of the interesting figures is Shukra, who is said to be the grandson of Hiranyakashipu, the evil demon king killed by the Narasimha avatar of Vishnu. Shukra is as knowledgeable as Brihaspathi (Lord of Prayer), and powerful, and is immortal, unlike the other asuras. Shukra has the secret of reviving the dead. He has many spiritual insights and was able to warn Bali when Vishnu appeared before him as the Vamana, a Brahmin boy, to bring about Bali's downfall, though his advice was disregarded. Bali is an asura but a virtuous one. His reign is said to be the golden age of the world, and that, too, within Kaliyuga, the age of evil. In Kerala the festival of Onam commemorates Bali's reign and is the national festival. Bali, though virtuous, was vanquished and sent to *Patala* (hell) by Vishnu, who appeared in the guise of a Brahmin boy. Bali readily granted the Brahmin boy's request to give him land which he could measure in three steps. Bali knew well who the boy was, but was said to be honoured that Vishnu had come personally to meet him. The boy grew and grew until his head was lost to view in the heavens. With his first and second steps the avatar measured the entire heavens and earth, and then asked Bali where he should measure the third step. Bali asked him to step on his own head, whereupon Vishnu stepped on Bali's head and pushed him to the nether world. Bali's removal from the world was deemed necessary because he was upsetting the established order by his virtue. His virtue had compromised the evil of Kali Yuga. One interpretation could, however, be that the touch of Vishnu conferred *moksha* on Bali, since the nether world could just be the sea of immortality, the primeval ocean, where Bali rightfully belonged as an asura. Bali, the virtuous asura, has no place in the world of *maya*, where suras and asuras have come to represent good and evil.

Prahlada is another outstanding example of the virtuous demon, especially in Bhakti texts, where he is portrayed as a devotee of Vishnu and is taken to task by his father Hiranyakashipu for not being true to his svadharma (true nature) as an asura. Prahlada remains loyal to Vishnu and faces the wrath of his father, who is eventually killed by Narasimha, the man-lion avatar of Vishnu. In the *Mahabharatha*, Prahlada is an asura who conquered all the three worlds (heaven, earth and hell) through his virtue, but Indra steals his virtue from him, disguised as a Brahmin, and Prahlada's powers are broken.

Similarly, Sukeshin the rakshasa taught virtue and *sanatana dharma* (the eternal righteousness) to demons, which caused an imbalance in the world. The brilliance of rakshasas, who practised dharma, is said to have paralysed the sun, moon and stars. The Sun god, angered by this, cast enemy-destroying rays on the rakshasa city and destroyed it.

The idea in some myths seems to be that when demons do not practise their own dharma, which in the case of rakshasas is to rape and steal, and begin practising the dharma of gods, there will be imbalance in the world order, which is based on the duality of sura and asura, and a disruption of the cosmic order, which seems to be reliant on the performance of *svadharma* by all.

The problem of the evil god

Myths abound in instances of gods who perform unethical and amoral actions. Indra was cursed by the sage Agastya when he entered into a liaison with the sage's unsuspecting wife Ahalya by taking Agasthya's form when the sage had gone for his morning ablutions. Indra becomes *sahasra bhaga* and Ahalya, though innocent, is turned into stone. Even Krishna, whose mission as an avatar of Vishnu was to uphold virtue, resorts to trickery in the slaying of Drona and Jayadhrada. He even coaxes Yudhishtira, the embodiment of dharma, to tell a lie regarding the death of Aswathama, Drona's son. Gods of pestilence, such as Rudra, Mariyamman, the smallpox goddess, and Bhadra Kali, often portrayed in horrifying forms (*paisachika*), are also instances of this ambivalence. These gods can curse as well as bless. For instance, Mariyamman can cause the dreaded disease of smallpox as well as cure it. The Atharvana Veda calls Rudra 'murderous and fearful' and the Vedanta Sutra calls him a robber, cheat and deceiver, whereas elsewhere his hand is described as 'soothing, healing and cool'. [14]

Generally Hindu myths portray both good and evil as originating in the creator god Brahma. Prajapati is said to be the progenitor of both the suras and the asuras, the asuras being the elder. The virtue of the sura and the evil of the asura are not so clear cut, even in the Smriti literature. The asuras seem to be in confrontation with the gods and seeking world domination rather than committing acts which are intrinsically evil. The evil actions they commit are in the course of their conflict with the gods. Even the sin of the egregious Mahisha – an asura for whose destruction the goddess Durga was created by the fusion of the powers of the Trimurthui – Vishnu, Shiva and Brahma – was dominating and reducing the gods to the rank of his servants.[15] Domination of the three worlds might be symbolic of attempts to revert the world order to its pristine, undivided form rather than the urge to conquer, rule, terrorize and persecute the denizens of the world. This is a debatable issue, but it conforms to the thesis stated at the outset of this chapter: that the suras and asuras belong to totally different world orders and epochs of time, rather than being opposing entities in confrontation in the contemporary world and age, representing absolutes of good and evil.

Sociological interpretation of the sura–asura divide

One interpretation of the sura–asura theme could be based on race, associating the two with the Dravidians and the Aryans. The Aryans, who were tall, fair and long-nosed, detested the shorter, snub-nosed and swarthy Dravidians, whom they termed as the Dasas (servants) and Dasyus. Nicholas Wyatt opines that the term 'Dasa' is related to the word *desha* (land) and refers to the original

---

14. Atharvana Veda 11.2.18; Vedanta Sutra 16.20–21; and Rg Veda 2.33.7, quoted in Zaehner, *Hinduism*, p. 33.
15. N. Wyatt, 'Devas and asuras in Early Indian Religious Thought', *Scottish Journal of Religious Studies* 7/1 (Spring 1986), p. 72.

inhabitants of the land. It is also possible that the term is related to *Varna dharma* (the caste system), and the Dasa or Dasyus might represent either the Shudra or the untouchable social categories. So the suras and asuras might be the reification of racial or social differences. Zaehner remarks that the rivalry between Varuna and Indra reflects the tensions between Brahmin priest and the Kshatriya kings in the social order.[16] Edward Hale opines that the word '*asura*' must originally have meant only 'Lord', and its use to indicate the lords of enemy forces, that is, leaders of the non-Aryan indigenous people of India, might have caused the eventual denigration of the term to mean 'evil beings'.[17] Alternatively, these might be the deities worshipped by the two races or castes. Thus the asuras who represent the Dasas and constitute a threat to Aryan hegemony might have been categorized as evil and demonic.

Conclusion

In conclusion, the sura and asura are two of the most misunderstood categories in Hinduism. This is to some extent due to the depiction of the two groups in later Hindu texts, and also the result of the rise of the Bhakti tradition. Moreover, a Hindu theodicy perhaps requires the existence of opposing forces in the world to account for the sin and suffering of the world. The Indologist Holwell writes: 'How much more rational and sublime the text of Brahman which supposes the deity's voluntary creation, or permission of evil for the exaltation of a race of beings, whose goodness as free agents could not have existed without being endued with the contrasted, or opposite powers of evil.' [18] Referring again to Samkhya philosophy, it may be possible to postulate that the states of *rajas* and *tamas* will necessarily involve evil.

---

16. Zaehner, *Hinduism*, p. 22.
17. W. E. Hale, *Asura in Early Vedic Religion* (Delhi: Motilal Banarsidass, 1986), pp. 180–181.
18. Quoted in O'Flaherty, *Origins of Evil*, pp. 46–47.

Only the state of Brahman, the state of stillness, the state of *sattva*, the state of non-duality, will be absolutely devoid of evil. If the asuras represent a state of tranquillity, a world order related to the *sattva guna*, then they certainly cannot be considered as evil beings. The fact that Varuna, the great asura, is normative of law, morality and order indicates the opposite. The metamorphosis of the asuras to demons happens only in the new world order of dualities or in *maya* when they are considered as evil beings in opposition to the holy suras and a threat to the new cosmos. But a closer examination reveals that they are evil only in relation to the ascendancy of the suras, and not from any intrinsic defect of their nature. Evil in Hinduism seems to be the result of the creation of a world of dualities from the world of undifferentiation.

7 THE MANTHIRAVADI: A SOUTH INDIAN WOUNDED WARRIOR-HEALER

Chris Gnanakan

'The world is, to a degree at least, the way we imagine it,' wrote Wink, and 'through the lens of our world view we make sense of our experiences.'[1] This statement rings true when discussing South Indian understandings of illness and healing. As Bergunder has observed, 80% of the Indian population follow popular religions and 'are looking for a power or person who is capable to save, heal and solve the problems of their lives'.[2] It is in this contextual situation that I explore the significant role of the *manthiravadi* – a Hindu shamanic healer who aids those afflicted with illness in the process of detecting its causes and offering remedies.

The manthiravadi as a traditional spiritual healer ritually uses mantras (incantations) to contact and control spirits. This exorcist

---

1. W. Wink, *The Powers That Be: Theology for a New Millennium* (New York: Augsburg, 1998), p. 14.
2. M. Bergunder, 'Miracle Healing and Exorcism: The South Indian Pentecostal Movement in the Context of Popular Hinduism', *India Church Growth Quarterly* 8/2 (2001), p. 12.

offers a focal point around which the aspirations of the sick with concepts of deliverance and care may be examined. After exploring the worldview, causative factors and curative means that warrant this healer's services, I will argue that this key figure is a wounded healer as much as a warrior-healer.

Spiritual powers in South India: Hindu deities, demigods and demons

In Indian cosmology all forms of existence, spirit or matter, inanimate stones or infinite reality, belong to *prana* – one unifying vital life force.[3] There is no categorical difference between creator and creature, seen and unseen, or human and non-human, and plausible boundaries are blurred. Hiebert's analytical framework usefully correlates the unseen (pure spirit) in the heavens/other world with lower empirical forms (pure matter) in the natural world. A Western dualistic, deterministic worldview often develops a 'blind spot' to a mezzanine level which Hiebert popularized as 'the flaw of the excluded middle'.[4] Within this category are supernatural but this-worldly spirits or demonic entities. These forces of evil come to the fore when analysing spiritual causes in the battle against *diseases*.

Hindu cosmology locates gods, goddesses and spiritual powers in a hierarchical system. Anthropologists like Weightman place them under four categories in relation to the South Indian socio-religious beliefs.[5] These can be discussed from the top down, where the lowest is regarded as most responsible for afflicting sickness. At the highest level is *Brahman*, the divine Lord Bhagvan,

---

3. A. Beal, *Gopalpur: A South Indian Village* (New York: Harcourt Brace College Publishers, 1980), p. 48.
4. P. Hiebert, *Anthropological Reflections on Missiological Issues* (Grand Rapids: Baker, 1994), pp. 189–201. See ch. 5 above for a fuller discussion of this theory.
5. S. Weightmen, *Hinduism in the Village Setting* (Milton Keynes: Open University Press, 1978), p. 26.

impersonal but considered as ultimate reality. Brahman is held in awe as sacred and unapproachable. No ritual worship is attached beyond recognizing it as the source and final goal for existence. Often whatever is accepted as fate is automatically associated with Brahman or unknownness.

Devas comprise a second level of mythological deities, like Rama, Krishna and Durga, who embody supreme reality. The mighty deeds of these gods call for human commemoration and celebrations. The celebrations are myriad, often customized and personalized for each tribe or family. In this way, popular Hinduism is polytheistic and henotheistic, that is, it allows a devotee the choice to venerate god/s after his or her own heart. Festivals surround the exploits of devas. But they are preoccupied with universal affairs and detached from the everyday anxieties of common folk, who consequently are reluctant to bother or upset the devas with their health or other existential needs.

Devatas or godlings constitute a third level and are deemed to be the community's territorial protectors and welfare controllers. These local gods are deified entities of the spirits of ancestors, the dead, historical heroes and natural forces. Demigods like Ganesha, Murugan and Kali, the mother goddess, are represented symbolically at village shrines or in sacred stones. Devatas expect worship and can bring misfortune, hence are revered and regularly propitiated. While they may possess humans, these dignified powers are normally benevolent.

Demons at the lowest level are uncouth, capricious ghosts called *bhuts* or, in Tamil, *peeys*.[6] As malevolent spirits they mischievously get involved in people's affairs, causing a whole host of trouble, misfortune and destruction. They are blamed for natural disasters, physical accidents and life's failures – the lack of harvest, barrenness in women or a child failing exams. Fundamental to the Indian aetiology is the conviction that *peeys* disrupt, create havoc and injure

---

6. The Tamil Bible uses *asutha avi* or *ketavi* for all kinds of evil spirits, or the Sanskrit derivative *pissacu*, but usually *peey* is employed to depict an afflicting spirit.

humans and are the main cause for sicknesses. They especially attack weak-willed and morally vulnerable people. Both illness and ill luck are consigned to this battalion of evil.

Popular spiritualities, Hindu, Muslim and Christian, recognize and respond to demons as a spiritual reality. As a phenomenon, Hindu demon possession has common features with Christian healing and deliverance.[7] Here, *peeys* function as entities with emotions and wills, albeit without a body. They have a definite mode of operation, and are identifiable – for instance as an afflicting demon from nature/forests (*kaattu picaacu*), an angry spirit (*muni*), a disturbed ancestral spirit, or a wandering spirit from an untimely death like drowning, suicide or murder, all seeking a body to inhabit. While notions of *peeys* differ slightly territorially, they are generally believed to oppress and take up residence within humans. Such a belief has been traced back to one of the earliest Hindu Artharvedas (c. 1500 BC).[8]

A South Indian worldview: conflicts and warfare

Indian religiosity is chiefly represented by popular folk forms, which emerge from tribal/ethnic communities with an underlying belief system that almost indelibly governs and guides one's faith. Hindus, even if not well versed in their scriptures, Thirumalai notes, 'build their own community/caste temples and offer all kinds of sacrifices; they believe in the ritual and they seek priests to perform them for their benefit'.[9]

---

7. D. Mosses, 'Catholic Saints and the Hindu Village Patheon', *Man in India* 29 (June 1994), p. 320; L. Caplan, *Religion and Power* (Madras: CLS, 1989), pp. 32–71; W. Hoerschelmann, *Christian Gurus* (Madras: Gurukul, 1998), pp. 378ff.
8. Cf. the Bhuta-Vidya form of exorcism, W. Wagner et al., 'The Modernisation of Tradition: Thinking about Madness in Patna, India', *Culture and Psychology* (Delhi: Sage, 1999), p. 419.
9. M. Thirumalai, *Sharing Your Faith with a Hindu* (Minneapolis: Bethany, 2002), p. 15.

Today 75% of India's people live in village settings and, despite urbanization and Westernization, maintain age-old folk beliefs, values and lifestyles.[10] In rural localities, medical aid is unaffordable in the rare instances when it is accessible and available. The Indian culture is diverse and plural and has been shaped historically by several religions. While there is an apparent threat by a globalized culture, India's stance is rather eclectic and, as Gurcharan Das points out, it is 'robust and should be able to maintain its richness and identity'.[11] This is equally true with regard to Indian notions of affliction healing.

Western forms of medical missions, Newbigin notes, became 'a powerful secularising force',[12] but they created conflict. Indian medical research has advanced in disease diagnosis, biochemical treatment and surgery. Yet the culture of scientific medicine is acutely aware of the danger of denying or excluding the spiritual or regarding non-medical healing as 'superstition'. Indian medics maintain an integrated and holistic view that considers the administration of medicine an expression of divine grace.[13] Subsequently, so-called supernatural as well as natural sources are associated with the idea of the sacred and seen as miraculous. Spirituality or faith aspects are a reality deemed essential within a socio-cultural construct of what it means to be healthy, that is, fully and truly human. Within this idea of health, the stress is on alleviating the symptoms, and relationships are vital.

The causes for sickness are many and varied and there are distinct approaches to discern remedial measures for what is perceived as illness. At the philosophical level, theories of good or bad deeds (*karma*) from past lives have explanations. This includes suffering as an illusion (*maya*) or non-reality. On the psychic level,

10. R. Ahuja, *Society in India: Concepts, Theories and Recent Trends* (Delhi: Rawat, 1999), p. 372.

11. G. Das, *India Unbound* (Delhi: Penguin, 2000), p. 349.

12. L. Newbigin, *Honest Religion for Secular Man* (Philadelphia: Westminster, 1966), pp. 18ff.

13. V. Thumbu, *Be Thou My Vision: Spiritual Resources for the Healing Ministry* (Delhi: TRACI, 1997).

there are mind-over-matter cures where therapeutic energies are channelled from an inexplicable life-force (*prana*). Creating balance or harmony in the vital life field (*aura*) of the sick body in a state of dis*ease* restores its one-with-ness and ensures healing.[14] However, I will focus on human well-being at the popular level, since it is pertinent to spiritual warfare and draws out the role of religious healers.

In India, there is always a need to experience the spiritual, almost as a *marga* or path to solve a host of personal, psychosomatic and social problems. Spiritual encounters are necessary, integrating forces located at the heart of what the community perceives as key to counteract misfortune. Without this outlook, the best of Western medical treatment or biological cure is fragmented, truncated and 'secular' – lacking balance, restoration and wholeness. The West increasingly admits to a transcultural reality, recognizing a common spiritual root in holistic forms of medicine.[15] Such a path to wholeness puts people in touch with their inner self and the cosmic powers. This has become the allure of the New Age movement and a reason why Westerners flock to ashrams or join guru movements like that of Rajneesh and Sai Baba.

Yet the spiritual quest is not merely to go within one's true self, but also to venture out into battle or war against those evil forces that bring the imbalance and conflict. With a dualism that treats ills as evil, a warfare worldview is adopted, which Boyd defines as 'a perspective on reality that centres on the conviction that the good and evil, fortunate and unfortunate aspects of life are to be interpreted largely as the result of good and evil, friendly and hostile spirits warring against each other and against us'.[16]

---

14. C. Gnanakan, 'Indian Notions of Illness and Healing', paper, Berlin Conference, Hirschluch, September 2003.

15. R. Ballentine, *Radical Healing: Integrating the World's Great Therapeutic Traditions* (New York: Harmony Books, 1999), p. 5. The concept of *sanus* (healthy) has direct coherence with *sanctus* (holy).

16. G. Boyd, *God at War: The Bible and Spiritual Conflict* (Downers Grove: IVP, 1997), p. 13.

Efforts have been made to improve medical missions from a mono to a holistic approach.[17] It is next to impossible to eradicate a sort of primal/animistic worldview that naturally seeks spiritual reasons for a physical problem. Questions abound in the mind of the sick and their family members: Has a deity been offended? Does an ancestral spirit feel neglected? Could this be the bewitching work of a sorcerer? In spite of medics' scientifically explaining that 'germs' were harmful bacteria, they are still considered to be evil forces at work in the human body and sent by someone. This socio-cultural logic has led to ethno-medical and indigenous treatments which correlate causes with ritualistic measures, to the patient's satisfaction. Here, a traditional healer is regularly consulted alongside medication. The focus of therapy for the sufferer becomes more on the containment and transference of the sickness through and out of the patient's body rather than its cure, in a strictly medical sense.

Sources of affliction and the demonization of disease

Three sources of affliction are commonly accepted and broadly categorized as (1) *natural*: disorders created within and by nature; (2) *spiritual*: both divine and demonic; (3) *human*: sorcery, black magic and spells and evil eye/mouth/actions. The emphasis is usually in the reverse order, yet a spiritual root is maintained. People are believed to bring sickness upon themselves in a number of ways. It could be a result of divine punishment for personal sin against a god, a broken moral code or violation of a religious sanction or taboo. Sins could be of *commission* (transgressing some social or moral norm) or of *omission* (failure to fulfil religious duties). In both ways rituals and sacrifices at once become obligatory and preventative.

At this point, some examples from my field research will help to illustrate how sickness is readily attributed to demons and calls for

17. V. Shah, report on the Indian health scenario, *The Church in India*, ed. F. Hrangkhuma and S. C. H. Kim (Delhi: ISPCK, 1999), pp. 152–156.

the caring service of the manthiravadi.[18] A baby, crying throughout the night with diarrhoea or colic, is often said to be possessed by a wandering *peey*. The mother, unable to pacify the crying, takes the baby to the manthiravadi, who intuitively identifies the spirit behind the diarrhoea and immediately gets to work. Mantras are chanted above the cries or at times simply whispered in the baby's ear. Often a lemon is circled three times around the baby's head. The manthiravadi then blows or spits on the lemon, which is cut up or crushed on the floor and carefully discarded. If by accident another child comes in contact with it, he or she is liable to exhibit the same symptoms.

On a psychological level, such empathetic objectification of disease that idealizes transference is important, as it signals the removal of illness.[19] Further, a sacred string is tied around the baby's neck or waist and a copperplate talisman around the arm to ward off and ensure that the *peeys* do not return.[20] After this exhaustive ritual, often the crying subsides and the child is breast-fed. As the mother and the family leave with a sense of relief, assurance and gratitude, a few rupees are placed in the manthiravadi's hand or that of his helper at the door. Then another mother brings her crying child in.

Children, especially good-looking boys, have a spot of black paste/powder (*mai*) put on their faces in order to avoid the evil eye.[21] There is a strong conviction in the idea of witchcraft – that humans possess invisible powers that they could project deliberately or unknowingly, to cause misfortune, harm or even death.

---

18. I have observed this process by visiting manthiravadis at Seppin's Road and Lingarajapuram, Bangalore. See also Brockman's experience in 'Possession and Medicine in South India', *JAPS* 2/3 (2000), pp. 303ff.
19. S. Kakar, 'Psychoanalysis and Eastern Spiritual Healing Traditions', *Journal of Analytical Psychology* 48 (2003), pp. 659–678.
20. S. Bhagwat and D. Chirmulay, 'Traditional Healing Practices in Rural Karnataka', *Man in India* 77/1 (1997), p. 74.
21. See D. Burnett, *World of Spirits* (Tunbridge Wells: Monarch, 2000), pp. 43ff., and P. Hiebert, *Understanding Folk Religion: A Christian Response to Popular Beliefs and Practices* (Grand Rapids: Baker, 1999), pp. 154ff.

These powers are thought to be concentrated in the human eye and made effective by an evil mouth, like a curse or something said out of avarice or jealousy that may have a reverse effect. Unfortunate events can be transferable by the evil touch of certain individuals; hence they are avoided or not invited to auspicious occasions. In order to remove, curb or prevent evil, the manthiravadi is consulted. A person's well-being – health, property and relationships, like marriage, family, education and business – become vulnerable if they are not, so to say, insured against these evil spiritual forces.

Because of an ingrained or *emic* aetiology, there is an established demonological basis for illnesses. Consequently *illness*, a culturally determined explanatory concept, is equated with the blanket term *sickness*, the real human experience of disease, and used interchangeably. Pilch points out that 'healing is directed toward illness, that is, the attempt to provide personal and social meaning for the life problems created by sickness'.[22] The diagnosis therefore includes interaction with spirits, and within South India this calls for the services of a shamanic agent – the manthiravadi.

The shamanic manthiravadi, spirit possession and exorcism

When constructing indigenous theologies, Hedlund reminds us, 'assumptions imported from Geneva or from the USA Bible-belt are far removed from the realities of India [where] animistic roots are found leading to concerns of power and the powers. A priest or Protestant preacher healer is a medium for access, hence a person of power.' Since there is a constant reference to God's presence 'in miracle working power', he rightly insists, 'an indigenous theology in the Indian context must address these and other issues'.[23] Hence,

22. J. J. Pilch, *Healing in the New Testament: Insights from Medical and Mediterranean Anthropology* (Minneapolis: Fortress, 2000), p. 25.

23. R. Hedlund, *Quest for Identity: India's Churches of Indigenous Origin* (Delhi: ISCPK, 2000), p. 212.

theological reflection on healing of illness takes place in the matrix in the form of power encounters.

Shamanism embraces the ancient healing practices of indigenous people worldwide with methods that communicate and interact with the spirit world. Rutherford makes it clear that it is not strictly a belief system but 'a path to knowledge, which is gained through experience of many facets of life through rituals, ceremonies, prayers and meditations, trial and tests. Knowledge is something that works; that stands up to the test of time that is known from the inside, unlike belief that is taken on from the outside, by others.'[24] Eliade has discussed the magico-religious life of societies centring on the shaman (derived from the Pali *samana*, Sanskrit *sramana*).[25] The Indian manthiravadi, folk doctor or spiritual healer, is believed to possess charismata, gifts (*fortuna*), that can bring about well-being. He is thus a strong link between the demonic, deliverance and restoration to health.

In the South Indian context, it is crucial to note that the wilful practitioner of harmful magic is another agent known as a *suniakaran*, who uses black magic to cause evil intentionally and to orchestrate or manipulate evil forces to control life events. The suniakaran, equivalent to the modern antisocial witch, resorts to sorcery to connect with spirit beings (divination) and to bring evil upon others (witchcraft). He inflicts pain on individuals and upsets community harmony. In contrast, the manthiravadi is 'the self-proclaimed guardian of the public against all manner of mystical attack'.[26] Yet, having chosen to be a sympathetic exorcist, he is socially regarded as benevolent, a people-helper and a protective agent for healing.

Concerning *peeys*, Caplan notes: 'They bring all kinds of misfortune at the command of the manthiravadi who control them, from infertility to cancer, to unemployment and even examination

---

24. L. Rutherford, *Principles of Shamanism* (London: HarperCollins, 1996), p. 4.
25. M. Eliade, 'Shamanism', *The Encyclopaedia of Religions* (London: Macmillan, 1987), p. 202.
26. L. Caplan, *Class and Culture in Urban India* (Oxford: Clarendon Press, 1987), p. 226.

failure.' He notes how 'manthiravadis are also assumed to control a number of spirits whom they can despatch to bring a variety of afflictions to their victims'.[27] Yet the manthiravadi, with the potential for sorcery that can serve evil ends, considers it his duty rather to champion the good of his fellow humans. Hence he is seen as a warrior-healer and a socio-religious advocate for personal well-being and community welfare.

The manthiravadi as a medicine man/woman is in essence a mysterious diviner who journeys into the spirit world through ecstatic experiences. Here, endowed with gifts to decipher mysteries, he effects the healing of 'dispirited' souls. His secret knowledge and spiritual powers make him a master of ecstasy and a healing agent. Yet he pastorally cares enough to address the existential questions of the common people and offers some meaning in their hurts from daily living. He is popularly known for his cunning ability to interact with the spirit world in order to restore the well-being of fellow human clients within his society. Hence, manthiravadis are readily associated with healing as well as reconciliation.

The manthiravadi as a warrior-healer

The manthiravadi is able to confirm whether a sickness, claimed to be medically incurable, is a spirit-connected aetiology. Healing is transactional and involves counter-transference of the afflicting spirits out of the sick person's body, at times through the manthiravadi, and into objects, which then are carefully discarded. For this therapeutic process, the manthiravadi requires the sufferer's co-operation as he enters into battle mode to confront ritually and vent off, or at times cajole or appease, but eventually to dismiss the disease-afflicting spirit(s). The concept of the 'warrior-healer' comes from this imagery of the possessed shaman going to battle against the sickness-inflicting *peeys*.

Several literal and cultural metaphors are examples of warriorship: the legendary Japanese Samurai, American Indians and

---

27. Caplan, *Religion and Power*, p. 41, 42.

British knights.[28] The Indian manthiravadi depicts a spiritual warrior, man or woman, who, without tangible weapons but with fearless bravery, is on the spiritual battlefront for the cause of the sick. He defends them against black magic and fights malevolent spirits that cause their illnesses. Like the polar shaman, who actually girds himself 'with the use of bows, lances and swords in their rites',[29] the South Indian manthiravadi often dresses up and makes facial gestures to frighten *peeys*. His deliverance ritual is an enactment of battle and conquest – the cunning capturing and casting out of evil spirits.

For effective exorcism the manthiravadi needs to be ritually pure. Before engaging in the agony of warfare, he himself is helpfully possessed by a stronger, familiar spirit as his ally. He struggles with pain and counters the effect of sorcery or breaks curses that have been cast on the sick victim. There is the added drumming, dance and chanting of mantras to bother and hopefully ward off the bad spirits as he challenges, irritates and threatens them. He fills the place with holy smoke and often consumes intoxicating drinks. These rituals are believed to arm him for battle and usher him into a trance during which he is able disarm their powers.

Anyone can aspire to be a manthiravadi, and the qualifications range from the bizarre to the arbitrary. Beyond a natural aptitude for ecstasy, manthiravadis are known to possess an extraordinary healing gift which, as it is exercised, simultaneously increases the healer's competence and fame. Determination and discipline are part and parcel of the development toward becoming a powerful warrior against evil spirits and a useful healer of humans wounded in their bodies, minds and spirits. There are three ways in which a potential candidate is initiated: by receiving a special 'call' in a vision; by hereditary transmission of shamanic powers or the healing gift; and by personal initiative. As Burnett notes, 'individuals who of their freewill choose to become shamans are rare and

---

28. S. M. S. Hiltunen, 'Warrior Mothers as Heroines and Other Healing Imagery in the Finnish National Epic of "Kalevala"', *Journal of Poetry Therapy* 15/1 (Fall 2001), pp. 7ff.
29. Burnett, *World of Spirits*, p. 189.

considered less powerful than those who are called or inherit the profession'.[30] Preparation for service can be likened to military training at a spiritual boot camp. The manthiravadi is always in demand to deal with mental and physical illnesses. His initiation process is not just informative but formative as it equips him with those essential virtues for his task as a healer and also gives him the credentials for his role as a health mediator within and on behalf of his society.[31] Hence the manthiravadi, for the sake of his own good value, seeks out an initiatory experience or gets tutelage from a renowned healer.

Hoerschelmann enumerates three basic types of exorcisms that the manthiravadi as a warrior-healer engages in: (1) *luring* of spirits with food or the like; (2) *expulsion* with threats, consecrated objects and violent blows; and (3) *capturing* spirits using a 'magical net' or the like while the victim is asleep and the spirit is hovering around the body.[32] His journey into the spirit world, called 'flight', is a universal shamanic rite, and this experience has to be recognized by the public if he is to be accredited as someone able to communicate with and control spirits. The nature of his endowment with power is beneficial, as it is used to heal and guide humans in crises. As far as society is concerned, it is proactive and protective in resisting, fending off and overcoming harmful forces. But, apart from confirming his fighting ability, there is yet another vital and pastoral significant element in the making of a manthiravadi.

The manthiravadi as a wounded healer

The manthiravadi's flight-fight experience legitimizes and authorizes his place in the world of spirits. Having triumphed through and over assaulting spirits, he now emerges with a new identity and a unique relationship, on the one hand with the

---

30. Burnett, *World of Spirits*, p. 176.

31. A. L. Siikala, 'Shamanism', in M. Eliade (ed.), *Encyclopaedia of Religions* 13 (London: Macmillan, 1987), pp. 201–215.

32. Hoerschelmann, *Christian Gurus*, p. 22.

spirits, and on the other with his community. In this way, his wounding has produced within him an empowerment to serve. Thus his initiatory experience has endued him with a capacity to heal. Put otherwise, he has become a wounded healer. This personal crisis and sickness-bearing experience is a vital part of the process of getting in touch with the source of his healing power and gaining the means by which he can tap into it. This helpful 'spirit possession' thus proves to be of good value for the fledgling shaman both spiritually and socially. The manthiravadi does not charge his clients financially, although he accepts the generous offerings and gifts in cash or kind whenever they are brought. His gift gives him his true identity and his honour rests in his curative services.

By experiencing intense forms of suffering at his initiation, the shaman develops a passion that moves him from pity to sympathy. His acquaintance with illness paradoxically generates for him a *spiritual power* that can bring about wholeness.[33] This is essential for his *pastoral formation*, since it subtly empowers him with the virtue of empathy to be a genuine caregiver. He understands human pain and from this vantage-point undertakes cure. Though given social prestige, the manthiravadi humbly acknowledges his struggles and feelings of weakness. The manthiravadi is thus known to be a vulnerable servant of society and respected for this. Kapur observed how, although he was at times 'wrong in his announcement of the complaint, the clients did not seem to mind and prompted him with their real complaints if he went wrong'.[34] Sufferers view the manthiravadi as a pastor who shows solidarity with them and looks out for their future well-being. Medical doctors often think of a manthiravadi as a clairvoyant or sham, but the manthiravadi considers hospitals complementary to and not in competition with his services. Along with his social-integration role, the manthiravadi often refers his clients to hospitals for further or even better

33. T. J. Csordas, 'The Raging and the Healing', *The Sacred Self* (Berkeley: University of California Press, 1997), pp. 228–275.

34. R. L. Kapur, 'The Role of the Traditional Healers in Mental Health Care in Rural India', *Social Science and Medicine* 13B (1979), p. 29.

treatment. In this way, he plays a key role in bridging the traditional arts and the modern medical sciences within his local community.[35]

The manthiravadi is a pastoral leader in his community inasmuch as leadership is about influencing, guiding and protecting. He possesses *charismata*, special abilities that induce confidence in the people who follow his advice and demonstrate his authority over *peeys*. He is also a *seer*, who can divine sources of misfortune. His enactments and ritual ministrations help his clients to experience relief from various forms of oppression. He is approachable and empathetic and administers *care* to humans, thereby effecting *cure* for their dispirited souls.

The source of power to heal or harm is a spiritual but also socially determined factor. Cultural norms dictate where exactly the loci of power reside and how it may be tapped and used.[36] Healing is not merely transactional, that is, objectifying and ejecting disease from a sufferer's body. It is profoundly relational, where trust is built between sufferer and healer to enable countertransference as the manthiravadi takes on the sufferer's affliction. For this, he exhibits genuine compassion, a rich and active pastoral term involving the heart ('compassion', *manadhurukkam* in Tamil, is derived from two words, *manathu* meaning 'heart' and *urrukam* 'to melt'.[37] The manthiravadi who experientially knows affliction can act with compassion (*passio*, to suffer; *com*, with). Both the sufferer and his family expect him to ritually bear away the weight of pain. Thus the manthiravadi is an effective healer, not just in spite of his wounds, but precisely because of them. Put another way, he is a wounded healer.

---

35. Brockman, 'Possession and Medicine in South Central India'.
36. L. Glick, 'Medicine as an Ethnographical Category', S. M. Channa (ed.), *Health and the Supernatural: Disease and Cure in Tribal Societies* (Delhi: Cosmos, 2002), p. 59.
37. M. Winslow, L. Spaulding and C. A. Pillai, *Winslow's English and Tamil Dictionary* (Delhi: Asian Educational Services, 1980), p. 227. NB other synonyms: *Irrakum*, *Karunai*, 'mercy', *Parithabam*, 'to pity', *Anbu*, 'love', *Anudhabam*, 'sympathy'.

As an archetype, the wounded healer uses his own affliction to provide inspiration, hope and healing to others, his own wounds being important to the healing process.[38] A Greek myth tells of Chiron, a centaur son of the Olympian god Kronos, who earned himself the reputation of being a great healer but all his life long suffered from a wound caused by an arrow in his own knee, which he could not heal.[39] Nouwen reminds the Christian minister that he 'must look after his own wounds, but at the same time be prepared to heal the wounds of others'.[40] Eliade views shamanic initiation as a 'paschal mystery', which in the history of religion finds a perfect example in Jesus' passion, death and resurrection.[41] The manthiravadi gains a rite of passage through a 'dying to self' experience. Having visited and talked with manthiravadis, I found them to be rather weak, anxious and poor, compared to the temple Brahmin priests. But this precisely what is winsome about them. Their own limitations and personal needs are not necessarily handicaps when it comes to healing; they are assets when comforting others.

Concluding remarks: the relevance of the manthiravadi

We have seen that while there is little explanation within the parameters of conventional science that adequately deals with the paranormal phenomenon of healing, on the popular level in Indian folk thinking two religious notions are well accepted within its culture. First, sickness is understood as a form of evil with

38. M. Kelsey, *Prophetic Ministry* (Dorset: Element Books, 1982), pp. 90–91.
39. Chiron taught the art of healing to Asklepios, who in turn taught Hippocrates, the father of medicine. James Watt (ed.), *What is Wrong with Christian Healing?* (London: Churches' Council for Health and Healing, 1993), pp. 5–6.
40. H. Nouwen, *Wounded Healer: Ministry in Contemporary Society* (New York: Image, 1979), p. 64; M. F. Foyle, medic and missionary, notes effects of stress in *Honourably Wounded* (London: MARC, 1987).
41. M. Eliade, *Zalmoxis: The Vanishing God* (London: Macmillan, 1972).

spiritual causes. Therefore sufferers are not treated merely in terms of biological disease or organic malfunction. Second, the predominantly Hindu-Indian religious psyche is well acquainted with earthly spirits as spiritual powers that are part and parcel of a system of evil that causes illnesses. A whole realm and hierarchical range of supernatural beings include evil spirits, astral forces, local deities and human influences. When the illness is perceived as the temporary dislocation of one's spirit from the body, the sick can be said to be literally dispirited.

The manthiravadi, generally considered a magico-religious practitioner, can be reckoned to be a sort of 'good' angel/messenger. He uses divination to heal demonized people and, through white or harmless magical means, offers them protection, guidance and good fortune. He is in the business of controlling and influencing unseen forces in the universe, yet is also intensely engaged in liberating individuals from mental, emotional and physical pain, and from the social stigma that accompanies and marginalizes them on account of their affliction. Serving best within folk religiosity and tribal-like societies, which place a high premium on cultural values and relationships, he responds to people's real-life problems, deep anxieties and felt needs. He deals with what really matters to make their life better in the here and now, yet his role seems to point to something beyond, the sacred.

The chief task of the manthiravadi is to bring comfort, healing and reconciliation to the sick individual on several levels. By virtue of his link with the spirit world, on the human level he exercises enormous authority and wields tremendous social influence. Of course, there are dangers that go with such a precarious duty – like the ever-present conflict between the power of love and the love for power. The real issue is how he chooses to use his powers: to control people for personal gain or to show compassion with a view to social transformation?

The manthiravadi's survival over the centuries and usefulness in society today stand as a firm reminder of human belief in the reality of the two worlds, the seen and unseen. In assisting fellow humans, he deals with the trans-empirical or supernatural world. Yet he functions as a human specialist, an intermediary channel for communication between the two. He is a living bridge, serving as a medium through which humans can ultimately get in touch with the spiritual within and beyond. In our mechanistic, materialistic and postmodern age, with the loss of spiritual relationships, his enduring presence is a sign of hope for religion. Both heavens and earth can share in goodness, and there is the possibility of harmony between the two and hope for healing in the midst of fears.

The manthiravadi as a caregiver offers spiritual experiences that address practical realities, emotional anxieties and, to some extent, remedy his client's sufferings. His initiation sets him apart for public service and is a sign that validates his powers. He is a pastoral leader with socially sanctioned authority due to his charismata. He is a prophetic leader and, as a seer, can foretell or forewarn of future calamities. His role has serious implications for pastoral care, as it takes compassion seriously and calls us to participate in the healing of a hurting world.

We have seen that the manthiravadi, portrayed as warrior-healer, provides a potent archetype for the imagination. It is evident that this powerful metaphor of a saviour figure makes his clients trust his services and experience some relief. Moreover, he is a wounded healer, and paradoxically this is where his strength lies. His healing is a form of taking on another's affliction, which results in spiritual deliverance and the social re-enfranchisement of sufferers. What is attempted and portrayed by the manthiravadi is significant. His shamanic role is a pointer to the idea of some sort of atonement and a dim reflection of the ultimate human need for meaningful relationships and wholeness.

8 HOW ALLAH COMMUNICATES: ISLAMIC ANGELS, DEVILS AND THE 2004 TSUNAMI

Peter G. Riddell

Those of us involved in scholarly engagement with the Islamic textual materials can easily become disconnected from the real world. Yet there are indisputable links between the recorded wisdom of Islamic scholars down the ages and Muslim interpretations of modern-day disasters such as the 2004 Asian tsunami. This chapter seeks to connect the two in ways which provide insights into Islamic understandings of angels, devils and the workings of Allah.

Islamic angels

Characteristics

Explorations into early writings by Muslim scholars, as well as the sacred texts of Islam, provide key insights into the characteristics of angels.

The great classical commentator al-Tabari (d. 923) states in his commentary on Qur'an 2:30 that most angels are created from light; only those of one tribe (*al-Hinn*, the guardians of paradise) are created from fire. These 'delicate bodies of light' are subtle forms which are capable of taking on various shapes.[1]

As created beings, the knowledge of angels is incomplete; for example, they did not know the names of the creatures when Allah tested them on this knowledge.[2] However, they are impeccable, or sinless, like prophets.[3]

In fact, angels are of one species with the *jinn* (genies) and the satans/devils (*shayatin*). However, this general shared feature does not carry through to specific detail. Nasir al-Din al-Tusi (d. 1274) informs us that the angels are distinct from *jinn* and devils in that angels are only good, whereas devils are only bad and the *jinn* can be good or bad.[4]

Angels are further distinct from the *jinn* in that the former are without gender, according to al-Laqqani,[5] and without offspring, according to al-Razi.[6]

Functions

A key function of Islamic angels relates to praising and serving Allah. In fact, angels exist to utter continuous praise of Allah, according to the canonical collection of Hadith by Muslim bin al-Hajjaj.[7]

1. A. Jeffery, *Islam: Muhammad and His Religion* (New York: Bobbs-Merrill, 1958), pp. 111–113, citing al-Laqqani, *Jawharat al-Tawhid*, and al-Razi, *Muhassal afkar al-mutaqaddimin wa al-muta'akhkhirin.*
2. Abu Ja'far Muhammad b. Jarir al-Tabari, *The Commentary on the Qur'an*, 1 (Oxford: Oxford University Press, 1987), pp. 206–227.
3. Jeffery, *Islam: Muhammad and His Religion*, p. 114.
4. Ibid., pp. 111–112.
5. Ibid., p. 113.
6. Fakhr al-Din al-Razi, *Mafatih al-ghayb* (Bayrut: Dar al-Fikr, 1981–3), commenting on Q2:30. Cf. T. Street, *Angels in Medieval Islamic Theology: A Study in Fakhr al-Din al-Razi* (PhD dissertation, Australian National University, 1988), p. 96.
7. Muslim 4.830.

Furthermore, in the Islamic scheme of things, while some angels bear the throne of Allah, others offer continuous salutations to those who bear the throne.[8] Given this role of subservience to their Creator, it is not surprising that Islamic angels accept Allah's decisions without question.[9]

However, angelic functions are also directed towards created beings, to fulfil the angelic role as Allah's administrators of the universe.[10] In carrying out their various functions in the earthly realm, angels must avoid houses with pictures, dogs or sexually defiled people.[11]

A key angelic role is to transmit messages through prophets to humankind, as Muslims believe to have occurred with the transmission of the Qur'an from Allah to Muhammad. But angelic errands do not end there. Angels also accompany believers in prayer.[12] This altruistic function is further evident in that the angels surrounding the throne of Allah intercede for believers on earth.[13]

Hence angels are intended to consider the welfare of people and to smooth the path of the believers. Angels are also reportedly responsible for the protection of Syria![14] This particular Hadith account probably dates back to the period when the Islamic Umayyad Empire (661–750) was centred on the Syrian capital of Damascus.

Hence Allah uses angels to make the way easier for those people who follow his injunctions. However, rewards must be earned,

---

8. Al-Zamakhshari, *al-Kashshaf 'an haqa'iq al-tanzil wa 'uyun al-aqawil* (Bayrut: Dar al-Fikr, 1981–3), commenting on Q40:7. Cf. H. Gatje, *The Qur'an and Its Exegesis: Selected Texts with Classical and Modern Muslim Interpretations* (Oxford: Oneworld Publications, 1996), p. 164.
9. Abu al-A'la Mawdudi, *Towards Understanding the Qur'an* (Leicester: The Islamic Foundation, 1988), p. 60 (commenting on Q2:30).
10. Mawdudi, *Towards Understanding the Qur'an*, p. 59.
11. Abu Dawud 1.227.
12. Ibn Malik, *al-Muwatta*, 9.24.85, 3.2.14.
13. Al-Zamakhshari, *al-Kashshaf* on Q40:7.
14. *Mishkat al-Masabih*, hadith 6224.

and, in order to gather sufficient data for the later judgment of each individual person, angels also meticulously record people's deeds.[15]

Angels also have a role to play at the end of people's lives. The angel of death draws out the souls of the dying, and angels carry the coffins of believers.[16] As for the realm of the afterlife, angels are sent by Allah to guard hell; they administer it and direct its affairs.[17]

Islamic devils

What of devils, those beings which wreak havoc in the created realms? In order to gain an insight into their functions and activities, we will focus upon a particular work by the seventeenth-century Acehnese scholar Abd al-Ra'uf of Singkel (c. 1615–c. 1693).

Abd al-Ra'uf is arguably the most important Islamic scholar from the Malay world to have lived during the formative stages of Malay Islam. He spent nineteen years (1642–61) studying with prominent Islamic scholars at key centres of learning in the Arabian peninsula, and incorporated what he learnt within his prolific literary output. His writings, in wide-ranging fields of Islamic learning, provided succeeding generations of Malay students of Islam with copious materials for study. His tomb and associated complex in Banda Aceh served as a site of pilgrimage for Muslim devotees until it was destroyed by the Asian tsunami on 26 December 2004.

One of his shorter works which bears directly on the subject of this chapter is *Lubb al-kashf wa al-bayan lima yarahu al-muhtadar bi al-'iyan*[18] ('Essential exposition and clarification on the visionary experience of the dying and what gladdens him'). This work

15. Muslim 1.233.
16. *Mishkat al-Masabih*, hadith 6228.
17. Al-Razi, *Mafatih al-ghayb* on Q2:30.
18. Voorhoeve 'Bajan Tadjalli', *Tijdschrift voor Indische Taal-, Land- en Volkenkunde* 23/1 (1952), pp. 91–93.

Abd al-Ra'uf's tomb, with its caretaker, 1982

describes the experience of death and the temptations to which the dying are subjected.

Abd al-Ra'uf wrote this as a reflection on another text in Jawi Malay,[19] manuscripts of which are held in collections in Calcutta and Paris. Abd al-Ra'uf described this work as being based on *Kitab al-tadhkira bi-umur al-akhira* by al-Qurtubi. This figure was a prominent Malikite scholar of Hadith and exegesis. He was born in Spain, and died in Upper Egypt in 1272.[20] Thus Abd al-Ra'uf's work is not merely the product of a single Malay scholar's reflections but provides a window into earlier generations of Islamic scholarly wisdom.

Annotated translated text of Lubb al-kashf

> In the name of Allah I begin reading this document . . . I found it within a Jawi text, addressing what happens to a person when he dies. It is as follows:

---

19. A copy of the Arabic text is catalogued in Leiden as Or. 5665(5) (P. Voorhoeve, personal communication).
20. R. Arnaldez, 'Al-Kurtubi', *EI*^{2}, 5, p. 512.

When a person is at the point of death[21] he experiences several visions.[22] When a vision of black appears to him, which is Satan, then he should utter [the creed] *There is no God but Allah and Muhammad is the prophet of Allah, He, He, He.*[23] When a vision of red appears to him, which represents the Christians, then he should utter *There is no God but Allah and Muhammad is the prophet of Allah, He, He, He.* When a vision of yellow appears to him, which represents the Jews, then he should utter *There is no God but Allah and Muhammad is the prophet of Allah, He, He, He.* When a vision of white appears to him, which represents the vision of our prophet Muhammad the messenger of Allah, then he should utter *By the will of Allah he was one of the true believers.*

After that, there comes [a vision] between the eyebrows of the person who is on the point of death, like the full moon in the evening [after a cycle] of fourteen days,[24] its brightness filling the Seven Heavens and Earth, containing a vision of ourselves. It proceeds with an exposition, the like of which I have never witnessed in all the books of Hadith and the writings of the Sufis[25] . . . I have only found such an exposition on the experience of death in the work *Tadhkira* by Shaykh Jamal al-Din . . . ibn Muhammad ibn Ahmad Qurtubi. Shaykh Jamal al-Din . . . relates in the work *Tadhkira* the following account from the scholars.

When a servant of Allah is at the point of death, two devils sit next to him, one on his right and one on his left. The devil on his right takes the form of his father, and says to him: 'O my child, I truly love and cherish you. Please die in the Christian faith, as it is the best of religions.' The devil on his left takes the form of his mother, and says to him: 'O my child, my womb was your shelter, my milk was your nourishment and my

---

21. Arabic *sakara al-mawt*, cf. Q50:19.
22. These represent temptations, designed to direct the Muslim away from Islam.
23. The third person singular pronoun is a further reference to Allah. Thus the Muslim avoids the tempter by pronouncing the Creed, which affirms his faith.
24. The full moon takes approximately fifteen days to appear after the sighting of the new moon.
25. Note the authority attributed to Sufi writings, alongside the Hadith collections.

lap was your place of repose. Please die in the Jewish faith, as it is the best of religions.'

Moreover, it states that Iblis[26] orders his soldiers to visit the person at the point of death and to confuse him. So they come to the person at the point of death, and they present themselves to the person in the form of all his loved ones who died before him, of those who guided him during his life, such as his father, mother, brothers, sisters, and friends who cared for him. They say to him: 'O so-and-so. You are dying. We have already undergone the experience of death before you. So please die in the Jewish faith, for it is the faith which is pleasing to Allah.' If the person turns away and does not wish to comply with the urgings of the devils, another group of devils comes to him and says: 'O so-and-so, please die in the Christian faith, for it is the religion of the Messiah, namely Jesus, which through him abrogated the religion of Moses.' These [devils] proceed to list for him all the beliefs of each religion.

Thereupon Allah inclines whoever He wishes towards faiths which have gone astray. This is in accordance with Allah's decree: *rabbana la tuzigh qulubana ba`da idh hadaytana*,[27] i.e. 'Our Lord! Do not incline our hearts to faiths which have gone astray at our moment of death after You have shown us the true faith beforehand, namely during our lives.' Whenever Allah wishes to show one of His servants the true path and to affirm him through statement of the Divine Unity, the angel of mercy comes to him – some scholars identify him as Gabriel – and he drives away from that person all the devils, and he wipes his face, and the person smiles from time to time. We can observe that the majority of people at the point of death smile in the grave while rejoicing at receiving the good account from Allah's angel of mercy. The angel of mercy says to him: 'O so-and-so, you do not know me. I am Gabriel, and they are your enemy, Satan. Please die in the faith which is pure and the law which is true.' Nothing is more cherished or more hoped for by a person than that the angel of mercy comes to him. This is in accordance with Allah's decree: *wahab lana min ladunka rahmatan innaka anta al-wahhab*,[28] i.e. 'My Lord, grant us mercy from Your presence. You alone are the Lord who is most bountiful.'

---

26. Satan.
27. Q3:8.
28. Q3:8.

Thereupon the angel of death draws out the soul of that person.

Reflections on the text

Lubb al-kashf is strongly determinist in orientation, as is evident in the penultimate paragraph: 'Allah inclines whoever He wishes towards faiths which have gone astray.' Hence the divine hand is central in the events described in this text. Just as angels were instrumental in the earlier discussion for the implementation of the divine plan for humankind, in *Lubb al-kashf* a series of devils appear as visions to test the dying person in his or her faith. This happens with divine assent.

Note also that *Lubb al-kashf* is not merely a document which provides insights into Islamic belief. It also addresses interfaith relations. Christianity and Judaism are presented clearly as having strayed from the true path. The Christians and Jews are presented, along with Satan, as those who tempt the dying to abandon Islam during the dying process.

This co-locating of Christianity and Judaism with demonic forces has a powerful impact. It serves to reinforce a clear demarcation between forces for good and forces for evil. This contrasts God and his angelic emissaries with Iblis and his agents: both are devils and competitor faiths.

This is significant, not so much on the basis of this particular text having an ongoing influence on Muslim readers, which is not the case because of its negligible distribution in the modern day, but rather because it provides a window into an exclusivist mindset which is interwoven throughout Islamic scholarly writings down the ages.

Also significant is the fact that this text opens the way for ordinary Muslims to see trials and tribulations as part of a celestial struggle. This theme is picked up in the next section of this chapter.

When communication breaks down between Creator and creature

The above discussion of characteristics and functions of angels and devils shows clearly that they are not acting on their own will, but are rather emissaries from Allah. Angels exist both to sing Allah's praises and to carry messages and guidance to people so the latter can also stay focused on their Creator. Devils wreak their havoc within a framework created by Allah, and in their own way assist in the fulfilment of the divine plan for the created world. Both angels and devils are instruments for Allah's communication with the world.

But what happens when the communication channels collapse, when people turn away from Allah and do not look for or listen to the messages brought by Allah's angelic emissaries? What other instruments are available for Allah to use when the temptation of the devils is too strong for some people?

On 26 December 2004, a giant earthquake off the Indonesian island of Sumatra triggered a series of tsunamis which devastated coastal areas in the Indonesian province of Aceh as well as parts of Thailand, Sri Lanka, India and even East Africa. The estimated death toll approached 250,000, of whom over one half died in Aceh.

Following the tsunami, many researchers attempted to find out how people in the devastated areas who survived the tsunami interpreted the disaster in terms of a divine plan. Several interviews were carried out with Indonesian Muslims in Aceh, spiritual descendents of earlier Acehnese scholars such as Abd al-Ra'uf of Singkel.

It is striking that the interviewees, whether benefiting from sophisticated Islamic theological training or rather drawing on popular religious perceptions, were essentially agreed in seeing the tsunami as a test or lesson sent directly from Allah. In this case, neither angels nor devils served as couriers of the message. Rather, the courier in this case was a massive tidal wave which was the instrument for Allah in communicating with the world.

Fadil, an Acehnese Muslim who lost all of his family in the tsunami, explained his understanding of the disaster in the following terms: 'I cannot be angry with my God because if the God take my family, I think it's the time for my family, they must die. [God is testing me] . . . now I have a link with God 100%.'[29]

---

29. *Tsunami: Where was God?* (3BM TV, 2005).

Similar views were heard in an interview with a group of other Acehnese Muslims who, like Fadil, were not formally theologically trained: 'Because of the power of God, we weren't crushed by the rubble. We were swept into the mosque. We prayed and prayed, glorifying Allah's name. We feared Judgement Day was coming. God did this because he loves us. It was a lesson to us. God didn't want us to become complacent.'[30] In other words, Allah allowed thousands to be killed so that the survivors would be chastened.[31]

Many Islamic relief and development agencies rushed to Aceh in the wake of the tsunami. These included a number of radical Islamic groups who saw the tragedy very clearly in terms of divine correction. Yusuf Al-Qardhawy, a spokesman for the radical Islamic Defenders Front, which has pursued an Islamic fundamentalist social and political agenda throughout Indonesia in recent years, explained the causes of the tsunami in the following terms: 'Islam forbids people to wear tight clothes. It forbids young people to go off to quiet places on their own; going off on motorbikes with someone who is not your husband . . . things that are prohibited by Allah. So all this had to be cleansed . . . What has hit them is a lesson so that we don't do it all again.' [32]

This message of tsunami as divine lesson was not merely a populist explanation preoccupying the masses. It also formed the core of the scholarly interpretation offered by Professor Yusny Saby, who took his PhD in Islamic Studies[33] at Temple University

---

30. Ibid.
31. This is reminiscent of the use of the flood to destroy wayward humanity, and the destruction of Sodom and Gomorrah, in Genesis. The difference is that the Old Testament depicts God as renouncing such punitive action in Gen. 8:21–22, whereas in Islamic thinking such divine retribution is regarded as still central to God's way of dealing with his creation.
32. *Tsunami: Where was God?*
33. His PhD dissertation was published as *Islam and Social Change: The Role of the Ulama in Acehnese Society* (Bangi: Penerbit Universiti Kebangsaan Malaysia, 2005).

and is currently Rector of the prominent Ar-Raniri Islamic State University in Aceh. He stated in interview:

> Anybody in the world . . . can be tested. What is in the mind of God . . . we don't know that. Men should be stronger and closer to God through testing if they pass. If they don't pass they may be farther from God. Because of this tragedy, they may even blame God. We are being tested by God. This is the very meaning of suffering. If you pass, you are closer to God. If you don't pass – you blame this, you blame that . . . maybe you are going to Hell.[34]

A series of natural disasters struck Indonesia following the 2004 tsunami. Floods, landslides and droughts preceded a large earthquake in July 2006. Many local Muslims interpreted these events as further evidence of Allah's anger, some even suggesting that the series of calamities was a divine statement against the rule of the incumbent president, Susilo Bambang Yudhoyono. In the words of Gendut Irianto, a Muslim car salesman in Jakarta, 'I think the earthquake was definitely a warning from God to all Indonesians so we should chant and pray for forgiveness.'[35]

Several observations can be made regarding the Islamic viewpoints expressed. A strong sense of fatalism is evident in the various Muslim comments. Allah controls everything, and used the natural disasters to give a lesson, so that humankind does not err again. Allah is thereby seen as judging, and humans cannot understand the divine mind. Finally, such tests distinguish between those headed for paradise and those going to hell.

The above viewpoints regarding the cause of disasters shows the widespread influence in Indonesia of Islamic scholars who take a more determinist approach to events of this world. Such a scholar was Muhammad al-Fadali al-Shafi'i (d. 1821), rector of Al-Azhar in Cairo and author of a theological treatise which had a

---

34. *Tsunami: Where was God?*

35. Tom McCawley, 'Indonesians Ask if Calamities Are a Divine Rebuke', *Christian Science Monitor* (24 July 2006), <www.csmonitor.com/2006/0724/p01s01-woap.html>

significant influence throughout the Muslim world during the nineteenth century and was translated into Malay and Javanese.[36] This treatise has the following to say regarding the causes of human suffering: 'If you are healthy it is that God wishes you to be so . . . If you suffer, God wishes to test you . . . no thing has its existence as a result of natural causality or force or nature.'[37]

Conclusion

The role of angels as intermediaries between Allah and His earthly creation is widely recognized and documented. We have seen that classical Islamic scholars identified a detailed list of characteristics and functions for angels. However, all the details presented can be condensed into two macro angelic functions: to praise and glorify Allah and to communicate his messages and injunctions to humankind.

We also saw that devils take various visionary forms in order to subject people to tests of faith during the dying process. This notion of testing, via satanic and demonic forces, is well attested within Islamic scholarly writing.

Scholarship has not been as energetic in identifying another key way in which Allah communicates with and tests humankind: through natural disasters. In addressing this issue, we have focused on the Asian tsunami of 2004. However, the Muslim masses themselves seem to be well aware of natural disaster as an instrument for Allah to express his displeasure with human behaviour.

Disasters such as the 2004 tsunami therefore can be seen as partners with angels and devils in providing Allah with a means to make his messages known to his often errant earthly creatures.

---

36. A. Rippin and J. Knappert (eds.), *Textual Sources for the Study of Islam* (Chicago: University of Chicago Press, 1986), p. 20. Cf. also J. Schacht, 'Al-Fadali', *EI*², II, p. 727.
37. Rippin and Knappert, *Textual Sources for the Study of Islam*, pp. 129–132.

9 ANGELS IN ISLAMIC ORAL TRADITION FROM THE QUR'AN TO THA'LABI

Andrew G. Bannister

Introduction

If one wanted evidence of the centrality of angels within Islam, a good place to begin would be with the creeds produced in the early formative centuries of Islam. Although they represent a wide range of individual scholars and schools, these creeds demonstrate a remarkable homogeneity on what were considered to be the core tenets of Islamic orthodoxy and orthopraxis. One such tenet was a belief in angels: 'The sum of what is held by those following the Hadiths and the Sunna is the confession of God, His angels, His books, His messengers, what has come as (revelation) from God, and what trustworthy (persons) have related from the Messenger of God.'[1]

The reference to the 'Hadiths and Sunna' is a salutary reminder that orthodox Islamic belief is not built on the Qur'an alone, but

---

1. The creed of al-Ash'ari (d. 935), cited in W. M. Watt, *Islamic Creeds: A Selection* (Edinburgh: Edinburgh University Press, 1994), p. 41.

rather the Qur'an read through the filter of later tradition. This chapter will reverse that hermeneutic by beginning with an angelology of the Qur'an, before exploring its development, especially its narrative development, in these later Islamic traditions. We shall also examine what light oral traditional studies can shed on this material.

An angelology of the Qur'an

Pre-Islamic beliefs about angels

The Qur'an is highly allusive, assuming a high level of background knowledge on the part of its audience; that it can afford to be allusive about angels points to existing beliefs about them in pre-Islamic Arabia, a religiously diverse milieu in which polytheists, Jews, Christians and pre-Islamic monotheists, *hanifs*, lived side by side. For example, the idea of angels as divine agents was apparently widespread, for the Qur'an reports Muhammad's opponents enquiring why no angel was sent to him:

> They say: 'O thou to whom the Message is being revealed! Truly thou art mad (or possessed)!
> 'Why bringest thou not angels to us if it be that thou hast the Truth?'
> (Q15:6–7)

This recurrent qur'anic motif contrasts with the well-attested Islamic stories, found throughout the Hadith, that depict Gabriel as heavily involved with Muhammad's mission from the very beginning. The Qur'an's failure to mention Gabriel's role in response to Muhammad's opponents suggests that these stories evolved later.[2]

Semantics

The Arabic word *malak* – which like its Hebrew cognate and the Greek *angelos* means 'messenger' – occurs ninety-four times in the

2. So F. E. Peters, *Muhammad and the Origins of Islam* (Albany: SUNY Press, 1994), p. 143. The name 'Gabriel' occurs only twice in the Qur'an.

Qur'an. Its usages can be divided into several key areas: God, creation, revelation, and eschatology.[3]

Angels and God

Several scholars have suggested that angel-worship was prevalent in pre-Islamic Arabia, and this seems to be an issue that the Qur'an attempts to correct, for example repeatedly stating that the angels are Allah's *servants*, not his equals or daughters (17:40; 34:40). Indeed, the angels sound the praises of Allah (13:13), surrounding his throne in adoration and worship (39:75; 42:5). Not arrogant in the slightest (16:49), angels are instead obedient, carrying out Allah's decrees (66:6).

Creation

The Qur'an describes the relationship between angels and the created order in several places, notably the story of Adam's creation and the rebellion of the devil, Iblis, who refused to bow before Adam along with the other angels. This narrative occurs seven times in the Qur'an,[4] raising many fascinating questions on which later commentators would expend much ink. (1) Given that Iblis is elsewhere described as a *jinn* (18:50), why did the command to the angels include him? (2) Why were the angels commanded to prostrate before Adam, a created being? (3) Who is ontologically superior, man or angels? This story suggests that the answer is Adam, yet other Qur'anic verses seem to reverse this order (e.g. 7:20).

Revelation

Another extremely important role of angels in the Qur'an is their function as agents of revelation, descending with scripture. But they can also carry other messages; thus angels come to Zachariah to tell him that John will be born (3:39–41), and to Mary to announce that Allah has chosen her (3:42) and to foretell the birth

---

3. Cf. G. Webb, 'Angel', in J. Dammen McAuliffe (ed.), *Encyclopedia of the Qur'an* (Leiden: Brill, 2001).

4. Q2:30–38; 7:11–18; 15:29–43; 17:61–64; 18:50; 20:116–117; 38:71–83.

of Jesus (3:45; 19:17–19). Some of the inspiration (*wahy*) which Allah gives to the angels consists of messages for a broader audience, for example news about the wonders of paradise for the believers in general (41:30).

Given this vital revelatory role, it is unsurprising that in lists of prescribed beliefs (2:285; 4:136) angels appear second, after Allah but before books and messengers. Given the Qur'an's emphasis upon Allah's transcendence, angels are arguably required to bridge the gap between Allah and his creation, just as the Spirit or divine Wisdom does in the Old Testament.

Eschatology

By far the most detailed information about the role of angels in the Qur'an concerns their eschatological function. Angels appear as soon as a person dies, their role being to remove the soul (6:61, 93); and later Islamic thinking would demarcate this task as the duty of one particular angel, the Angel of Death, mentioned in the Qur'an just once (32:11). If the deceased is a believer, the angels will greet him (21:103), one imagines positively. Unbelievers, however, will have their faces struck and they will be told about the flames of hell awaiting them (8:50) before their souls are violently ripped out (79:1).

The Qur'an is silent concerning the deceased's fate between death and the Day of Judgment itself, an event in which angels play an important role. On that day they will appear with Allah, eight of them bearing the divine Throne (69:17). When the final trumpet is blown, it seems to be angels who will lead each soul forward to be judged (50:21). The Qur'an also hints at the role of the two recording angels who sit on a person's left and right throughout life and whose reports will be important on the Day of Judgment (50:17; cf. 89:22).

Following judgment, angels will lead the disobedient to hell (16:28–29), a terrible place policed by stern angels (66:6) who guard the flames (74:31), dealing severely with the wicked (96:18). Conversely, angels also lead the believers into the joys of paradise (16:32), a beautiful abode in which other angels wait to warmly greet the faithful (13:23).

Other Qur'anic references to angels

These major themes aside, there is a wealth of other minor references to angels throughout the Qur'an. For example, we read how angels fought alongside the Muslims in the battle of Badr (3:124), and that they protect and oversee believers in this earthly life (41:31). Finally, four angels are named: Gabriel (2:98; 66:4), Michael (2:98), Harut and Marut (2:102).

Conclusion

Throughout this material, the Qur'an remains highly allusive, assuming that the reader is familiar with the realities being described. From these verses the more systematized Islamic understanding of angels would develop.

The post-Qur'anic Islamic tradition

In the first few centuries of the Islamic era, other strands of tradition developed alongside the Qur'an, most notably biographical traditions about Muhammad: the *sira-maghazi* literature and the Hadith. There was also *tafsir*, commentary on the Qur'an. But often neglected is a fourth category, popular-level stories, the so-called *qisas al-anbiya'*, or 'Stories of the Prophets'. Angels feature heavily in all these traditions, from the highly scholarly down to the most popular.

Angels in the sira-maghazi and Hadith traditions

The sira-maghazi *traditions*

The most prominent and authoritative attempt to compile the independent traditions about Muhammad into a unified biography was by Ibn Ishaq (d. AD 767). Among the many traditions he reports are a few stories concerning angels; all feature Gabriel as the main protagonist, connecting him directly to Muhammad's ministry.

One such account concerns the beginning of Muhammad's prophetic vocation. Ibn Ishaq tells how Muhammad was a devout man who regularly prayed and meditated. One night in a cave on Mount Hira, Gabriel appeared, carrying some writing, and said,

'Read!' Muhammad replied, 'What shall I read?', and Gabriel squeezed him so tightly Muhammad feared he would die. This was repeated three times before Gabriel revealed the opening verses of Sura 96. The following morning Muhammad descended the mountain and halfway down had a dramatic vision of Gabriel.[5]

This particular story has assumed near-canonical status for Islam and it is repeated in various forms in the later traditions. Its importance and function rest upon its providing the all-important prophetic-call narrative, underpinning the divine authority behind Muhammad's mission. The same is true for a second angel story that Ibn Ishaq reports, namely the tale of Muhammad's 'Night Journey', his trip with Gabriel on the winged half-mule, half-donkey Buraq from Mecca to Jerusalem. There Muhammad met Abraham, Moses and Jesus and, after he had talked with them, a ladder descended from heaven. Gabriel led Muhammad up to the gate of the lowest heaven, where they met Adam, then upwards to the second heaven, where they met Jesus and John. In the third heaven, they met Joseph; in the fourth, Idris; in the fifth, Aaron; in the sixth, Moses, and in the seventh, Abraham. Finally, Muhammad met God, who laid a duty of fifty daily prayers upon the Muslim community. On the trip back down, Moses discovered this and insisted that Muhammad return and ask for a reduction; repeated haggling resulted in five daily prayers being agreed upon.[6]

What is striking about this material in Ibn Ishaq is that we are clearly in the realm of narrative, demonstrably a genre different from much of the Qur'an. Ibn Ishaq's failure to divulge his sources in detail makes it difficult to trace the genesis of this material in the two generations after Muhammad's death in AD 632, but what we see in the generation *after* Ibn Ishaq is tremendous growth in the number of *sira-maghazi* traditions. This is best seen by comparing Ibn Ishaq's work with that of Waqidi (d. AD 823), which contains considerably more material. Careful

5. A. Guillaume, *The Life of Muhammad* (Karachi: Oxford University Press, 2001), pp. 105–106.

6. Ibid., pp. 181–187.

analysis of Waqidi's work reveals how his style represents that of the popular storytellers of his day, the *qussas*.[7] In short, it is probably the *qussas* to whom we can trace many of these angel traditions. Many of them may also have been influenced by the Jewish and Christian communities in the fledgling Islamic empire. This is not to accuse these Islamic stories of being copied, but it is to recognize that oral, narrative traditions are fluid, dynamic and open to a myriad influences.[8]

Angels in Hadith traditions

The Hadith are a large and disparate corpus of sayings and deeds of Muhammad, transmitted over several hundred years before being gathered into the various canonical collections.[9] There is a wealth of angel stories to be found in the Hadith.

Many such traditions in the Hadith relate angels to Muhammad's prophethood, exploring the origins of his prophetic office and seeking to push its beginnings back beyond his calling on Mount Hira'. Muslim reports how one day when the young Muhammad was playing with some boys, Gabriel appeared and tore open Muhammad's chest, removed his heart and squeezed out a clot of sin. Gabriel then proceeded to wash the heart in holy Zamzam water before replacing it. By this point, the boys had fled and reported Muhammad dead.[10]

Further traditions record Muhammad explaining the various ways in which revelation would come: sometimes Gabriel would appear in human form,[11] sometimes Muhammad would hear a

---

7. J. M. B. Jones, 'Ibn Ishaq and al-Waqidi, The Dream of Atika and the Raid to Nakhla in Relation to the Charge of Plagiarism', *Bulletin of the School of Oriental and African Studies* 22 (1959), pp. 41–51.
8. R. Firestone, *Journeys in Holy Lands* (Albany: State University of New York Press, 1990), p. 18.
9. The most famous collections are those compiled by Muhammad Ibn Ismail al-Bukhari (AD 810–870) and Muslim ibn al-Hajjaj al-Qushayri (AD 821–875).
10. Muslim 1.311.
11. Bukhari 1.1.2.

voice like a ringing bell,[12] at other times he would experience vivid dreams.[13] But the angelic revelatory experience *par excellence* in the Hadith is the same as that recorded in the *sira*, namely Muhammad's journey through the seven heavens led by Gabriel.[14] All these traditions serve to underline the divine nature of Muhammad's prophetic office, reinforcing that the Qur'anic revelations did not have a human source. The Hadith also relate how angels guarded Muhammad constantly, enabling him to threaten his enemies with immediate angelic revenge.[15]

A second major role of angels in the Hadith is eschatological. For example, the interrogation in the grave, merely alluded to in the Qur'an, is here expounded in detail for the first time. Two angels (as yet unnamed) appear to the deceased and ask him about Muhammad. If the deceased replies that Muhammad is Allah's apostle, he will enjoy a peaceful rest until the Day of Judgment.[16] On that Day, faithful believers will go to paradise while unbelievers will be punished in hell, overseen by the fierce angel Malik.[17] Muhammad will be astonished to see some of his community in the flames, but Allah will inform him that these were hypocrites.[18] Others, weak believers, will have to endure hell briefly in a kind of purgatory experience, before those whose foreheads bear the marks of prostration in prayer are plucked from the flames.[19]

For orthodox Islam, the fate of each person both in the grave and on the Day of Judgment depends upon his or her behaviour during life, and according to the Hadith it falls to angels to maintain a good and accurate record of each person's deeds. This recording process commences before birth, when an angel asks

---

12. Bukhari 4.59.3215.
13. Bukhari 7.67.5125.
14. Bukhari 9.97.7517; Muslim 1.313.
15. Bukhari 6.65.4958.
16. Bukhari 1.3.86.
17. Bukhari 4.59.3236.
18. Bukhari 6.65.4625.
19. Bukhari 8.81.6574.

Allah the newly conceived child's sex, fate and the age to which it will live.[20] Then throughout life, each person is assigned two angels to record everything they do.[21]

The Hadith also deploy angel stories to underpin Muslim orthopraxis, showing that everything from prayer to pilgrimage is divinely ordained and either monitored by or mirrored among the angels. For example, not only do angels gather at the times of prayer and report to Allah if you were praying when they left,[22] but they pray themselves, and if your 'amen' coincides with theirs all your sins will be forgiven.[23] In a similar vein, angels ask Allah's forgiveness while you are prostrated praying at the mosque – provided you do not break wind.[24] The Muslim practice of reciting the Qur'an is also angelically supported, with Bukhari reporting how Usaid bin Hudair's horses were disturbed when his night-time recitation of Surat al-Baqara drew the angels near.[25] Other Hadith explain that whichever of the seven vocalizations one chooses to recite the Qur'an is largely irrelevant, since Gabriel himself taught Muhammad all of them.[26]

A further type of angel story in the Hadith concerns angelic blessings and curses, several traditions warning that angels have the power to curse powerfully those who commit certain specific sins. For example, we are informed that anyone who cuts down a tree in Medina or invokes a heresy will be cursed by both Allah and the angels.[27] Betraying a Muslim will also lead to angelic curses, as well as the removal of any good deeds accredited to the betrayer.[28] Finally, anybody who introduces an innovation into Muslim belief or praxis, or who protects an innovator, stands under the curse of

20. Bukhari 1.6.318; Muslim 33.6395.
21. Bukhari 8.81.6491.
22. Bukhari 1.9.555.
23. Bukhari 1.10.780–781.
24. Bukhari 1.8.477.
25. Bukhari 6.66.5018.
26. Muslim 4.1785.
27. Bukhari 3.29.1867.
28. Bukhari 8.85.6755.

Allah and the angels.[29] Indeed, the formulaic phrase 'Allah and his angels' occurs frequently in the Hadith, often in the context of curses, blessings and oaths.

The final category of angel material in the Hadith worthy of note is a number of lengthy tales in which angels play a major feature, stories which often have no apparent connection to Islam. These are potentially *isra'iliyyat*, stories which made their way into Islam via Jewish and Christian Jewish converts. For example, there is the story of the Angel of Death being sent to Moses, who slaps him and sends him away. The Angel of Death returns to Allah and complains that Moses is not ready for death. Allah instructs Moses to place his hand over the back of an ox; the number of hairs he covers will dictate how many more years he will be permitted to live.[30]

To summarize the angel traditions in the Hadith, we can make several observations. First, there was a tremendous explosion of material between the time when Ibn Ishaq wrote his *sira* and when the canonical Hadith collections were recorded. These Hadith traditions are narrative in form, like the *sira*, and were probably generated by the same forces: the work of storytellers. This may also suggest that the Hadith angel traditions are more popular-level stories, not scholastic expositions of Islamic theology.

Furthermore, what we find in the Hadith is the expansion in story form of themes and topics that the Qur'an only alluded to. We shall shortly see a similar phenomenon in the *tafsir* writers, for whom narrative was often the way the Qur'an was exegeted. This common use of narratival material suggests that trying to separate out the early Islamic traditions into distinct genres – *sira*, Hadith and *tafsir* – may result in an imposition of a later taxonomy on an earlier amorphous tradition.[31] Rather, in the early period there was simply a deep and growing pool of common narrative material

29. Ibid.

30. Bukhari 2.23.1339; Muslim 30.5851.

31. Cf. J. Wansbrough, *Quranic Studies* (Oxford: Oxford University Press, 1977), p. 127; C. Adang, *Muslim Writers on Judaism and the Hebrew Bible* (Leiden: Brill, 1996), p. 14.

from which different tradition writers could fish, reshaping it to suit their purpose and audience.

Angels in tafsir

Narrative is by far the dominant form in which angel material is cited by the *tafsir* writers, even among later commentators, probably because it was in the form of stories that most angelic material was known, and removing it from this form was all but impossible.

We commence our survey with Tabari (d. 923), a commentator of tremendous importance since he purports to preserve earlier *tafsir* material that is no longer extant. Tabari favours long narratives and often cites multiple stories in discussing a single Qur'anic verse. For example, in exegeting Q2:30, Tabari wishes to explain why the angels are worried about Allah's creating mankind on the earth. Tabari reports a tale concerning the creation of the *jinn*, another class of spiritual being, who were created before mankind and who caused much bloodshed on the earth. The angels had to fight against and subdue them and were worried that man would act likewise. Tabari also reports how the clay from which Allah created man was fetched from the earth by the Angel of Death – Allah had first dispatched Gabriel and Michael, but both had felt sorry for the earth when it had expressed reluctance to give up her soil.[32]

Turning to Zamakhshari (d. 1144), a writer whose overall narrative content is lower, we discover that stories still dominate his material on angels. To cite just one example, in commentating on Q53:4–10, Zamakhshari reports a story that tells how Gabriel, rather than Allah himself, carried out the destruction of the people of Lot, carrying up their villages to heaven before casting them down again.[33]

Angel stories also appear extensively in both Razi (d. 1209) and Baidawi (d. 1286). For example, Razi records the story of

---

32. Abu Ja'far Muhammad b. Jarir Tabari, *The Commentary on the Qur'an*, 1 (Oxford: Oxford University Press, 1987), pp. 209–220.

33. Helmut Gätje, *The Qur'an and Its Exegesis* (London: Routledge, 1976), p. 166.

Abraham and Ishmael building the Ka'ba with Gabriel acting as architect, instructing them so that the earthly copy followed the heavenly archetype;[34] while Baidawi, commenting on Q2:97, reports the story of the Jews telling Umar that Gabriel is their enemy (since he helped Muhammad) and explaining that Michael is far more trustworthy. On being further informed that Gabriel stood on God's right and Michael on his left, Umar retorted that Michael and Gabriel must therefore share a unity of purpose.[35]

Such polemical use of angel stories can also be found in intra-Islamic debate, a good example occurring in Tabarsi (d. 1153), a classical Shi'ite commentator. His commentary on Q3:122 includes a story in which Muhammad reports seeing Gabriel sitting on a throne, announcing that there was no true sword except the sword of Muhammad and no true young fighter except Ali.

What we find, therefore, in examining this third strand of Islamic tradition is that angel stories continue to be transmitted in narrative form. However, in contrast to the Hadith, the focus is less on angel stories *per se*; rather, these stories are so deeply embedded in the tradition that they can be quoted to support a wide range of exegetical positions. The Shi'ite example from Tabarsi is particularly revealing; so widespread is the motif of Gabriel's appearances to Muhammad that when one wants to advance a sectarian position, to do so through the mouth of Gabriel is the obvious approach.

Angels in the qisas al-anbiya'

The term *qisas al-anbiya'* was possibly first used by Ibn Qutayba (d. 889), who deployed it to describe histories of the world in which tales of the pre-Islamic prophets were arranged chronologically.[36]

---

34. Mahmoud M. Ayoub, *The Qur'an and Its Interpreters*, 2: *The House of 'Imran* (Albany: State University of New York Press, 1992), p. 259.

35. Gätje, *Exegesis*, p. 47.

36. J. Pauliny, 'Some Remarks on the Qisas al-Anbiya Works in Arabic Literature', in A. Rippin (ed.), *The Qur'an: Formative Interpretation* (Aldershot: Ashgate Variorum, 1999), p. 313.

Arguably the best examples of this narrative genre are the works of Tha'labi (d.1035) and al-Kisa'i, (c. AD 1200), both of whom drew from multifarious sources, including pre-Islamic traditions and biblical material.[37] Angel stories are scattered liberally throughout the *qisas al-anbiya'* collections and are frequently told to fill in the background of a person, episode or fact to which the Qur'an simply alludes. But, unlike the *tafsir* writers, the *qisas al-anbiya'* writers usually wrote for a popular audience.

Many *qisas al-anbiya'* collections begin with creation, expanding upon the Qur'anic account of the creation of Adam and the rebellion of Iblis. Ibn Kathir tells the story of how the angels were frightened when Adam was first created from clay and disliked having to file past him before he was brought to life. Iblis was the most terrified and his fear made him lash out and strike Adam, causing a sound like ringing pottery.[38] Other legends tell of Iblis's subsequent attempts to tempt Adam and Eve, an exercise that first required Iblis to sneak back into paradise. One such tale explains how Iblis did this by flattering the peacock, who agreed to hide him under his wings and carry him in past the angel Ridhaun, guardian of paradise.[39]

Other tales in the *qisas al-anbiya'* collections pick up on the Qur'anic allusions to pre-Islamic prophets. A popular candidate for such tales was Idris (biblical Enoch), for the lack of biblical source material to draw upon allowed storytellers something of a free reign. For example, Tha'labi tells how the sun blazed down so hard on Idris that he cried to Allah who sent the Angel of Death to carry him directly on his wing to heaven.[40] Stories were also told of prophets not mentioned by name in the Qur'an: Wahb b. Munabbih reports how the Angel of Death caused Ezekiel to die and remain dead for a hundred years, after which he awoke to find

---

37. Firestone, *Journeys*, p. 4.
38. I. Kathir, *Stories of the Prophets* (Riyadh: Darussalam, n.d.), p. 31.
39. J. Knappert, *Islamic Legends*, 1 (Leiden: Brill, 1985), pp. 36–37.
40. B. M. Wheeler, *Prophets in the Qur'an: An Introduction to the Qur'an and Muslim Exegesis* (New York: Continuum, 2002), p. 47.

his donkey turned to bones. Allah then brought the creature back to life in front of him.[41]

Arguably the most popular candidate for this kind of story was Jesus, with Khalidi's 2001 volume recording many such tales.[42] Since angels were also tremendously popular figures, it is unsurprising that several stories combine the two motifs. One popular story, probably also traceable to Wahb b. Munabbih, tells how, when Jesus was born, all the idols fell over. The devils panicked, fleeing to Iblis to ask him what was occurring. Iblis flew around the world until he found a spot entirely surrounded by angels. He tried to get in at their head, feet and middle but failed, making Jesus the only infant not touched by Iblis at birth.[43]

The *qisas al-anbiya'* collections are full of such stories, few of which also appear in the *sira*, Hadith and *tafsir* literature. While the *sira* and Hadith traditions sought to tie stories to Muhammad, and the *tafsir* writers to particular Qur'anic verses, the *qisas al-anbiya'* collectors were free to draw upon everything that the storytellers had to offer, thus offering a tremendous window into popular belief and piety.

Common features

The appearance and use of angels across all these literary streams of the Islamic tradition have a number of features in common. First, most of the material is narrative-based, reflecting the narrative-primacy of all three genres, including *tafsir*, which was predominantly narrative in its earliest form.[44] Indeed, the *Sitz im Leben* of much of the Islamic tradition in the early period was probably the popular sermon;[45] such sermons were

---

41. Ibid., p. 287.
42. T. Khalidi, *The Muslim Jesus* (Cambridge, MA: Harvard University Press, 2001).
43. Ibid., p. 63; cf. Wheeler, *Prophets*, p. 302.
44. The type of *tafsir* termed 'haggadic' by Wansbrough. See Wansbrough, *Studies*, pp. 122–148.
45. Ibid., p. 145.

spread by *qussas*, storytellers, whose activity was responsible for circulating large amounts of tradition in the growing Islamic empire.[46]

In many of these angel stories there is the apparent influence of biblical material, for, as the Islamic empire rapidly grew, Muslims found themselves interacting with Christian and Jewish communities, and stories would naturally have been swapped. It is noteworthy that among the transmitters of many of these angel stories one frequently finds the names of Jewish converts to Islam, such as Wahb b. Munabbih, Abd Allah b. Salam and Ka'b al-Ahbar;[47] such stories would eventually acquire the label '*isra'iliyyat*'. This material was slowly Islamicized, with the removal of elements offensive to Muslim sensibilities, geographic and cultural adaptation to fit a Muslim milieu, and the insertion of formulaic Islamic elements.[48]

When the tradition began to crystallize as the Muslim empire shifted from a primarily oral to a literate culture, oral growth and development ceased. It is also around this time that we see a growing concern with the activity of the *qussas* and the spread of *isra'iliyyat.* Since many *tafsir* writers had also written *qisas al-anbiya'* works, this had also resulted in a blurred boundary between the genres and there was a desire to halt this process. This blurring is especially noticeable in the case of Tha'labi, whose commentary was unpopular in later years because it included this *isra'iliyyat* material.[49]

---

46. Adang, *Muslim Writers*, p. 9.
47. Ibid., pp. 7–12; Schmitz, 'Ka'b al-Ahbar', in *EI*², 4, pp. 316–317.
48. Firestone, *Journeys*, pp. 19–21; N. Calder, 'From Midrash to Scripture: the Sacrifice of Abraham in Early Islamic Tradition', *Le Muséon* 101 (1988), pp. 81–108.
49. P. G. Riddell, 'The Transmission of Narrative-Based Exegesis in Islam', in P. G. Riddell and T. Street (eds.), *Islam: Essays on Scripture, Thought and Society* (Leiden: Brill, 1997), p. 62; A. Rippin, 'Al-Thalabi', in *EI*², X, p. 434.

Oral narrative traditions and the Qur'an

Islamic tales and biblical traditions

Angel stories were popular in all the strands of Islamic tradition in the post-Qur'anic period. They grew through the work of generations of storytellers, who created a common pool of narrative stock from which the writers and collectors of *sira*, Hadith, *tafsir* and *qisas al-anbiya'* material could fish, finding stories which they could shape to fit their purposes. Narrative and theology are tightly interwoven in Islam, not least because in oral cultures stories are the means by which beliefs and values are preserved and transmitted.

We have also seen how the storytellers freely drew on biblical and other traditions in telling their angel stories and this leads us to a thorny question in scholarship. If these later traditions freely drew on non-Islamic sources, what about the angel material in the Qur'an? Here one enters a scholarly minefield: for a whole generation of Western scholarship, it was axiomatic that the Qur'an had copied earlier writings, Jewish and Christian; and, particularly in German Qur'anic scholarship, source-criticism held sway. We are now experiencing something of a backlash, with many Western scholars loath to apply any critical scholarship to the Qur'an. However, there may be an alternative way to explore the Qur'an's relationship to earlier narrative traditions without resorting to the somewhat positivistic and simplistic methods of source criticism, a methodology that allows for both influence and originality in the construction of the Qur'an. One such method is oral-formulaic theory. It is also a method to which the angel material in the Qur'an, especially the Iblis and Adam stories, is particular suited.

Oral-formulaic theory

Oral-formulaic theory is a comparatively new field of research whose inception can effectively be traced back to two scholars, Milman Parry (1902–35) and Albert Lord (1912–91).[50] Parry was a

---

50. J. M. Foley, *The Theory of Oral Composition* (Bloomington: Indiana University Press, 1988), pp. 19–56.

classicist, concerned particularly with the so-called Homeric question, the question whether the *Iliad* and the *Odyssey* were the work of one poet or several. Parry came to the conclusion that the answer was effectively *both*; Homer had been an oral poet, drawing upon the tradition that lay before him and retelling it afresh to audiences of his day.[51]

Central to Parry's argument was Homer's highly formulaic language, and Parry realized that this was the key to the work of the oral poet. It is formulaic language that allows the oral poet to compose live in performance, fluently in the traditional way. Formulas are groups of words regularly deployed to express a key idea; think of a repertoire of clichés and stock phrases. This does not limit the oral performer to mechanical reproduction:

> When we speak a language, our native language, we do not repeat words and phrases that we have memorized consciously, but the words and sentences emerge from habitual usage. This is true of the singer of tales working in his specialized grammar. He does not 'memorize' formulas, any more than we as children 'memorize' language. He learns them by hearing them in other singers' songs, and by habitual usage they become part of his own singing as well . . . The learning of an oral poetic language follows the same principles as the learning of language itself, not by the conscious schematization of elementary grammars but by the natural oral method.[52]

Developing this theory on inert texts was one thing, but Parry's particular genius was to look for a contemporary comparative that would enable him to undertake live fieldwork. He found this in Yugoslavia, where, working with his research assistant, Albert Lord, they studied a tradition of oral epic poetry that was still alive, enabling Parry to test and refine his theory of oral-formulaic composition.

---

51. See A. Parry (ed.), *The Making of Homeric Verse: The Collected Papers of Milman Parry* (Oxford: Clarendon Press, 1971).
52. A. B. Lord, *The Singer of Tales*, 2nd edn (Cambridge, MA: Harvard University Press, 2000), p. 36.

Lord and Parry concluded that the term 'original' is meaningless in oral tradition, belonging instead to a literary paradigm. The 'author' of an oral epic is both the performer (because the text is created in performance) and the traditional material and prosody which he deploys to tell his tale. This combination of creativity and tradition leads to a degree of fluidity; a story or poem's essence may remain constant, yet this stability is not reflected at the level of the wording for each telling is unique.[53]

Since Lord and Parry's work, oral-formulaic theory has been applied to hundreds of different cultures around the world, from *Beowulf* to the Hindu Vedas; from African Xhosa praise poetry to women's songs in the South Pacific Islands; from the pre-Islamic oral poets to Black Pentecostal preaching in Southern America. Scholars have consistently found that the insights of Parry and Lord have shed new light on texts that are or were created orally.

Oral-formulaic theory and the Qur'an

The Qur'anic story of the angels being commanded to bow down to Adam and Iblis's refusal to do so is ripe for exploration using oral-formulaic techniques. Its appearance seven times in the Qur'an means that, formulaic language aside, one is immediately alerted to the possibility that these stories may be performance-variants, alternative versions of the same oral story told on different occasions. The Hadith claim that Muhammad preached his revelations orally, so the suggestion that he was an oral performer is one that orthodox Muslims would affirm to an extent. But we can take things further by comparing these seven stories with each other and the wider Qur'an, analysing them for formulaic language. Space permits us to look briefly at just one account, in this case Q38:71–83.

> Behold, thy Lord said to the angels: 'I am about to create man from clay:
> '*When I have fashioned him (in due proportion) and* **breathed into him of My Spirit,** *fall* ye down in obeisance unto him.'

---

53. Ibid., pp. 99–101; cf. K. E. Bailey, 'Informal Controlled Oral Tradition and the Synoptic Gospels', *Asia Journal of Theology* 5/1 (1991).

So the angels *prostrated themselves, all of them together*:

Not so Iblis: he was *haughty*, and became one of those who reject Faith.

(Allah) said: 'O Iblis! *What prevents thee from prostrating thyself* to one whom I have created with my hands? Art thou haughty? Or art thou one of the high (and mighty) ones?'

(Iblis) said: '*I am better than he: thou createdst me from fire, and him thou createdst from clay.*'

(Allah) said: 'Then get thee out of here: for **thou art rejected, accursed**.

'And My *curse shall be on thee till the Day of Judgment*.'

(Iblis) said: '*O my Lord! Give me then respite till the* **Day the (dead) are raised**.'

Allah said: 'Respite then is granted thee –

'Till the **Day of the Time Appointed**.'

(Iblis) said: 'Then, by Thy power, I will put them all in the wrong,

'*Except Thy Servants amongst them, sincere and purified (by Thy Grace)*.'

Italic text represents phrases that appear more or less exactly in one or more of the other six Qur'anic accounts of this story, while that which is in bold type appears elsewhere in the Qur'an. In each case, what we have identified is formulaic material, clues that the text before us was created live, in performance, by an oral performer, drawing upon traditional material.

This analysis reveals that 21.5% of the text consists of formulas that occur elsewhere in the Qur'an, while 64% are formulas shared between the Iblis and Adam stories, making a total of 67% formulaic content overall. This is highly significant, for scholars have suggested that 20% marks the lower threshold of formulaic density – the further one goes beyond this figure, the more certain one can be of a text's oral provenance;[54] a figure of 67% is unusually high.

---

54. J. J. Duggan, *The Song of Roland: Formulaic Style and Poetic Craft* (Berkeley: University of California Press, 1973); cf. A. Dundes, *Fables of the Ancients?* (Oxford: Rowan and Littlefield, 2003), p. 65.

Conclusions

The idea that at least some of the angel material in the Qur'an was generated by live, oral storytelling removes the false disconnect that is often set up between the Qur'an and the later *sira*, Hadith, *tafsir* and *qisas al-anbiya'* works. Instead, we see that all Islamic traditions, from the canonized to the tightly controlled and scholarly and to the popular, drew upon the work of the storytellers, the *qussas*. The pre-Islamic Arabia into which Islam emerged was an oral, preliterate culture, and it was in oral form that tradition, culture and lore were transmitted and told; the storytellers and poets were important figures in their communities. The allusive nature of the Qur'an has long been recognized, and it is an oral culture to which it stands in intertextual relationship.

That angel material is narrative, story-based material, be it in the Qur'an or elsewhere, is profound and testifies to an important fact; Islamic angelology is a popular, narrative theology; it is theology from the bottom up, not imposed from the scholarly elite downwards. The predominance of angel stories in Islam demonstrates that theological ideas and categories transfer not merely from the clerical class down, but also from the popular level up. In the Qur'an, *sira*, Hadith and *tafsir* we see the same stories that grew so wildly in the *qisas al-anbiya'* works picked up, cited and deployed, in the case of *tafsir*, often to serve scholastic ends.

Despite the attempts around the time of Tha'labi to clamp down on this kind of material, it may in fact be that scholastic theology actually fuelled popular level angelology. With Allah so transcendent and the arguments of the classical scholars so far removed from the average Muslim, angels were a connection between ordinary Muslims and the divine; watching over them, protecting them, warning them to be pious and obedient, encouraging them and praying for them, just as they had done for Muhammad and the previous prophets. In short, Islamic angelology is not just narrative theology, it is also theology democratized.

10 ANGELS AND DEMONS IN FOLK ISLAM

Bill A. Musk

Friend and foe

Angel and demon together make their appearance in an amulet commonly purchased by Muslims in the Middle East. After acquisition, that amulet is sewn into clothing or encased in a leather pouch and hung round the neck or carried within a purse. The words and symbols copied on to the paper forming the amulet tell a powerful story. Two main characters are quickly introduced; the well-loved prophet Suleiman (Solomon) and the widely feared *jinni* Umm al-Subyan (literally 'Mother of Children'). An encounter between these two protagonists is described. Umm al-Subyan boasts real power to badly damage human beings, male and female – especially with regard to fertility and the humans' ability successfully to produce or sustain babies. Prophet Suleiman overwhelms the evil *jinni*, refusing to release her until she has sworn some seven times to a self-limiting contract with him. That contract promises safety from Umm al-Subyan for all who will carry on them this special amulet. The seven covenants comprising the contract between the prophet and the *jinni* constitute the main body of the charm. The first covenant exemplifies all seven. The 'voice' is that of Umm al-Subyan:

> In the name of God the Merciful and Compassionate. By God and there is no god but He, the Seeker, the Sought-after, the Victor over the vanquished, the Intelligent, the Destroyer, the Holder of dominion and Master of this world and the next, the Restorer of rotting bones, the Guide to the misbelievers, the Despiser of him who follows his own caprices, the Conqueror, the Ruler, from whom no one can escape, and whom no one can overcome or outwit. I shall not come near the person upon whom this amulet has been hung, neither in travel nor in rest, neither in studiousness nor in stupidity, neither in sleep nor in solitude, and God is witness to what I say.

Elsewhere in the amulet, God and the Prophet (Muhammad) are invoked, as are four archangels – Jibra'il (Gabriel), Mika'il (Michael), 'Azra'il (Azrael) and Israfil (Israfel). The famous Qur'anic verses known as 'the verse of light' (Q. 24:35) and 'the verse of the throne' (Q. 2:255) conclude the contract as recorded in the amulet. The aim of this amulet or charm – often referred to as 'The Seven Covenants of Suleiman' – is to protect Muslims from the feared *jinni*, Umm al-Subyan, especially around the vulnerable period of childbirth.

Umm al-Subyan is a frequently encountered and much feared *jinni*, female and very powerful. She is known by personal experience or reputation throughout a considerable part of the Muslim world. The existence of *jinn* such as Umm al-Subyan is firmly established by the Qur'an. We are told that *jinn* are just as surely created by God from fire as man is from clay: 'We created man from sounding clay, from mud moulded into shape; and the *jinn* race, We had created before, from the fire of a scorching wind' (Q. 15:26–27).

One *hadith* or tradition relates that Prophet Muhammad identified three kinds of *jinn* – the kind that flies through the air, the kind that finds expression as snakes or dogs, and the kind that is based in one place but travels about.[1] Muslims therefore need

---

1. Abu Tha'laba al-Khushani said: 'The messenger of Allah said: "The jinn are of three types: a type that has wings, and fly through the air; a type that

to be wary of dogs and snakes. Another *hadith* picks up this concern:

> Narrated Abu Sa'id al-Khudri:
> Muhammad ibn AbuYahya said that his father told that he and his companion went to Abu Sa'id al-Khudri to pay a sick visit to him. He said: Then we came out from him and met a companion of ours who wanted to go to him. We went ahead and sat in the mosque. He then came back and told us that he heard Abu Sa'id al-Khudri say: The Apostle of Allah (pbuh) said: Some snakes are *jinn*; so when anyone sees one of them in his house, he should give it a warning three times. If it return (after that), he should kill it, for it is a devil.[2]

In both West and East Africa today, the purchase and keeping, or sudden appearance, of certain kinds of snakes is often interpreted as the manipulation or intrusion of *jinn*. Loren Entz records part of the story of Abou Traoré, a Muslim and a traditional sorcerer in Burkina Faso. After his conversion to Christianity, Abou Traoré developed a reputation as a Christian exorcist. One day he was challenged by Makoura, a powerful sorceress whose 'source of power was that of a special evil spirit which had enabled her to kill hundreds of people through the years'.[3] Abou Traoré won the ensuing encounter with Makoura's evil spirit and Makoura discovered to her horror 'that her evil spirit which normally took on the form of a snake had been sighted dead in the bush'.[4] The snake's corpse rebuked Makoura for giving it too difficult an assignment!

Footnote 1 (*cont.*)

looks like snakes and dogs; and a type that stops for a rest then resumes its journey."' Reported in *Mushkil al-Athar* 4:95 by Imam Abu Ja'far al-Tahawi, one of the most outstanding authorities of the Islamic world on *hadith* and *fiqh* (jurisprudence). He was a contemporary of the great traditionists al-Bukhari, Muslim and Abu Dawud.

2. Abu Dawud 41.5236.
3. Loren Entz, 'Challenges to Abou's Jesus', *Evangelical Missions Quarterly* 22/1 (1986), p. 49.
4. Ibid., p. 49.

Makoura lost her sanity. Snakes are often perceived to be metamorphosed *jinn*.

Umm al-Subyan constitutes an example of a named *jinni*. A Kenyan Adventist pastor recently told me about a colleague of his in East Africa who has for many years exercised a powerful ministry of evangelism, which has on different occasions included exorcism. This evangelist, he told me, maintained that two of his front teeth had been knocked out of his mouth during a violent encounter with Umm al-Subyan. Umm al-Subyan is well known in the Middle East and East Africa, in experience or by reputation, and she is feared as a powerful harmer of human beings.

And the angels mentioned in the amulet? Those archangelic beings are invoked because of their perceived authority under God in the affairs of human beings. Jibra'il, of course, is the conveyor of God's word to Muhammad. The Prophet caught a glimpse of this holy being on two occasions, on at least one of which he lost consciousness, overwhelmed by the glorious form of the angel. Mika'il, mentioned once by name in the Qur'an, is charged with providing nourishment for bodies and knowledge for souls. 'Azra'il is identified in the Qur'an by the ascription 'Angel of Death', with his name supplied only by commentators on the sacred text. He collects the souls of all creatures at the time of their dying. Israfil delivers commands from God, places spirits within human bodies and will blow the trumpet on the Last Day. He has twelve wings and lives within touching distance of the very throne of God. These are very special angelic beings, powerful with God, and authoritatively engaged in the lives of human beings. The amulet seeks to engage their assistance for its carrier against the named *jinni* who would cause that person harm.

Powerful beings

Belief in angels comprises one of the requirements of Muslim believing, as the Qur'an forthrightly declares: 'The Messenger believeth in what hath been revealed to him from his Lord, as do the men of faith. Each one (of them) believeth in Allah, His angels, His books, and His messengers' (Q. 2:285).' Al-Bukhari records the following complementary tradition or *hadith*:

> Narrated Abu Huraira:
> One day while the Prophet was sitting in the company of some people, (the angel) Gabriel came and asked, 'What is faith?' Allah's Apostle replied, 'Faith is to believe in Allah, His angels, (the) meeting with Him, His Apostles, and to believe in Resurrection.'[5]

The Arabic word for 'angel', *malak*, whose root meaning is 'messenger', occurs more than eighty times in the Qur'an (usually in a plural sense) and repeatedly in the traditions (*ahadith*). Angels are intertwined with all the dimensions of human life, including original creation and subsequent continuing events that occur in the world. Angels are intimately involved with the key occurrences of Islam's sacred history – from the giving of revelation via mighty Gabriel to the Prophet's nocturnal ascent to heaven, to the famous battle of Badr, when God reputedly sent down as many as a thousand angels to help the outnumbered Muslims. Muslims know that a guardian angel is appointed to each person, while the deeds of every individual, from birth to death, are subject to angelic monitoring. Recording angels sit – one at each of a person's shoulders – constantly keeping account of acts good and bad (Q. 50:17). Pious Muslims regularly greet these angels, after completing their formal prayers, by bowing to the right and the left. At a person's death, his recording angels return to heaven from whence they will appear to act as witnesses for and against him on the Day of Judgment. The night of power, during the fasting month of Ramadan, marks the moment when the angels and the Spirit descend from heaven to earth to engage believers to God's will for the coming year: 'The Night of Power is better than a thousand months: Therein come down the angels and the Spirit by Allah's permission, on every errand' (Q. 97:3–4).

By God's leave, angels govern all macrocosmic and microcosmic forces in the world. In the Qur'an, the theme of power is strongly associated with the angels:

---

5. Bukhari 1.2.47.

> Praise be to Allah, Who created (out of nothing) the heavens and the earth, Who made the angels, messengers with wings, – two, or three, or four (pairs): He adds to Creation as He pleases: for Allah has power over all things (Q. 35:1).

> He was taught by one Mighty in Power,
> Endued with Wisdom: for he appeared (in stately form);
> While he was in the highest part of the horizon:
> Then he approached and came closer,
> And was at a distance of but two bow-lengths or (even) nearer;
> So did (Allah) convey the inspiration to His Servant – (conveyed) what He (meant) to convey (Q. 53:5–10)

The juxtaposition of Gabriel's power and the size of his wings is a frequent theme in the *hadith* literature:

> Narrated Abu Huraira:
> The Prophet said, 'When Allah ordains something on the Heaven the angels beat with their wings in obedience to His Statement which sounds like that of a chain dragged over a rock. His Statement: "Until when the fear is banished from their hearts, the Angels say, 'What was it that your Lord said?' 'They reply, '(He has said) the Truth. And He is the Most High, The Great'"' [Q. 34.23].[6]

In later texts the linkage between wings and power is developed further – Gabriel has six wings, each composed of a hundred smaller wings; or Gabriel has 1,600 wings all covered with saffron hair, from which fall drops that form other, lesser angels. Angels will accompany a man to the next abode on his departure from the earthly sphere. Sufis, especially, have tended to connect angels and human ecstatic experience:

> When you have travelled from man, you will doubtless become an angel;
> After you are done with this earth; your station is heaven.
> Pass again from angelhood; enter that ocean,

---

6. Bukhari 9.93.573.

That your drop may become a sea which is a hundred seas of Oman.[7]

Al-Ghazali identified three classes of angels: terrestrial, celestial and the archangels.[8] The terrestrial angels are those who concern themselves with the bodily processes of human beings. They get involved with dust, with blood and water, with sex. In the popular imagination:

> The angels bring a little dust from three places: from the place where he is created and from the place where he is born and from the place where he dies. The angels are present at the sexual connection. The angel brings this dust and kneads it and puts it into the woman, in her body – and also the dust from the place where he is born and also dust from the place where he dies. Angels are to be found in all three places.'[9]

Conception, birth and death – all times of sacred vulnerability – are viewed by many Muslims as moments when the angels willingly involve themselves with the human creation. Such terrestrial angels (reverting to al-Ghazali's typology) receive assistance from their celestial counterparts, who in turn are sustained by the

---

7. A. Iqbal, *The Life and Work of Jalaluddin Rumi* (Oxford: Oxford University Press, 1999 [1956]), p. 268. Rumi's point in this poetry is that human beings should not fear death because a person has already passed through a series of deaths in progressing from mineral to plant to animal to human. 'When was a person ever "less" by dying?' he asks. Now, we humans may expect the death of our earthly bodies so that we might be released into a stage where death itself dies – a joyous expectation!
8. See M. E. Marmura, 'Ghazalian Causes and Intermediaries', in *Journal of the American Oriental Society* 115/1 (Jan.–Mar. 1995), pp. 89–100. Marmura's article comprises a review of R. M. Frank's monograph *Creation and the Cosmic System Al-Ghazali and Avicenna* (Heidelberg: Carl Winter Universitätsverlag, 1992).
9. Thus speaks Hamdiye in Hilma Granqvist's record of conversations with Muslim women. In H. Granqvist, *Birth and Childhood Among the Arabs* (New York: AMS Press, 1975), p. 36.

archangelic throne-bearers. Al-Ghazali suggested that the being closest to God, closer even than Gabriel, is Seraphiel.

There is, evidently, a considerably developed taxonomy of angels within Islam, and it is little wonder that ordinary Muslims seek to attract their assistance in their search for advantage, or at least equilibrium, in a personal world that all too often seems subject to powerful malevolent forces.

For demons also are real in Islam! If you live in Morocco, it will not be Umm al-Subyan that will concern you so much as 'Aisha Qandisha:

> A man is walking along a road, and suddenly his vision blurs. He thinks there is something wrong with his eyes, but in fact it is Lalla 'Aisha Hasnawiyya [one of 'Aisha Qandisha's manifestations]. He sees only her in front of him, and he looks on and sees only her. When he comes to an isolated crossing or path, she takes him by the hand. She asks him why he is following her and where he knows her from. The man tries to excuse himself and says that he thought she was a woman he knew. She says, 'Fine. Welcome. Come with me. But we must go into a garden, and not into a house.' 'I'll even go beyond the garden,' the man answers. Lalla 'Aisha agrees and tells the man to follow her. Because he follows her, he sees only clouds. He alone sees her. Suddenly they find themselves in a big garden with a lot of food, near a well-furnished house. Lalla 'Aisha takes the shape of a woman the man loves and desires. She has the same features as the beauty, but they are slightly exaggerated. Her bust is eighty centimetres. They make love. Afterward she asks him what he wants to do. The man says he is single and wants to marry. Lalla 'Aisha says she wants to do the same. 'We'll make a vow [*ahd*] to God,' she says. She tells him not to tell anyone, not even his mother. If he does, she'll have his throat.[10]

Vincent Crapanzano describes the universe in which such a Muslim lives in his book *The Hamadsha*. It is a universe known to many Muslims, especially men. 'Pleasure at a price' is frequently

---

10. V. Crapanzano, *The Hamadsha: A Study in Moroccan Ethnopsychiatry* (Berkeley: University of California Press, 1973), pp. 152–168.

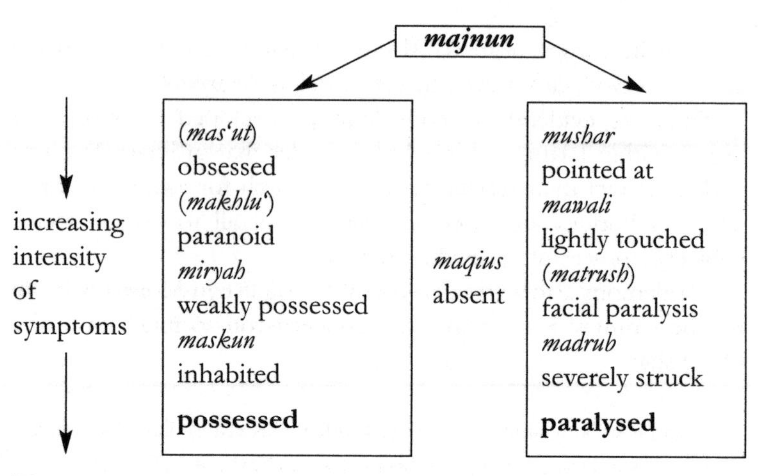

Figure 10.1 Crapanzano's taxonomy of *jinn*-produced illnesses

offered by female *jinn* to human males in many parts of the Muslim world.[11] Elsewhere, Crapanzano produces a taxonomy of *jinn*-produced illnesses (see Figure 10.1). His research unveils just how all-embracing and complex is the interacting of the malevolent spiritual world on the everyday human world. For a start, there are two distinct species of illness: the species that results in possession and the species that results in paralysis. In each kind of illness, an increasing intensity of symptom indicates the greater severity with which the *jinn* attacks the human being concerned. Different remedies (if the illness is treatable) need to be applied to different states or degrees of paralysis or possession. The general term *majnun* (often translated into English as 'mad') literally means 'to be be-*jinn*ed' or 'affected by *jinn*'.

---

11. See the parallel experience described by Shahhat, an Egyptian male, as recorded in R. Critchfield, *Shahhat: An Egyptian* (New York: Syracuse University Press, 1978), pp. 43–46. The biographer comments: 'No one was surprised. Many village men had been visited by such genii in their sleep, and it was not unknown for a man to even take one for a wife. One sorcerer in El Kom had done so and had been forced to stop sleeping with his real wife altogether because his genie warned she would kill him if his wife conceived a child' (p. 43).

Some of the states of illness are temporary, some are permanent, while a person who is at first only 'struck' or paralysed may progress to a state of being 'inhabited' or possessed. Some effects of a *jinn* attack always occur in the same part of the body, others can vary. A variety of potential remedies may be applied to those who have been subject to demonic attack. Those remedies aim either to drive out the offending *jinn* or to establish a symbiotic relationship with the *jinn* concerned.

The symbiosis-type of treatment that sometimes applies in the North African response to *jinn* activity is reminiscent of the handling (in the Middle East and Sudan) of infiltration by *zar* spirits into women or (in Pakistan and Bangladesh) of attacks upon females by *bhuts* or ghosts. These latter types of spirits seek a give-and-take relationship with the woman concerned, or perhaps, in the case of the *bhut*, with the husband of the woman concerned. From Kafr el-Elow in Egypt comes the following description of a woman caught up with a *zar* spirit. The symbiotic nature of the relationship (or damage resulting from a lack of commitment to it from the human party) is well illustrated:

> PATIENT NUMBER ONE. This is a woman in her forties who has been married twice. As a child she fainted of fright in a cemetery. Her mother used incense to help her recover from the experience and then took her to a male *zar* practitioner (*shaik*), who prescribed the sacrificing of a pair of pigeons and the blessing of the child with their blood. The mother was also advised to buy her daughter ornaments specifically designed to repel the evil spirits that were causing her headaches and her troubles with her brothers and sisters. The ornaments consisted of two silver rings engraved with the words, *Allah Akbar* (God is great), a fetish made from a brown stone to be pinned in her hair, and a necklace with a red stone to protect her heart. During her first marriage, the young woman's internal problems manifested themselves again. This time, she was in continuous conflict with her husband and she imagined that Negroes were trying to kill her. Upon consulting another *shaik*, she was told that she was possessed by the spirit *Abdel Salam El-Soudani* and that to satisfy him she had to sponsor or attend a *zar* ceremony, wear a white dress, sacrifice a sea pigeon and a red rooster, put their blood on her head, and not go out for a week. She felt so much better after participating in a *zar* as the *shaik* had recommended

> that she has not missed a single one since that time. During her first pregnancy she sacrificed several fowl, hoping to thereby prevent the evil spirits from killing her baby at birth. Now that the patient is older, however, she suffers from pains in her head and legs which, she contends, are punishment because she has not obeyed her spirit's directives. Now she is willing to do anything to please the spirit and to secure relief from her distress, because doctors are not able to cure her and only make her feel worse.[12]

In the *zar* cult, the spirit world and the human psychological world become entwined. The possessing spirit demands certain sorts of behaviour from the afflicted woman in order for the woman 'possessed' to live at peace. Often, such a woman may find considerable 'healing' in attending *zar* ceremonies where she can dance and express herself in an uninhibited manner. Treatment, in such cases, is not focused on acts of exorcism but rather on finding the means to a symbiotic relationship between human protégé and infiltrating spirit. So, as we have seen, a practitioner in the Middle East may discern that a woman is possessed by a certain *zar* spirit, and announce that the pathway to peace of mind for her will be for her to wear clothes of a certain colour, for her to sacrifice a certain kind of animal or to fulfil other obligations. In Pakistan or Bangladesh, an equivalent practitioner may declare that a *bhut* troubling a female patient will quieten down only if the woman's husband stops beating her. The *bhut*–human relationship is a complex one requiring wisdom at a psychological as well as at a purely spiritual level.

The world of demons as a whole is an intricate one. It requires the careful discernment of skilled practitioners to diagnose exactly what has happened to the human victims concerned. Affected people look to practitioners of proven ability to access the kind of power required to counteract such invasions of evil into their everyday lives. Such practitioners retain authority with people precisely because they exhibit authority within the world of spirits. Frequently, those practitioners are women. They are usually people

---

12. As described by H. Fakhouri in *Kafr El-Elow: An Egyptian Village in Transition* (New York: Holt, Rinehart and Winston, 1972), p. 95.

somewhat removed from the official hierarchy of the Islamic faith – though not always so. Some local imams may well supplement their meagre incomes by involvement in this area of peoples' everyday lives. In this world, 'payment by results' dominates the exchange of funds for positive help received. Those involved in acting within this world – both patients and practitioners – see nothing in it contradictory to their profession as faithful Muslims.

One of the main female characters in Nawal El Saadawi's *The Innocence of the Devil* is Nefissa. Nefissa is incarcerated in the Yellow Palace, an asylum for the insane. At night in her dreams, Nefissa takes on the character of her Aunt Zanouba, her favourite relative from childhood days. Aunt Zanouba represents freedom to Nefissa – not just the freedom of non-confinement, but also the freedom of being a woman on equal footing with men. Zanouba owns such freedom because of her familiarity with the spirit world. She is called 'El Alma', 'the lady who knows' – one who has access to spirit-inspired sources of information:

> During the day she saw her Aunt Zanouba sitting amongst the men. She smoked the water pipe and blew the smoke into the Headman's face. The Headman threw his head back and laughed, and the men around him called her El Alma. Her house was built of red brick. It rose two storeys higher than the house of the Headman, and was three metres higher than the House of God [the mosque]. She moved her arms and legs freely in front of the Headman. She feared no one, not the King, nor the President, nor the General. She stamped on the ground and her voice rose in song. Everyone acclaimed her name and called her Zanouba El Alma. Their eyes gleamed and their irises trembled in the whites of their eyes. Their hearts beat under their ribs and in their hearts was hidden a feeling like awe, a fear mingled with lust. She knew their secrets. She knew what was hidden, what was beyond ordinary understanding. God had revealed things to her. She read the cup and the palm of the hand. She could decode the signs in the palm and understand the language of shells. She mingled with spirits and sirens.[13]

13. N. El-Saadawi, *The Innocence of the Devil* (London: Methuen, 1994), pp. 177–178.

Saadawi's aim in her novel is to illustrate some of the cracks she discerns in the patriarchal, male-oriented world of the Muslim Middle East. She is writing in support of a movement for women's liberation. In the process she identifies a major theme in most Muslims' lives: they are caught up in attempts to manipulate the spirit world. The universe of the unseen – of *jinn* and angels, blessings and curses – is familiar territory to them. Some of them, such as Zanouba – potent woman in a man's world – have incredible power in that universe. All of them fear it.[14]

I have attempted elsewhere[15] to delineate a cosmology of popular Islam (see Figure 10.2). In such a cosmology, concepts of personal being that are trans-empirical in nature but that inhabit this world are many – and the majority of them are hostile to human beings. We have considered *jinn* (including the concept of specific, named *jinn*), and the *zar* spirits plus their equivalents. The *qarinat* comprise another genus of spirit (authenticated again by the Qur'an) that impinge on every human being. For every human has a twin-spirit that was born into the 'parallel' world at the same time as the human was born into this world. The *qarinat* constantly interfere in the lives of their human 'twins' – especially if they are not pleased with the human persons' actions. Thus it may be believed that a child is having constant night terrors because its spirit equivalent is not pleased with how the human child is being treated, or because its *qarin* (male spirit for female human) or *qarina* (female spirit for male human) is jealous of the human child. Ruses are indulged in – such as calling a beautiful child 'ugly' or dressing a boy in girls' clothing – in order to pre-empt hostile spirit action that is born of envy or jealousy. *The Story of Zahra* is considered to be a largely autobiographical life story written by Hanan Al-Shaykh, a Lebanese Shi'a woman. In this sad account, multiple crises throughout the young woman's life lead inexorably to a

14. See the sobering account of accurate predictions of respective marriage and remarriage for Sultana and her sister Sara through palmistry by Huda, their Sudanese slave, in J. P. Sasson, *Princess* (London: Bantam Books, 1993), pp. 144–148.

15. B. A. Musk, *The Unseen Face of Islam* (London: Monarch, 2003), p. 174.

	Concepts of 'Power' (Impersonal)	Concepts of 'Being' (Personal)	
OTHER WORLDLY REALM	*qadr*	God	
		archangels: Sarafiel Gabriel others	
	books: especially Qur'an	angels: no gender; created of light	
THIS-WORLDLY REALM	magic	devils: Iblis others	TRANS-EMPIRICAL PHENOMENA
	sorcery		
	astrology	jinn: have gender usually bad	
	divination	prophets: apostles prophets messengers	
	baraka		
	dhikr	dead saints: good	
	evil eye		
	omens	*zar* spirits	
	vows	named jinn	
	curses	*qarinat*	
	blessings	ancestors	
	prophylaxes	souls of recently dead	
	{ dreams visions sleep }		
		living holy men	EMPIRICAL PHENOMENA
	herbs	humans: Muslim: male female others	
	drugs	animals	
	other natural forces	plants: wheat (bread) others	

Figure 10.2 Cosmology of popular Islam

tragic conclusion. Zahra's mother has an affair that is uncovered by her violent father, who is a ticket operator on the Beirut tramlines. Zahra herself gets involved with Malek while working in a cigarette factory, and ends up undergoing two backstreet abortions. Later, Zahra is given a chance of a peaceful life, away from a country embroiled in civil war and away from a history that has damaged her. She stays with her uncle in Africa, eventually marrying a friend of his there, a man called Majed. Within that relationship, Zahra's past catches up with her and she suffers some breakdowns. In those breakdowns, she experiences flashbacks to events with Malek, with her parents, and with her spirit-double, or *qarina*: 'When I was a girl, whenever my struggles began with my *Qarina*, I would be unable to open my eyes. I would try to shout and release myself with all my strength, but my vocal cords would be paralysed. The *Qarina* stood between me and my sight, my voice, my thoughts.'[16]

In the end, Zahra returns to Beirut. In some senses, she has become 'insane' but the book ends with a twist by suggesting that actually Zahra has a 'sanity' in the midst of the civil war – a sanity which those fighting that war deny. She befriends and 'services' a sniper from an opposing faction. She loves across the confessional and ethnic divides: that is her 'sanity' in the midst of the hatred that dominates the society. Zahra inevitably becomes pregnant and is in the end killed by the very sniper whom she has loved because, for him, his 'insanity' outweighs the 'sanity' that she offers in her body. In some ways the book might be seen to be asking whether recourse is needed to evil spirit-beings, like the *qarinat*, when human beings can do one another so much damage.

Contrasting with hostile, trans-empirical beings are other, more benign – though equally trans-empirical – beings, such as ancestors or dead saints. Such beings are the focus of invocation and pilgrimage on a massive scale in many Muslim contexts. Angels constitute a distinct kind of benign, trans-empirical being. They exist in a variety of species and are far more powerful than any 'this-worldly' trans-empirical beings (both beneficial and hostile),

---

16. H. Al-Shaykh, *The Story of Zahra* (London: Pavane, 1986), p. 82.

because they live not in this world but in the 'other world', closer to God himself. Their engagement on a believer's part promises real potential. Angels of all species constitute a tremendous force for good. Moreover, because angels are known to act only in obedience to divine decrees, their value as protectors and overseers of human beings is inestimable. Angels do not act capriciously or seek, out of their own will, to afflict people. Rather, if they can be invoked, they promise real protective help to human beings exposed on every quarter to evil.

Taking sides

> Longingly, I dreamed of finishing my book in secret and returning to Venice. I approached the grave, which had been carefully covered with dirt. At this moment, angels are interrogating him above, asking him whether he is male or female, his religion and whom he recognizes as his prophet.[17]

Beyond the grave, it is with the powerful angels that mankind will have to contend. So why not recruit them to assistance in this life also? For many Muslims, the 'terrestrial' world they live in is a complex place, full of unseen, competing beings and subject to the effects of powerful forces. Angels and demons constitute some of the major players in that larger-than-human drama. In such a complex world, survival seems frequently to depend upon discovering help – from whatever source – for recovering equilibrium in life. Too often, evil invades peoples' families or circumstances. Knowledge and power are the prerequisites for recovering health or sanity, or for inflicting revenge upon a human enemy. The world of angels and demons, as it finds contemporary expression in ordinary Muslims' lives, is an amoral world. Pragmatism determines peoples' practices: what works is what is seized upon. Whoever has the needed deposit of knowledge or

---

17. O. Pamuk, *My Name is Red* (London: Faber and Faber, 2001), pp. 116–117.

power will be appealed to in order for life to continue as bearable. Often, the holder of that deposit will be a living human being, a practitioner of some kind. Sometimes, the holder will be a dead saint or an esteemed prophet or an angel; such beings may be approached directly by the supplicant. Usually, any human practitioner worth their salt will in any case appeal beyond himself or herself to beings or forces of a trans-empirical nature. So, angels or *jinn* will be recruited to accomplish positive or negative ends. Approaches may be made to saints, prophets, angels and archangels for protection and help against malevolent demons and spirit-beings. Or, malevolent beings may be engaged to wreak vengeance on some human rival. The taking of sides is, in essence, amoral. The means are justified by the end. Precisely because of that, one can never know when one might be subject to attack. An unknown rival might be jealous of one's own success, or of one's pretty, marriageable daughter. An enemy might want to take vengeance for an offence committed, wittingly or unwittingly. Or, someone might just be evil, out to wreak havoc. Or perhaps the *jinn* are feeling mischievous or the *qarinat* jealous? Who knows? The best solution for a Muslim caught up in such a changeable and chancy existence is to purchase a renowned amulet, telling the story of a famous prophet gaining advantage over an abhorrent *jinni*. Wear that amulet, and one might just be able to survive the day and the night. Wear that amulet, and one might just be able to secure some balance in a universe peopled by angels and demons.

11 COPING WITH THE NON-EXISTENT: *A COURSE IN MIRACLES* AND EVIL

Ruth Bradby

Introduction

In the recently published *Encyclopedia of New Religions*, the article on *A Course in Miracles* states that spiritualities[1] based on the *Course*

---

1. I use the plural of 'spirituality', as *A Course in Miracles* has spawned many forms of spirituality with various understandings of *Course* teaching and various emphases. At one end of the spectrum is the Trappist monk, John Jacob Raub of the Abbey of Gethsemani [*sic*] in Kentucky, USA, who combines the wisdom of orthodox Christian spirituality with insights from the *Course*. See J. J. Raub, *Who Told You That You Were Naked? Freedom from Judgment, Guilt and Fear of Punishment* (New York: Crossroad, 1992). Kenneth Wapnick, the final editor of the *Course* and believed by many to be its official interpreter, views *Course* spirituality as a unique spiritual path which stands alongside the great religious and philosophical traditions of the world. His most scholarly volume on the *Course*, the 600-page *Love Does not Condemn: The World, the Flesh, and the Devil according to Platonism, Christianity, Gnosticism and 'A Course in Miracles'* (Roscoe, New York:

deny the presence or possibility of evil.[2] Therefore, a discussion of how devotees of the *Course*, as it is popularly known, cope with evil appears to be a non-starter: why develop strategies for coping with that which does not exist? On a deeper level, however, the *raison d'être* of the *Course* can be understood as a self-help textbook providing a metaphysical system and a metanarrative which answers the perennial problem of theodicy. The *Course* combines teaching with exercises in disciplined mind-training designed to enable the devotee to apply the spirituality of this metaphysical system to the situations of daily life.

My purpose in this chapter is, first, to examine the context of *Course* spirituality, that is the phenomenon of channelled literature, distinguishing between intentional and spontaneous channelling. The widespread practice of channelling in the new holistic spiritualities reveals much about the participants' beliefs concerning good and evil in the universe. Secondly, I shall examine in some detail the spirituality of *A Course in Miracles* as an example of an influential text which owes its origin to spontaneous channelling. I shall focus on the *Course's* attitude towards evil, which the *Course* claims to be non-existent. In the final section, I shall look briefly at the practical problems this strand of *Course* teaching throws up for participants in *Course* spiritualities.

Footnote 1 (*cont.*)

Foundation for *A Course in Miracles*, 1989), appears to be written for the future, when scholars and academics will view the *Course* as something more than pop psychology. Another *Course* interpreter, Robert Perry, provides an interpretation of *Course* teaching which differs from that of Wapnick. See R. Perry, *Path of Light: Stepping into Peace with 'A Course in Miracles'* (Sedona, Arizona: Circle of Atonement, 2004). While most *Course* devotees sustain their spirituality through individual practice, meeting in study groups and conferences and using the internet, the Revd Tony Ponticello has founded the Community Miracles Center, which meets and organizes itself as a church and ordains *Course* clergy.

2. R. Bradby, 'A Course in Miracles', in C. Partridge (ed.), *Encyclopedia of New Religions* (Oxford: Lion, 2004), pp. 248–249.

The background of channelled literature

A Course in Miracles, published in 1975, is part of a genre of esoteric texts called 'channelled literature', which emerged in the late 1960s and '70s and influenced the emerging New Age spiritualities[3] of the 1980s. The Dutch New Age scholar Wouter Hanegraaff has argued that many of the core beliefs of the New Age network of spiritualities of the 1980s were first formulated in channelled messages. He writes 'In spite of the tendency among

---

3. Use of the term 'New Age' for the new spiritualities which emerged at the end of the twentieth century has become problematic and unfashionable in both popular and academic writing, although it continues to have currency on the European continent. During the 1970s and '80s many (including some of the devotees themselves) regarded the new spiritualities as alternative spiritual paths associated with the counterculture movement of young people. Since then the new spiritualities have evolved into a commonplace feature of today's culture and have ceased to be alternative. Furthermore, many of those involved in the new spiritualities (including the publishers of *A Course in Miracles*) object to the term because they associate the 'New Age' with superficiality, celebrity glamour and commerce-driven motives which seem alien to the idea of sincere spirituality. For a discussion of the problems involved in using the label 'New Age', written in the early 1990s, see J. R. Lewis, 'Approaches to the Study of the New Age Movement', in J. R. Lewis and J. G. Melton (eds.), *Perspectives on the New Age* (Albany: SUNY Press, 1992). More recently, Paul Heelas, who wrote a book called *The New Age Movement* in 1996 (Oxford: Blackwell), has substituted the term 'holistic milieu' for 'New Age' in his recent book, co-authored with Linda Woodhead, *The Spiritual Revolution* (Oxford: Blackwell, 2005). Another scholar of contemporary spiritualities, Christopher Partridge, uses the term 'occulture' in his *The Re-Enchantment of the West*, 1 (London: T. and T. Clark, 2005). However, the expression 'New Age' continues to be useful to describe alternative spiritualities which emerged in the 1980s, because the term was common currency at that time and continues to differentiate these spiritualities from other popular spiritualities also emerging at the time: paganism, heathenism and Satanism, for example.

New Age believers to emphasize personal experience as the exclusive basis of religious truth, New Age religion must, to a large extent, be considered a religion of revelation, *Offenbarungsreligion*.'[4] In order to understand the context of *A Course in Miracles* and its attitude towards evil, one must look briefly at the phenomenon of channelling.

Hanegraaff defines channelling as 'the belief of individuals that they are able to act as a channel for information from sources other than their normal consciousness. This source is believed to represent a level of wisdom superior to that of humans.'[5] Writing from an emic perspective, Jon Klimo defines channelling as 'the communication of information to or through a physically embodied human being from a source that is said to exist on some other level or dimension of reality than the physical as we know it, and is not from the normal mind (or self) of the channel'.[6] Klimo stresses the importance of the phrase 'is said to' in his definition and argues that one's own intuition and inspiration are potential sources for channelling.[7] Given that two important beliefs within holistic spiritualities are (1) in the interconnectedness of all life and (2) in the Self (or Higher Self) as in some sense divine, one's intuition and inspiration could also be viewed as sources of divine wisdom coming from that which is greater than the individual self. Hanegraaff makes the same point when he quotes the famous lines from George Bernard Shaw's play *Saint Joan*:[8]

> *Joan*: I hear voices telling me what to do. They come from God.
> *Robert*: They come from your imagination.
> *Joan*: Of course. That is how the messages of God come to us.

---

4. W. J. Hanegraaff, *New Age Religion and Western Culture: Esotericism in the Mirror of Secular Thought* (New York: Brill, 1996), p. 27.
5. Ibid., pp. 23–24.
6. J. Klimo, *Channeling: Investigations on Receiving Information from Paranormal Sources* (Berkeley: North Atlantic Books, 1998), p. 2.
7. Ibid. p. 4.
8. Hanegraaff, *New Age Religion and Western Culture*, p. 23.

Channelling may be intentional or spontaneous. In the latter, the channeller is at the mercy of the revelation, while for the former, there are techniques taught in spiritual self-help books, tapes, seminars and workshops to show people how to become channels. These channelling manuals have become in themselves a genre of spiritual self-help literature.

Information gained from intentional channelling is often claimed to be specifically helpful and authoritative to the person acting as channel. The activity of channelling itself is said to have a beneficial effect on the channeller. One author of a channelling manual writes that 'typically people who channel become more self-confident, happier, clearer about their path and their choices, less selfish, less stressed over life's problems, calmer, more loving and psychologically much stronger'.[9] The literature on channelling, as well as the stories of channelling experiences told to me by devotees, suggest that many see channelling as central to their spiritual experience. They claim that the messages they have received have helped them over specific difficulties, helped them in relationships and sometimes given them confidence by showing them that they are cared for by their own spirit guide. Thus, intentional channelling has become an important feature for many practising one of the new holistic spiritualities. I have spoken to individuals who say that channelling has helped them to cope with evil in the guise of negative thoughts or external difficulties. They speak of gaining confidence when struggling with feelings of hopelessness. The channelling experience, they say, has shown they are not helpless in the face of external events and forces beyond their control. There is benevolent, personal help available for the asking.

The widespread practice of intentional channelling also shows how sensitive those in the holistic milieu (including non-pagans) are to what might be called a spirit world. Significantly for this chapter, the seemingly universal assumption among those involved in intentional channelling is that the entities channelled – whether they be ascended masters, spirit guides, angels, extraterrestrials,

---

9. L. De Alberdi, *Channelling: What It Is and How to Do It* (London: Piatkus, 1998), p. 8.

historical personalities, gods or goddesses – are benign beings. The information channelled is seen as helpful, healing, affirming and transforming. The channelled message may offer help about a specific problem or suggest ways of creating more healthy mental attitudes. The point is, channellers perceive themselves as inhabiting a loving universe, peopled by higher beings eager to help them on the path of spiritual evolution. During the five years in which I have spoken to those involved in channelling, I have not encountered anyone who spoke of receiving a message of evil or harmful intent. The large body of literature which has come out of channelling also suggests that the entities channelled are believed to be benign, helpful beings.

However, messages from intentional channelling, helpful and authoritative though they may be for the individual, have not commanded the teaching authority which messages from spontaneous channelling have achieved for many followers of holistic spiritualities. Most of the core beliefs which were central to New Age spiritualities in the 1980s were first articulated, not in intentional channelling, but through spontaneous channelling. While intentional channellers have control over the phenomenon, and indeed try to induce the practice by various techniques, spontaneous channellers have been taken by surprise by the 'dictation' coming from a source outside their consciousness. This was true of the genesis of three of the most influential channelled texts in holistic spiritualities from the 1970s: the material from the entity 'Ramtha' channelled by J. Z. Knight, Jane Roberts' 'Seth' texts, and *A Course in Miracles*. The story of how *A Course in Miracles* was scribed illustrates how authoritative spiritual entities appear to invade the ordinary existences of the channellers in this second form of channelling.

The history of *A Course in Miracles*

The history of the writing of *A Course in Miracles* is well known to all *Course* devotees. They attach great importance to the story of the *Course* for at least two reasons. First, the manner in which the material was received and written down is believed to place the

Course on a par with the revealed scriptures of the great world religions. Secondly, the story of how the *Course* came to be written is thought to provide a living example of the spiritual principles of the *Course.*

A Course in Miracles was scribed by Helen Schucman, a research psychologist and associate professor in the Department of Psychiatry at Columbia University in New York. As a lapsed Jewish atheist, she viewed the hearing of 'voices' as pathological behaviour and found the experience of channelling a disturbing one. In her unpublished autobiography, she describes how she resisted the process and only allowed the material to be published anonymously, fearful that it would damage her professional reputation.[10] After going through a disquieting period of receiving dream-like visions, in October 1965 Schucman heard an inner voice commanding her, 'This is a course in miracles. Please take notes.' As Schucman later wrote, 'That was my introduction to the voice. It made no sound, but seemed to be giving me a kind of rapid, inner dictation which I took down in a shorthand notebook. The writing was never automatic. It could be interrupted at any time and later picked up again. It made me very uncomfortable, but it never seriously occurred to me to stop. It seemed to be a special assignment I had somehow, somewhere agreed to complete.'[11] The text implies that the voice is that of the biblical Jesus.

Schucman's head of department at Columbia University, Professor William Thetford, was more open to paranormal phenomena than Schucman, and gladly undertook the task of typing Schucman's manuscript. Photocopies of the manuscript were shown to a few friends who embraced its teaching with enthusiasm. One friend, Kenneth Wapnick, also a psychologist, helped Schucman to edit the *Course* into its present form. In 1975, another

10. K. Wapnick, *Absence from Felicity: The Story of Helen Schucman and Her Scribing of 'A Course in Miracles'* (Roscoe, New York: Foundation for *A Course in Miracles*, 1999), pp. 183–187.

11. Anonymous, *A Course in Miracles: Text, Workbook and Teacher's Manual* (New York: Viking Penguin, 1996 [1976]), p. viii.

friend, Judith Skutch, formed the Foundation for Inner Peace and published the first 1,200-page edition of *A Course in Miracles*, consisting of three volumes: *Text, Workbook for Students* and a *Manual for Teachers*. Since then over a million copies of the *Course* have been sold in English and it has been translated into the major languages of the world. Thousands of *Course* study groups have grown up around the globe together with hundreds of websites and organizations formed to support students of the *Course* and to emphasize one or another aspect of *Course* teaching. A new edition of *A Course in Miracles* for Great Britain was launched in May 1985 in the Jerusalem Chamber of Westminster Abbey by Lillian Carpenter, wife of the Dean at that time and herself a *Course* teacher. At present there are over a dozen *Course* organizations in the UK, running workshops, conferences, church services, study groups, websites and counselling services. All are loosely linked through the Miracle Network in London, directed by Ian Patrick, who edits *The Miracle Worker* magazine. In October, 2004, the Miracle Network celebrated its tenth anniversary with a weekend conference in London in which most British *Course* groups participated.

Hanegraaff has referred to *A Course in Miracles* as the closest thing the New Age network of spiritualities has to a widely revered 'sacred scripture'.[12] The Swedish scholar Olav Hammer finds 'distinct signs that *A Course in Miracles* has entered the process that leads to the creation of a canonical scripture'.[13] Few reading this chapter will have heard of *A Course in Miracles;* yet it is equally unlikely that anyone reading this has not, unknowingly, encountered the teaching and spirituality of the *Course* in one guise or another, most probably through the self-help books inspired by *A Course in Miracles*. There are now hundreds of such spiritual self-help books based in whole or in part on the *Course*. They are found on the 'spirituality', 'self-help' and 'body, mind and spirit' shelves of major bookshop chains across the country. Many of them have

12. Hanegraaff, *New Age Religion and Western Culture*, pp. 37–38.

13. O. Hammer, *Claiming Knowledge: Strategies of Epistemology from Theosophy to the New Age* (Leiden: Brill, 2001), p. 459.

reached the top of the bestseller lists on several continents and now have a life of their own quite apart from the various *Course* organizations.[14]

Given that *Course* spiritualities deny the existence of evil, how do they help devotees to live in a world where evil appears to triumph more often than not? To accomplish this, *A Course in Miracles* offers its readers a logical metaphysical system based on non-dualism overlaid with a metanarrative of fall-redemption derived from the Bible.

A metanarrative of fall-redemption

While the *Course* does not recognize the presence or possibility of evil, it does acknowledge 'mistakes', 'obstacles to peace' and

14. For example, M. Scott Peck's *The Road Less Travelled* (London: Rider, 1978) was in part inspired by his study of the *Course* soon after its publication and has sold over ten million copies. G. Jampolsky's *Love Is Letting Go of Fear* (London: Bantam Books, 1980 [1979]), also an international bestseller, was based on his use of *Course* principles to help dying children. See also two bestsellers by S. Jeffers, *Feel the Fear and Do It Anyway: How to Turn Your Fear and Indecision into Confidence and Action* (London: Ryder, 1991), and *Embracing Uncertainty: Achieving Peace of Mind as We Face the Unknown* (London: Hodder and Stoughton, 2003); C. Spezzano, *If It Hurts It Isn't Love: Secrets of Successful Relationships* (London: Hodder and Stoughton, 1999); E. Tolle, *The Power of Now: A Guide to Spiritual Enlightenment* (London: Hodder and Stoughton, 1999). N. D. Walsch's *Conversations with God* books, beginning with *Book One: An Uncommon Dialogue* (London: Hodder and Stoughton, 1995), now take up an entire bookshelf in my local Borders store and have been bestsellers for ten years. M. Williamson, *A Return to Love: Reflections on the Principles of 'A Course in Miracles'* (London: Thorsons, 1996 [1992]), was the first *Course*-related self-help book to be published by a mainstream publisher; it continues to be popular. L. Hay, *You Can Heal Your Life* (London: Eden Grove, 1984), has sold over three million copies. Its success encouraged Hay to form her own publishing firm, Hay House, to publish her books and those of other spiritual self-help authors.

'blocks to the awareness of God's love'.[15] The Introduction to the *Course* states its purpose clearly: 'The course . . . does aim, however, at removing the blocks to the awareness of love's presence.'[16] *Course* ontology posits two levels of reality. Level one is God (the real), and level two is the material world (the unreal). In a much-loved and much-quoted passage from the Introduction, this teaching is laid out with simplicity.[17]

> Nothing real can be threatened.
> Nothing unreal exists.
> Herein lies the peace of God.

All that is wrong in the individual and in society can be traced back to the false belief that separation from God the creator (level one) is possible; the answer to the problem lies in a return to God/level one (which in reality one has never left) by renouncing the false belief in separation. In *Course* cosmology, all humankind was in union with God (the real), who is love. The *Course* does not define love: 'The course does not aim at teaching the meaning of love, for that is beyond what can be taught.'[18] However, God and love are seen to be synonymous and 'all-encompassing'; both are beyond human definition. The *Course* teaches that the opposite of love is fear, the key attribute of level two (the unreal). Logically, what is 'all-encompassing' (God/love) can leave room for no other presence: 'The opposite of love is fear, but what is all-encompassing can have no opposite.'[19] If separation from God is impossible, what went wrong? When all were joined as 'Sons of God', having one mind, the Son of God is said to have come to believe during a 'mad moment' in the possibility of separation from God. 'You have chosen to be in a state of opposition in which opposites are possible.'[20] This

---

15. Anonymous, *Text*, p. 1.
16. Ibid.
17. Ibid.
18. Ibid.
19. Ibid.
20. Ibid., p. 76.

moment of 'madness' caused him to forget his true reality as God's perfect creation and to enter the unreal dream (or nightmare) of level two. Level two is the physical material world of bodies, our natural earthly environment, a place where there is a belief in separation. This false belief in the possibility of separation from God results in other false beliefs besides fear: in sin, guilt and evil in oneself and in others.

This false belief in separation is seen as the source of all that we perceive as evil. The 'fall' from level one to level two can be seen as a metanarrative derived from the biblical fall-redemption metanarrative. The pre-separation state is described with words which describe the reality of level one: God, love, Father, Christ, Kingdom of Heaven, spirit, truth, being, innocence, life, knowledge, light, peace, grandeur, eternity and joy. Conversely, the unreality of level two is described with contrasting words: fear, sin, guilt, body, existence, ego, the world, perception, war, time and scarcity. The *Course* metanarrative appears not only to derive from the biblical fall–redemption model, but to correct it:

> We have discussed the fall or separation, but its meaning must be clearly understood. The separation is a system of thought real enough in time though not in eternity. All beliefs are real to the believer. The fruit of only one tree was 'forbidden' in the symbolic garden. But God could not have forbidden it, or it could not have been eaten . . . The 'forbidden tree' was named the tree of knowledge. Yet God created knowledge and gave it freely to His creations. The symbolism here has been given many interpretations, but you may be sure that any interpretation that sees either God or his creations as capable of destroying Their Own purpose is in error.[21]

The *Course* metanarrative is compared to Jesus' earthly life, his birth (leaving level one by believing he could have a body) and suffering: 'You have nailed yourself to a cross and placed a crown of thorns upon your own head.'[22] At the low point the student of the

21. Ibid.
22. Ibid., p. 209.

Course is urged to make the choice to turn from crucifixion: 'You will not find peace until you have removed the nails from the hands of God's Son, and taken the last thorn from his forehead.'[23] The trip back to God involves choosing to undo the crucifixion: 'Teach not that I died in vain. Teach rather that I did not die by demonstrating that I live in you. For the undoing of the crucifixion of God's Son is the work of the redemption, in which everyone has a part of equal value.'[24] Finally, the resurrection is the means of the return to level one (redemption). However, this can happen only when the devotee perceives the resurrection in everyone, thus combining the *Course* metanarrative with the *Course* ontology of monism (which will be considered in the following section): 'I am *your* resurrection and *your* life. You live in me because you live in God. And everyone lives in you, as you live in everyone. Can you, then, perceive unworthiness in a brother and not perceive it in yourself? And can you perceive it in yourself and not perceive it in God?'[25]

The belief in separation also provides *A Course in Miracles* with the *raison d'être* for its alternative metanarrative of humankind's choice to believe in the existence of level-two values and 'falling' from level one, which is God/love/the real. This 'fall' is described in many ways. It is a falling asleep to be reawakened to one's unchangeable position in level one,[26] it is becoming mad and regaining sanity, [27] a journey into darkness and a return to the light of level one,[28] a forgetting one's true identity with God and then remembering one's identity (along with everyone else's) as God's perfect Son in level one.[29] In Freudian terms, it is a denial of the reality of level one and a projection of one's false identity in level two on to others (by believing that they are separate from us),

23. Ibid.
24. Ibid.
25. Ibid., p. 208 (italics original).
26. Ibid., pp. 182, 252–253.
27. Ibid., pp. 459, 492.
28. Ibid., pp. 198–199, 520–522.
29. Ibid., pp. 112, 146, 182–184.

followed by the choice to deny the error of belief in a false identity of unreality, bringing a return to level one.[30] In every model, there is a descent from level one, at the low point of which one chooses to view oneself as God's perfect creation, and the ascent back to one's true identity as part of the universal Sonship of level one (which in reality one has never left).

In this metanarrative, the low point in the journey brings the person to the moment of choice. 'Choice' becomes a leitmotif throughout the *Text*: 'You are free to believe what you *choose*, and what you do attests to what you believe.'[31] The final chapter of the *Text* brings the theme of 'choice' to a climax with the chapter title 'Choose Once Again'. The choice offered is not the bleak existential choice for individual authenticity in the face of all the evidence against such a choice, an outlook which was popular during the 1960s and '70s when Schucman scribed the *Course*. The reader is urged to choose that which is the only logical possibility and is offered God's power to make the choice in favour of God's reality. Throughout the *Text*, the individual's power of choice is emphasized. Here its empowering attributes are explained: 'Do you not see that all your misery comes from the strange belief that you are powerless (that is, without the power of choice)? Being helpless is the cost of sin. Helplessness is sin's condition; the one requirement is that it demands to be believed. Only the helpless could believe in it.'[32]

The final passage on 'choice' at the end of the *Text* focuses on the causes of human suffering and evil while reminding the reader of what is 'real' as set out in the Introduction:

> You always choose between your weakness and the strength of Christ in you. And you choose what you think is real. Simply by never using weakness to direct your actions, you have given it no power . . . or you have brought your weakness into Him, and He has given you His strength instead. Trials are but lessons that you failed to learn presented

---

30. Ibid., pp. 382–384.

31. Ibid., p. 7 (emphasis original).

32. Ibid., p. 461.

> once again, so where you made a faulty choice before, you now can make a better one, and thus escape all pain that what you chose before has brought to you. In every difficulty . . . Christ calls to you and gently says, 'My brother, choose again.' He would not leave one source of pain unhealed, nor any image left to veil the truth . . . Learn then the happy habit of response to all temptation to perceive yourself as weak and miserable with these words: I *am* as God created me. His Son can suffer nothing. And I am His Son.[33]

The *Text* links the power of 'choice' with strength. This theme of power through choice has become an important empowering theme in popular spiritual self help books drawn from the *Course* where readers are encouraged to 'create their own reality'.

The *Text* ends with prose reminiscent of Revelation 21:3, which draws down the curtain on the panorama of the biblical fall–redemption narrative. 'And so we say "Amen." For Christ has come to dwell in the abode You set for Him before time was, in calm eternity. The journey closes, ending at the place where it began. No trace of it remains . . . Not one illusion is accorded faith, and not one spot of darkness still remains to hide the face of Christ from anyone.'[34] The reader is reminded that the *Course* offers an alternative metanarrative, not God coming to earth to 'dwell' with humankind, but Christ coming to 'dwell' in the abode the reader has set for him.

A metaphysical system of monism

As noted in the previous section, the belief in the possibility of separation from God is the source of all that is perceived as evil. This belief in the possibility of evil, sin, guilt and fear can be undone, the *Course* teaches, only by removing the 'blocks to the awareness of love's presence which is your natural inheritance'.[35]

---

33. Ibid., pp. 666–667 (emphasis original).
34. Ibid., p. 669.
35. Ibid., p. 1.

The *Course*, then, defines all negative impulses as being a part of level two and therefore unreal. At the heart of the *Course's* metaphysical system is the bedrock belief that the only reality is God and God's love, from which it is impossible to be separate: 'What is all-encompassing can have no opposite.'[36]

Thus the *Course* represents a form of monism: reality begins and ends with God; God is the only reality: 'The first in time means nothing, but the First in eternity is God the Father, Who is both First and One. Beyond the First there is no other for there is no order, no second or third, and nothing but the First.'[37] The *Course* teaches, 'We say, "God is" and then we cease to speak, for in that knowledge words are meaningless.'[38] God is believed to be pure, loving motionless Mind, outside the realm of time and space. Even use of the word 'outside' does not do justice to the *Course's* radical teachings about the all-encompassing nature of God, for nothing can be 'outside' of what is 'all-encompassing'. If someone is perceived to be less than the perfect love and purity of God, this is shown to be a logical impossibility because nothing can exist beyond God's all-encompassing infinity. The *Course* states: 'Oneness is simply the idea God is. And in His Being, He encompasses all things. No mind holds anything but him.'[39] In the *Course* scheme, then, reality is not a realm of time and space, a place where things exist separate from each other, in short the world which we perceive with our senses. As people we think, wrongly, that we are limited, separate, temporary, mind/bodies.

The *Course* teaching on reality is uncompromisingly otherworldly. It does not say that reality is the opposite of unreality because that would give dignity to the world of illusion; to use the word 'opposite' implies a comparison of like with like. It teaches that reality is unrelated to the world we believe we inhabit. While there is much teaching about the nature of reality, the *Course* also

---

36. Ibid.
37. Ibid., p. 279.
38. Ibid., p. 323.
39. Ibid.

admits that reality is impossible for us to describe as long as we are in this physical world:

> It would be impossible to be in the world with this knowledge. For the mind that knows this unequivocally, knows also it dwells in eternity and utilises no perception at all. It therefore does not consider where it is, because the concept 'where' does not mean anything to it. It knows that it is everywhere, just as it has everything.[40]

The world we believe we inhabit, the world of form, time and space, is a dream. 'Look at the world, and you will see nothing attached to anything beyond itself. All seeming entities can come a little nearer, or go a little farther off, but cannot join.'[41] Since any form of separateness is less than God's whole, the physical individual and the realm of nature are seen to be part of level two and unreal. On the other hand, the 'Mind' of an individual is the creation of God, or, in *Course* vocabulary, 'an extension' of God.

Individuals in time and space are seen to be pitted inevitably in conflict against each other. The *Course* paints a picture of separate wills striving against each other and against the whole. God's creation is not the physical universe; indeed he does not know of its existence. It does not exist except in the mind of the dreamers. God's creation (or extension) is God's Son. All minds are part of the Sonship of God and thus are one:

> It should be noted that God has only one Son. If all His creations are His Sons, every one must be an integral part of the whole Sonship. The Sonship in its Oneness transcends the sum of its parts. However, this is obscured as long as any of its parts is missing. That is why the conflict cannot ultimately be resolved until all the parts of the Sonship have returned. Only then can the meaning of wholeness in the true sense be understood.[42]

---

40. Ibid., p. 258.
41. Ibid., p. 542.
42. Ibid., p. 33.

Jesus, who is believed to have authored the *Course*, is seen as the Son of God in exactly the same way as all minds are. The only difference between Jesus, the Son of God, and all of us as parts of the 'Sonship' is that through his resurrection Jesus proved that death cannot ultimately hurt our true mind identity, which is the Son of God, the creation of God.

If the metanarrative of the *Course* derives from the biblical fall–redemption narrative, the metaphysical system of the *Course* can be shown to derive from Advaita Vedanta, as described by Theodore Gabriel earlier in this volume. Schucman loved and read the King James Version of the Bible and the overarching metanarrative of the *Course* can perhaps be traced to her knowledge of biblical themes. Thetford, who assisted her in scribing the *Course*, had studied Advaita Vedanta and loved the writings of Vivekananda who was the first Hindu 'missionary' to the West at the beginning of the twentieth century. Thetford preferred to see the *Course* as a restatement of Advaita Vedanta spirituality, which he believed to be the perennial philosophy behind all great religious traditions.[43]

How does *Course* metaphysics echo the monism of Advaita Vedanta? One of the earliest statements of Hindu monism is found in the Mandukya Upanishad. This text begins with the famous statement, 'OM. This eternal Word is all: what was, what is and what shall be and what beyond is in eternity. All is OM.' Gaudapada, an early teacher of Vedanta, argued that if only the Transcendent One is real, then it logically follows that everything else is unreal, *maya*,[44] what the *Course* refers to as illusion, the dream and unreality. The inevitable corollary of this concept of *maya* is that logical thought and sensory perception are untrustworthy agents for experiencing union with the Transcendent.[45]

43. R. Skutch, *Journey Without Distance: The Story Behind 'A Course in Miracles'* (Berkeley: Celestial Arts, 1984), p. 72; interview, Judith Skutch, 23 September 2005.

44. R. Reyna, *The Concept of May from the Vedas to the 20th Century* (London: Asia Publishing House, 1962), pp. 14–15.

45. P. D. Devanandan, *The Concept of Maya* (London: Lutterworth Press, 1950), pp. 20–24, 87–90.

Building on Gaudapada's work, the eighth-century Hindu philosopher Shankara constructed a coherent system of thought whereby the Transcendent One, Brahman, could be directly experienced at a level beyond reason and sensory experience.

Shankara's Advaita differed from other systems of Vedanta in his belief that ignorance (*avidya*) was the cause of the false awareness of this world of distinctions as separate from Brahman.[46] This seems to parallel the *Course*'s teaching on the 'choice' to believe in the error of separation which leads to the opposite of love, namely fear, sin and guilt. In both systems, it is the belief in the possibility of separation from God which is the source of all error. Like the *Course*, which seeks to 'remove' the blocks to the awareness of God's love,[47] Shankara taught that the 'removal' of ignorance (*avidya*) can bring a mystical experience of oneness with Brahman and liberation from the rebirth cycle (*samsara*). Shankara's frequent use of a text from the Chandogya Upanishad (6.2.1), 'Being only was this in the beginning, one, without a second', and his commentary on this text link the Advaita concept of God with that of the *Course*:

> There can exist nothing different from Brahman, since we are unable to observe a proof for such existence . . . Nor can there exist, apart from Brahman, something which has no beginning since scripture affirms that 'Being only was this in the beginning, one, without a second'. The promise moreover that through the cognition of one thing everything will be known renders it impossible that there should exist anything different from Brahman.[48]

This passage from Shankara's commentary links closely with the *Course's* description of God: 'The first in time means nothing, but the First in eternity is God the Father, Who is both First and One.

---

46. E. Lott, *Vedantic Approaches to God* (London: Macmillan, 1980), p. 43.
47. Anonymous, *Text*, p. 1.
48. G. Thibaut, *Vedantasutras with Sankara's Commentary*, 2 (Oxford: Clarendon, 1890), pp. 176–177.

Beyond the First there is no order, no second or third, and nothing but the First.'[49]

Lastly, to deal with the physical world in which people live their lives, Shankara posited two levels of reality. First, there is Brahman, who is identical with the universal Self (*atman*) and thus never separate from it. Second, there is the lower level where individual selves exist, a world of illusion but also a place of learning for those with lower levels of understanding. *Course* metaphysics, as noted above, is founded on two levels of reality, the real and the unreal. The lower level, the unreal, becomes the arena in which to unlearn false perceptions and make the 'choices' that remove the 'barriers to the awareness of love'.[50]

Coping strategies in the *Workbook*: overcoming the obstacles to God's love

While the *Text* emphasizes the individual's freedom to 'choose again' between the contrasting features of level one and two, the *Workbook*, containing a lesson for each day of the year, emphasizes a daily practice of the principles of the *Text*. The daily discipline of mind-training (of unlearning illusion and learning truth) makes possible the 'miracle' of the shift from living in the values of the 'illusory' level two back to the 'reality' of level one. The word 'miracle' in the title does not refer to external supernatural intervention to change the natural course of events, but to one's own decision to change one's false perception of a situation. 'The miracle does not awaken you from the ego's dreams of separation and victimisation, but merely shows you who the dreamer is. It teaches you there is a choice of dreams while you are still asleep.'[51]

The daily mind-training exercises, through which the *Workbook* takes the student in a year, are based on the practice of forgiveness. Early lessons help the student to unlearn false assumptions

49. Anonymous, *Text*, p. 279.
50. Ibid., p. 1.
51. Ibid., p. 593.

and begin to exercise the power of choice. Lesson 1, for example, states: 'Nothing in this room means anything . . . this table does not mean anything', etc.[52] Lesson 2 continues the idea: 'I have given everything I see in this room all the meaning that it has for me',[53] as does lesson 3: 'I do not understand anything I see in this room . . . The point of the exercises is to help you clear your mind of all past associations, to see things exactly as they appear to you now, and to realise how little you really understand about them.'[54]

By Lesson 62, positive learning has begun: 'Forgiveness is my function as the light of the world . . . remember that in every attack you call upon your own weakness, while each time you forgive you call upon the strength of Christ in you.'[55] As the year progresses through the *Workbook*, some lessons are used to review and summarize past themes: Lesson 120, for example, is simply: 'For morning and evening review: "*I rest in God. I am as God created me*. I lay aside all sick illusions of myself and let my Father tell me Who I really am." On the hour: "*I rest in God*." On the half hour: "*I am as God created me*."'[56]

Conclusion: critiques of *Course* spiritualities

It is not the purpose here to present a detailed critique of *Course* attitudes towards evil. However, one or two points should be made. *Course* spirituality has been criticized from several perspectives. Christian critics are offended by the *Course's* co-opting of biblical vocabulary for a system that draws on Hinduism (in its view of the world as illusion, *maya*), Gnosticism (in its uncompromising otherworldliness), Platonism (in its view of the physical as evil and the spiritual as good) and Christian Science (in its denial of the possibility of evil). Non-Christian critics accuse it of trying

52. Anonymous, *Workbook*, p. 3.

53. Ibid., p. 4.

54. Ibid., p. 5.

55. Ibid., p. 104.

56. Ibid., p. 213 (emphasis original).

to slip a version of Christian fundamentalism in through the back door by using obscure language and tortuous logic. Others see it as a superficial exercise in denial and positive thinking with a dash of Buddhist detachment from the real world of suffering.

The *Course's* emphasis on the power of choice, the idea that every situation presents a person with the stark choice between the values of level one and level two, has become an empowering device for many who view themselves as victims. The *Course* presents the victim and the victimizer, the abused and the abuser, as equally innocent in God's eyes; the cause of abuse, for example, rests with the 'choice' made (on some level) by the abused. There can be no distinctions where God is 'all-encompassing'. Through *Course* organizations and self-help books based on the *Course*, prisoners, the abused and those caught up in various addictions tell how they have been helped. *Course* teaching trains the mind, on the one hand, to refuse to see oneself as a victim and, on the other hand, to believe that one has the power to choose how one lives and to take responsibility for oneself. However, the application of this teaching to abused children must be questioned. More generally, in a system of monism (such as that propounded by Shankara and the *Course*), where there are no 'distinctions' and there is a denial of 'separateness', is there a logical basis for any distinction between good and evil, whether in theory or in practice?

Course teachers argue that the large problems of today's world – poverty, war, nuclear weapons and terrorism – all begin with people's attitudes towards themselves and others. Therefore *Course* spirituality is relevant far beyond the realm of helping relationships between middle-class professionals, where it has proved to be successful and transforming. They cite victims of the Holocaust who have been brought to a place of forgiveness through applying *Course* principles. But the question remains: can a starving Darfur tribesman in Sudan, who has been driven from his home, be helped by the understanding that he has a choice of how to view his situation? Kenneth Wapnick, the final editor of the *Course*, replies:

> The *Course* is strictly a mind-training system . . . it is meant to be lived in the world, but since it says that there is literally no world, only a dream

> of one, the *Course* is not interested in trying to improve the dream. It only wants to change the mind of the dreamer. When that happens the dream will automatically change in some way, but it is the mind of the dreamer that is the focus of the *Course*.[57]

A Course in Miracles is unflinchingly consistent in its attitude towards evil. However, its very rigour may in some cases make its message hard to accept for those for whom the reality of evil in the world and in their own experience is only too painful and palpable.

---

57. D. Patrick Miller, *The Complete Story of The Course* (London: Ryder, 1997), p. 119.

12 SATANISM AND THE HEAVY-METAL SUBCULTURE

Christopher Partridge

If belief in demons in the modern period in Western societies has significantly retreated before the forces of rationalism and empiricism, it has not disappeared entirely.[1] Indeed, interest in the demonic is experiencing something of a revival. This has been particularly evident in popular culture, in which the flow of films with demonological content has remained steady, largely – and significantly – because they consistently prove to be successful at the box office.[2] Again, several music subcultures, most notably the 'heavy-metal' subculture, have found Satanism and, more broadly, Christian demonology a particularly rich religio-cultural vein to mine. However, before turning to the satanic themes in heavy

1. See J. B. Russell, *Mephistopheles: The Devil in the Modern World* (Ithaca: Cornell University Press, 1986).
2. See C. Partridge, *Re-Enchantment of the West: Alternative Spiritualities, Sacralization, Popular Culture and Occulture*, 2 vols. (London: T. & T. Clark/Continuum, 2004–5), 2, pp. 239–246. See also Amy Summers-Minette's contribution to this present volume (ch. 13).

metal, something needs to be said of the principal spirituality that has been a source of fascination and inspiration within this subculture, namely Satanism.[3]

The advent and evolution of modern Satanism

In San Francisco, on the evening of 30 April 1966 – '*Walpurgisnacht*, the most important festival in the lore of magic and witchcraft – Anton LaVey (the principal architect of contemporary Satanism) ritualistically shaved his head in accordance with magical tradition',[4] announced the formation of the Church of Satan, and declared the arrival of 'the Age of Satan'. Describing himself as 'the Black Pope', he founded the best-known and influential Satanist organization. Indeed, LaVey's *The Satanic Bible* – which has been translated into several languages – remains a key text for many Satanists (whether they belong to the Church of Satan or not).[5] Interestingly, the idea for a *Satanic Bible* came not from LaVey, but from Peter Mayer, an editor with the publishers Avon Books. 'As a direct result of the success of the popular film *Rosemary's Baby* and the subsequent increase of popular interest in Satanism and the

---

3. Perhaps the best history of Satanism and perceptions of Satanism is G. Medway's enjoyable *The Lure of the Sinister: The Unnatural History of Satanism* (New York: New York University Press, 2001).
4. B. H. Wolfe, 'Introduction', in A. S. LaVey, *The Satanic Bible* (New York: Avon Books, 1969), pp. 13–14.
5. A survey of Satanists conducted by Lewis 'consistently indicated the centrality of LaVey to modern Satanism . . . Furthermore, however one might criticise and depreciate it, *The Satanic Bible* is still the single most influential document shaping the contemporary Satanic movement. One of my informants noted, "I do not think Satanists can get away from LaVey, although some seem to take a real issue with him or try to downplay his importance. He wrote the book that codified Satanism into a religion, and for that he should be considered a central figure of the religion.' J. R. Lewis, *Legitimating New Religions* (New Brunswick: Rutgers University Press, 2003), p. 116.

occult, Mayer decided that "the time was right for a 'Satanic Bible'," and he approached LaVey about authoring it.'[6] This is interesting, in that, as I have argued elsewhere, it indicates the influence of popular culture on the emergence of new religious belief.[7] Essentially, *The Satanic Bible* was the result of a commercial decision made by an editor who recognized an increased market for such a volume, which, in turn, was the direct result of popular culture. Bearing this in mind, the influence of popular music on world-views and 'plausibility structures'[8] should not be underestimated.

It was not too long before the charismatic LaVey was gaining considerable publicity by performing satanic weddings and satanic baptisms of children, as well as attracting a number of notable celebrities (including Sammy Davis Jr, Christopher Lee, Laurence Harvey, Jayne Mansfield, Barbara McNair, and Kim Novak). In the words of Burton Wolfe (who wrote the 'Introduction' to *The Satanic Bible*), 'the alternative rites that LaVey worked out, while still maintaining some of the trappings of ancient ceremonies, were changed from negative mockery to positive forms of celebrations and purges: Satanic weddings consecrating the joys of the flesh, funerals devoid of sanctimonious platitudes, lust rituals to help individuals attain their sexual desires, destruction rituals to enable members of the Satanic church to triumph over enemies.'[9] He continues:

> On special occasions, such as baptisms, weddings, and funerals in the name of the devil, press coverage, though unsolicited, was phenomenal. By 1967 the newspapers that were sending reporters to write about the Church of Satan extended from San Francisco across the Pacific to Tokyo and across the Atlantic to Paris. A photo of a nude woman, half covered by a leopard skin, serving as an altar to Satan in a LaVey-conceived wedding ceremony, was transmitted by

6. Lewis, *Legitimating New Religions*, p. 112.
7. See Partridge, *Re-Enchantment of the West*, 1, pp. 119–188.
8. See P. L. Berger, *The Heretical Imperative* (London, Collins, 1980), pp. 17–22.
9. Wolfe, 'Introduction', p. 14.

> major wire services to daily newspapers everywhere; and it showed up on the front page of such bulwarks of the media as the *Los Angeles Times*. As the result of the publicity, grottoes . . . affiliated with the Church of Satan spread throughout the world, proving one of LaVey's cardinal messages: the Devil is alive and highly popular with a great many people.[10]

Central to the beliefs of the Church of Satan and much subsequent contemporary Satanism is an emphasis on the 'animal' or physical appetites of humans, which are to be indulged, rather than denied. LaVey is particularly critical of Christianity for suppressing this side of humanity by labelling it 'sinful'. Indeed, *The Satanic Bible* contains an assault upon the morality associated with Christianity and, while we shall see that LaVey denies that he worships an actual entity called Satan, he argues that Satan is nevertheless a powerful symbol of opposition to all traditional, institutional authority: 'Before none of your printed idols do I bend in acquiescence, and he who saith "thou shalt" to me is my mortal foe.'[11] As with many forms of Satanism, the implications of LaVey's social Darwinism are brutal. For example, it is taught that a principal law by which life should be lived is the survival of the fittest. The human is understood to be an animal that should strive to overcome the weak. Such 'human garbage' should be pushed aside in the interests of attaining one's own potential. Indeed, Satanists are encouraged to distance themselves from 'the common herd':

> Blessed are the strong, for they shall possess the earth – Cursed are the weak, for they shall inherit the yoke! Blessed are the powerful, for they shall be reverenced among men – Cursed are the feeble, for they shall be blotted out . . . Blessed are the iron-handed, for the unfit shall flee before them – Cursed are the poor in spirit, for they shall be spat upon![12]

---

10. Wolfe, 'Introduction', pp. 14–15.
11. LaVey, *Satanic Bible*, p. 30.
12. LaVey, *Satanic Bible*, p. 34.

That said, this brutal philosophy should be understood in the context of the Church of Satan's explicit forbidding of murder and cruelty to animals.

As to Satanist spirituality, most forms can be described as self-spirituality that encourages egocentricity and personal development, rather than being a belief system which is explicitly opposed to Christianity. Indeed, some Satanists would insist that their religion has little direct interest in Christian doctrine and practice. 'My brand of Satanism', says LaVey,

> is the ultimate conscious alternative to herd mentality and institutionalized thought. It is a studied and contrived set of principles and exercises designed to liberate individuals from a contagion of mindlessness that destroys innovation. I have termed my thought 'Satanism' because it is most stimulating under that name. Self-discipline and motivation are effected more easily under stimulating conditions. Satanism means 'the opposition' and epitomizes all symbols of nonconformity. Satanism calls forth the strong ability to turn a liability into an advantage, to turn alienation into exclusivity. In other words, the reason it's called Satanism is because it's fun, it's accurate, and it's productive.[13]

That said, while much Satanism is not explicitly anti-Christian, LaVey specifically sought to construct an 'atheology', which, as he says above, 'epitomizes all symbols of nonconformity'. 'Satanism means "the opposition".'[14] In other words, it *stands against* much that the Christian tradition morally *stands for*. This is clearly evident in a survey conducted by James Lewis. For example:

> The Devil represents much more than absolute evil. By default, the Prince of Darkness has come to embody some very attractive attributes. For example, because traditional Christianity has been so anti-sensual, Satan represents sex. The Christian tradition has also condemned pride, vengefulness and avarice, and, when allied with the status quo, has

---

13. A. S. LaVey, *The Devil's Notebook* (Portland: Feral House, 1992), pp. 9–10.
14. LaVey, *Devil's Notebook*, p. 9.

> promoted conformity and obedience. The three former traits and the antithesis of the latter two traits thus became associated with the Devil. (As one respondent wrote, 'Satan stands for all that Christians deem wrong in the world.') LaVeyan Satanism celebrates such 'vices' as virtues, and identifies them as the core of what Satanism is really all about.[15]

More specifically, LaVeyan Satanism is an atheistic, self-centric philosophy that claims to be at home in a rationalist, secular age. This is evident in Wolfe's 'Introduction' to LaVey's *Satanic Bible*:

> The intent of some . . . secret orders was to blaspheme, lampoon the Christian church, and address themselves to the devil as an anthropomorphic deity that represented the reverse of God. In LaVey's view, the devil was not that, but rather a dark hidden force in nature responsible for the workings of earthly affairs, a force for which neither science nor religion had any explanation. LaVey's Satan is 'the spirit of progress, the inspirer of all great movements that contribute to the development of civilization and the advancement of mankind. He is the spirit of revolt that leads to freedom, the embodiment of all heresies that liberate.' . . . He saw the need for a Church that would recapture man's mind and carnal desires as objects of celebration. Rational self-interest would be encouraged and a healthy ego championed.[16]

Hence, LaVeyan Satanism is very much an egocentric spirituality, based on an atheistic worldview and critical of those belief-systems that stand at odds with modern science and progress. 'Satan', proclaims LaVey, 'represents vital existence, instead of spiritual pipe dreams!'[17] Hence, when LaVey writes about invoking Satan[18] or practising 'magick', he is simply referring to the development of

---

15. J. R. Lewis, 'Who Serves Satan? A Demographic and Ideological Profile', *Marburg Journal of Religion* 6/2 (2001): <http://www.uni-marburg.de/religionswissenschaft/journal/mjr/lewis2.html> (accessed 7 November 2002).
16. Wolfe, 'Introduction', pp. 13–14.
17. LaVey, *Satanic Bible*, p. 25.
18. See his 'Invocation to Satan', in LaVey, *Satanic Bible*, p. 144.

our natural potential as humans. He defines magick as 'the change in situations or events in accordance with one's will, which would, using normally accepted methods, be unchangeable'.[19] Using rituals, understood as psychodramas, LaVey simply seeks to stimulate emotions and elevate the self,[20] all occult forces being understood by LaVey as fundamentally natural and open to scientific scrutiny – although, he believes that, to a large extent, science hasn't quite reached the stage at which it is able to investigate these dark, natural forces.

Reflecting the influence of LaVey, Lewis's survey found that 'most Satanists are humanistic (atheistic/agnostic) Satanists . . . Sixty percent of respondents (84) said that Satan was a symbol, an archetype, myself, nature, or some other anti-theistic understanding of Satan. Twenty-five percent indicated that Satan was an impersonal force. (Though not regarded as "supernatural", this force is something not adequately understood by current science.)'[21] Claims by some scholars, therefore, that Satanism is 'the worship of the Christian Devil',[22] or that it 'is dependent upon Christianity, accepting its traditional belief in a devil who rebelled against God, and continues to engage in combat with him', or that 'explicit worship of Satan . . . is the hallmark of the Satanist',[23] are, to some extent, misunderstandings.

Having said that, while LaVey and particularly his *Satanic Bible* are important to many within the Satanist network, as Lewis notes, 'few movement participants outside the Church of Satan would regard themselves as "orthodox Laveyans"'.[24] Hence, for example, there are those, sometimes referred to as 'traditional Satanists', who clearly do believe in some form of satanic being. Lewis's

19. LaVey, *Satanic Bible*, p. 110.
20. See A. S. LaVey, *The Satanic Rituals* (New York: Avon Books, 1972), pp. 15–27.
21. Lewis, 'Who Serves Satan?'
22. J. R. Lewis, *Witchcraft Today: An Encyclopedia of Wiccan and Neopagan Traditions* (Santa Barbara: ABC-CLIO, 1999), p. 260.
23. G. D. Chryssides, *Exploring New Religions* (London: Cassell, 1999), p. 341.
24. Lewis, *Legitimating New Religions*, p. 104.

survey, for example, found that a small minority of respondents were 'theistic Satanists' – 'although even most of these respondents did not have what one would call a traditional view of Satan/god/demons'.[25] One such Satanist, Amy Krieytaz, makes the following comment: 'My experiences have convinced me that Satan is more than just a symbol and deserves to be treated with respect – yes, even "worship".'[26] Similarly, according to a 1995 survey of Temple of Set initiates, Set/Satan is variously understood: 'Some say that Set is a "real being", "an incorporeal entity", "a metaphysical reality" . . . "Lord of this world" . . . Others consider Set to be "the archetypal rebel", "the ultimate male principle", "a figure representing pride, self-interest, and self-gratification" . . . "the driving force in human evolution".'[27] Moreover, while many traditional Satanists understand Satan to be a rebellious, self-serving being, they also, quite naturally, do not see him as the demonic other. That is to say, they often do not view him in the sinister way that Christians do, believing him to be a deity who can be 'approached as a friend'[28] and who, sometimes with reference to the serpent in Genesis 3, dispenses knowledge ('the Black Flame') to those who strive for it.

The principal theistic Satanist organization and the main rival to the Church of Satan is the Temple of Set, founded by Michael Aquino, a former US army officer who left the Church of Satan in 1975. The Temple of Set is hierarchically ordered: the ruling body is called 'the Council of Nine' and the smaller groups are known as 'Pylons' (of which there are several outside America). In a way that reminds one of Gnostic initiation, there are six 'degrees' (levels) of membership. Beginning with the lowest, these are as follows: Setian; Adept (the status of most members); Priest/Priestess;

25. Lewis, 'Who Serves Satan?'

26. Quoted in J. K. McRitchie, 'A Critique of Evangelical Understandings of Satanism' (unpublished MTh dissertation, University College Chester, 2001), p. 57.

27. G. Harvey, 'Satanism in Britain Today', *Journal of Contemporary Religion* 10 (1995), p. 288.

28. Ibid.

Magister/Magistra Templi; Magus/Maga; and Ipsissimus/ Ipsissima. Falsely describing itself as 'the only legally recognized "Satanic" institution in the world',[29] although it shares some beliefs with the Church of Satan and reveres *The Satanic Bible*,[30] it is arguably a more intellectual form of Satanism. Whereas the Church of Satan stresses the continuity between animals and humans, and emphasizes evolutionary development, the Temple of Set insists that humans are distinct from animals by virtue of their intellect and that this enquiring intellect is *not* simply the result of evolution, but is rather the gift of Set/Satan to humanity. The Temple of Set seeks to exercise this gift, symbolized as 'the Black Flame' – 'the symbol of knowledge and scepticism towards the received wisdom of established religions'.[31] As its 'General Information and Admission Policies' state, 'The Temple is designed as a tool for personal empowerment and self-cultivation.'[32] The increase in knowledge leads, in a Gnostic-like way, to self-development and spiritual progress: 'As Set was, we are; as Set is, we will be.'[33] The aim is, therefore, not to worship Set, but rather to learn from him and eventually become like him. Preferring the description 'the Left-Hand Path' to 'Satanism', the organization's website points out that following the path is 'a process for creating an individual, powerful essence that exists above and beyond animal life . . . Initiation begins with denial and rejection of the herd-mentality . . . The Initiate . . . seeks continuous, positive self-evolution.'[34] This transcendence above animal life is summed up in the term *xeper*, 'an Egyptian verb which means "I

29. <http://www.xeper.org/pub/gil/xp_FS_gil.htm> (accessed 5 May 2004).

30. See Lewis's comments on Aquino's understanding of *The Satanic Bible* as an 'inspired' text: *Legitimating New Religions*, p. 121.

31. J. La Fontaine, 'Satanism and Satanic Mythology', in B. Ankarloo and S. Clark (eds.), *Witchcraft and Magic in Europe: The Twentieth Century* (Philadelphia: University of Pennsylvania Press, 1999), p. 101.

32. <www.xeper.org/pub/gil/xp_FS_gil.htm> (accessed 5 May 2004).

33. Quoted in Harvey, 'Satanism in Britain Today', p. 288.

34. <www.xeper.org/pub/gil/xp_FS_gil.htm> (accessed 5 May 2004).

Have Come Into Being". This word, which is the eternal Word of Set, reflects the consciousness-worshipping nature of our religion and the source of ultimate responsibility in all things – the self.'[35] Hence, even theistic Satanism can be understood as a form of detraditionalized, self-spirituality. Several studies have shown the powerful, apparently positive psychological effects of such belief: reduction of fear, increase in self-esteem, removal of feelings of guilt, and decrease in self-doubt.[36]

Detraditionalization is evident in their beliefs about Set, in that reading through the Temple's official general information does not give one the impression that it is, strictly speaking, a theistic or traditional Satanist organization – although it does sometimes speak of Set in such terms. As with LaVey's understanding of Satan, the figure of Set is described as 'the archetype of isolate self-consciousness'.[37] Hence, although Graham Harvey's survey does indicate that some Setians view Set as an ontological reality, the official documentation appears not to encourage this view, describing him more in terms of archetype, image and symbol. For example, we read that

> Set is a more complex, less stereotypical metaphysical image than that of the Judaeo/Christian Satan. Satan, the archetype of rebellion against cosmic order and stasis, may be the symbol for many people's initial commitment to initiation, but this symbol is too tied to conventional religions and their moral codes to be an effective representation of the richness, subtlety, and complexity of the Left-Hand Path.

As with many Satanists and Left-Hand Path practitioners (who, to some extent, follow the practices and theories of Aleister

---

35. Ibid.

36. E.g. A. Moriarty, *Psychology of Adolescent Satanism* (Westport: Greenwood, 1992); E. J. Moody, 'Magical Therapy: An Anthropological Investigation of Contemporary Satanism', in I. I. Zaretsky and M. P. Leone (eds.), *Religious Movements in Contemporary America* (Princeton: Princeton University Press, 1974), pp. 355–383.

37. < www.xeper.org/pub/gil/xp_FS_gil.htm> (accessed 5 May 2004).

Crowley), there is an emphasis on ritual and ceremonial magick (sometimes – not always – spelt by Satanists with a 'k' to distinguish it from conjuring trickery).[38] In a way similar to LaVeyan Satanism and in accordance with the principles of Left-Hand Path magick generally,[39] it is understood in terms of the operations of the will in order to effect change in the world. Of particular note is the distinction Aquino makes between 'an "objective universe", the natural world, and the "subjective universe", which is the individual's personal perspective'.[40] Essentially, the two universes are understood to be continuous and thus, he argues, by effecting a change in the inner, subjective universe, one causes 'a similar and proportionate change in the objective universe'.[41] Ceremonial magick, particularly 'Black Magick' – as described in Aquino's book, *Black Magic in Theory and Practice*[42] – has an impact upon the subjective universe, 'raising power' within the individual, and thereby increasing the effect of the will upon the 'objective universe'.

Other theistic Satanists include what Harvey has called '*ad hoc* Satanists'. Such practitioners are usually adolescent, and inspired by gothic imagery, horror texts, and certain like-minded musicians – particularly those of a subgenre of heavy metal, known as 'black metal'. Because they define themselves very clearly by opposition to current social mores and particularly Christianity (symbolized by the wearing of inverted crucifixes), such Satanists do experiment with 'devil-worship'. In other words, wanting to offend and shock, they quite naturally turn to popular notions of Satanism

---

38. While the Temple of Set tends to use a 'k' regularly, the earlier writings of LaVey tend not to do so. That said, it is almost *de rigueur* nowadays within the ritual 'magick' community.
39. For an excellent discussion of Left-Hand Path magick see P. Sutcliffe, 'Left-Hand Path Magick', in G. Harvey and C. Hardman (eds.), *Paganism Today* (London: Thorsons, 1996), pp. 109–137.
40. La Fontaine, 'Satanism and Satanic Mythology', p. 102.
41. M. Aquino, *Black Magic in Theory and Practice* (San Francisco: Temple of Set, 1992), quoted in Harvey, 'Satanism in Britain Today', p. 289.
42. Aquino, *Black Magic in Theory and Practice.*

inspired by Christian anti-Satanist rhetoric and popular culture, rather than to the beliefs of official Satanist organizations.[43] For example, one Norwegian black-metal fan involved in church-burning, interviewed by Fin Bjørn Tønder for the newspaper *Bergens Tidende*, distanced himself from Satanism and explicitly allied himself with 'devil-worship': 'We worship the Devil, but prefer not to use the term Satan. That name has been made ridiculous by foolish groups of poseurs.'[44] Still others reject what they term 'liberal Satanism' and, we will see, turn to a form of far-right political Satanism, 'fascist Satanism'. While much of this is still of the *ad hoc* type, as Massimo Introvigne has noted, there are small Satanist organizations which do attract far-right Satanists: Black Order, Order of the Nine Angles, Ordo Sinistra Vivendi (formerly Order of the Left-Hand Path), Order of the Jarls of Balder. All of these groups are small and belong to a network called the Infernal Alliance.[45]

Finally, partly because of the secretive nature of some of the groups and partly because there is a paucity of serious academic research in this area, there is no consensus regarding the numbers involved in Satanism. While those who are convinced of the existence of a massive underground network of organized satanic groups permeating all levels of society are certainly mistaken, it does seem clear that this is a growing phenomenon. Indeed, in 1992, LaVey noted that 'interest in the Church of Satan has never been greater'.[46] However, even so, those interviewed by Lewis estimated that there were perhaps as few as 700–800 self-identified Satanists within North America. That said, even if those who

---

43. See M. Moynihan, and D. Søderlind, *Lords of Chaos: The Bloody Rise of the Satanic Metal Underground* (Portland: Feral House, 1998); G. Baddeley, *Lucifer Rising* (London: Plexus, 1999).
44. F. B. Tønder, 'We Lit the Fires', *Bergens Tidende* (20 January 1993). Trans. D. Søderlind. Reproduced in Moynihan, *Lords of Chaos*, p. 333.
45. M. Introvigne, 'The Gothic Milieu: Black Metal, Satanism, and Vampires', <www.cesnur.org/testi/gothic.htm> (accessed 27 September 2004).
46. LaVey, *Devil's Notebook*, p. 29.

belong to particular groups such as the Church of Satan and the Temple of Set are still comparatively small, there are almost certainly larger numbers of solitary *ad hoc* practitioners who consider themselves Satanist and who make use of the writings of LaVey and Aquino.[47]

Satanism and the heavy-metal subculture

A particular focus of concern for many embroiled in satanic moral panics has been the popular music genre 'heavy metal', particularly the subgenres of 'black metal' and 'death metal'.[48] 'By far one of the most popular types of music among white adolescents', it has been dogged by allegations that it encourages delinquency, Satanism, and even satanically inspired suicide.[49] Although many of these allegations were (and still are) made by right-wing Christian organizations, in the late 1980s they began to filter into mainstream culture. As James Richardson observed,

---

47. On the problems estimating numbers of Satanists, see La Fontaine, 'Satanism and Satanic Mythology', pp. 107–109.
48. On death metal, see N. J. Purcell, *Death Metal Music: The Passion and Politics of a Subculture* (Jefferson: McFarland and Company, 2003). On heavy metal *per se*, see D. Weinstein, *Heavy Metal: The Music and Its Culture* (New York: Da Capo Press, 2000). However, her argument that heavy metal is 'playful' in its use of satanic imagery is, while true on one level, a little naïve on another. While it is certainly correct to argue that 'the use of satanic symbols reflects the ambivalence of the proud pariah' (p. 262), this needs to be balanced with some discussion of self-professed Satanist groups and of the cultural impact of the use of satanic symbolism. As we shall see, the devotion of some fans and artists does go beyond the 'playful'. Indeed, although earlier in the book she acknowledges that there is heavy metal 'for practicing Satanists' (p. 96), the significance of this is not discussed.
49. J. S. Epstein and D. J. Pratto, 'Heavy Metal Rock Music: Juvenile Delinquency and Satanic Identification', *Popular Music and Society* 14/4 (1990), p. 67.

even those opposed to fundamentalist agendas and the anti-cult movement are beginning to accept popular beliefs about heavy metal. He notes, in particular, an editorial that appeared in the *Religious Freedom Alert*, a periodical opposed to the anti-cult movement, which makes the following claim: 'There is a Satanism problem in America. It involves teenage drug users who are instructed in satanic symbols and practices by the music recording industry and, to a lesser extent, the motion picture industry.'[50] The point is that, 'What musicians and producers may be using as a marketing tool to increase sales to rebellious teenagers, others view as thorough-going evangelism for an international satanic conspiracy.'[51]

Clearly, the demonization of 'the other' and the subversive values provided by Western demonology and Satanist mythology are enormously attractive to those wanting to construct counter-cultural identities. This, of course, is explicit in the various manifestations of heavy metal. Hence, while many of the claims made against heavy-metal musicians are ridiculous, one can understand why their work is antagonistic to the religious right and worrying to the parents of the teenagers who buy it. Take, for example, Brian Warner, who took the name Marilyn Manson – a name constructed from those of his icons Marilyn Monroe and, controversially, Charles Manson.[52] Although Manson is clearly more interested in shocking and, he argues, thereby encouraging listeners to question the dominant religion and culture (particularly

---

50. J. T. Richardson, 'Satanism in the Courts: From Murder to Heavy Metal', in Richardson, Best and Bromley (eds.), *Satanism Scare*, p. 213.
51. Richardson, 'Satanism in the Courts', p. 211.
52. On the adoption of this name, see G. Baddeley, *Dissecting Marilyn Manson* (London: Plexus, 2002), pp. 19–33. Charles Manson was the leader of a group, the 'Family', involved in multiple murders, including that of Roman Polanski's pregnant wife, Sharon Tate. Although probably not a member of a satanic organization, he and several of his followers had several connections with satanic groups (as well as with Scientology), most notably the Process Church of Final Judgment, which, following the murders, sought to distance itself from him.

institutional Christianity), and although he claims that he has 'never been and never will be a Satan worshipper, or someone who worships the Devil',[53] and 'still considers himself a member of St Paul's Episcopal Church in his home town of Canton, Ohio',[54] he was nevertheless ordained an honorary minister of the Church of Satan by LaVey in 1994, is a keen student of Aleister Crowley,[55] and has said that Satanism is one of the philosophies on which he bases his belief system.[56] Of course, since much Satanism – particularly LaVeyan Satanism – is not theistic, and thus does not understand itself to be 'devil-worship', Manson's denials of devil-worship, while accurate, may not necessarily be denials of Satanism *per se*.[57] Indeed, 'elements of LaVeyan Satanism', Gavin Baddeley reminds us, 'were all-pervasive in Marilyn Manson's early material: the distinctive face of LaVey appeared on newsletters and his books on recommended reading lists for Spooky Kids [his fans] . . . Distinctive LaVeyan phrases peppered Marilyn's lyrics and speech during interviews.'[58] As well as having the Church of Satan's baphomet insignia tattooed on his arm, his videos, CD covers and lyrics all draw heavily on Christian imagery and Western demonology. This theme reached its apex with his third album, *Antichrist Superstar* (1996) – a conscious spoof of Andrew Lloyd Weber's idealistic musical *Jesus Christ Superstar* (1970).[59] Highly critical of organized religion, he has, as Robert Wright points out,

---

53. Manson, quoted in Baddeley, *Dissecting Marilyn Manson*, p. 141.
54. On the Judas Priest case, see Richardson, 'Satanism in the Courts', pp. 211–213; M. Billiard, 'Heavy Metal Goes on Trial', *Rolling Stone* (12 July, 1990), pp. 83–88, 132; R. Wright, '"I'd Sell You Suicide": Pop Music and Moral Panic in the Age of Marilyn Manson', *Popular Music* 19 (2000), pp. 374–375.
55. See Baddeley, *Dissecting Marilyn Manson*, pp. 73–82.
56. See ibid., pp. 141–155.
57. See M. Manson (with N. Strauss), *The Long Dark Road Out of Hell* (London: Plexus, 1998), pp. 163–176.
58. Baddeley, *Dissecting Marilyn Manson*, p. 141.
59. See Manson, *Long Dark Road Out of Hell*, pp. 218–244.

> ingeniously . . . constructed for himself an elaborate autobiographical mythology in which his personal transformation from obscurity into superstar is fulfilled . . . Manson's messianic complex is animated by his remarkable fluency with the concepts and especially the jargon of conservative evangelicalism, which helps to explain why the religious right find him 'dangerous' and 'evil'. Indeed, Manson's 'Antichrist' persona is chilling – and brilliant – because he has so thoroughly appropriated the language of the New Testament, not only in scripted performances, but in casual conversation.[60]

Although Manson is, as Wright comments, 'clearly interested in mystifying his own image and rhetoric', it is nevertheless clear from his autobiography (and other sources) that he 'takes himself and his music very seriously, that his critique of organised religion is both personal and ideological'.[61]

Manson may be one of the best-known metal musicians, but he is only one of a long and growing list of artists who are working with ideas and images drawn from Western demonology and contemporary Satanism. Certainly it is the case that, for several decades, 'the Devil and all his evil doings have provided rock with some of its most potent images'.[62] For example, the lyrics of the Brazilian 'extreme metal' band, Sepultura, are, certainly on their earlier albums, focused firmly on the celebration of violence, Satan, and opposition to Christianity. The track 'Bestial Devastation' speaks of 'a legion of demons', a vision of 'Satanas', and 'the beast of son of evil tormenting the preacher of Christ'.[63] Likewise, the lyrics of the group Deicide – the lead singer of which, Glen Benton, has an inverted crucifix burned into his forehead and claims to conduct authentic black masses – drink from a common pool of popular Western demonology and *ad hoc*

---

60. Wright, 'I'd Sell You Suicide', p. 377.
61. Ibid., p. 375.
62. P. Wilding, 'Lucifer Rising', *Classic Rock* 31 (September, 2001), p. 53.
63. Sepultura, 'Bestial Devastation', quoted in K. Kahn-Harris, '"Roots"? The Relationship Between the Global and the Local Within the Extreme Metal Scene', *Popular Music* 19/1 (2000), pp. 27–28.

Satanism. 'Travel unto Satan,' Benton declares. 'Bring forth the blood red sea.'[64] Indeed, by the early 1990s, not only had *ad hoc* Satanism become part of heavy-metal chic, but so had explicit opposition to Christian belief. Slogans such as 'Support the War Against Christianity' began to appear on flyers and CD covers and, as Keith Kahn-Harris comments, 'the sheer level and venom of the anti-Christian abuse displayed in black metal took it to a new level'.[65]

However, again, it is important to understand that this explicit anti-Christian content (such as inverted crucifixes and exaggerated blasphemy), while central to satanic panic mythology, is often not part of organized Satanism. The subculture of 'rock Satanism' is more concerned with Hammer Horroresque demonology and adolescent shock value. That is to say, like Manson, such musicians are aware of what sells records to rebellious teenagers and, very likely, they themselves enjoy offending mainstream values and particularly right-wing Christians. Hence, while it would be erroneous to claim that all heavy-metal musicians and their followers are simply out to shock, with little interest in Satanism or other forms of demonological religious belief, it is hard to avoid the conclusion that, for many, such interest is either staged or temporary and superficial. For example, this was certainly the case for Ozzy Osbourne, who once responded to accusations that he conjured up demons, with 'It takes me all my time to conjure myself out of bed.'[66] Indeed, his former band, Black Sabbath, which has been central to the popularization of Western demonology in rock music, claimed that it was actually opposed to the emergent fascination with Satanism in the 1970s. As Philip Wilding comments,

> They were the first band to seriously toy with satanic imagery, crucifixes and relentlessly doomy, evil-laden lyrics. Sabbath bassist and lyricist Terry 'Geezer' Butler admitted to a morbid interest in the then fashionable subjects of occultism and mysticism, and painted his flat black and

---

64. Quoted in P. Sutcliffe, 'Go Forth and Rock', *Q* 140 (May 1998), p. 78.
65. K. Kahn-Harris, 'Meaning of Strife', *Terrorizer* 128 (2005), p. 40.
66. Quoted in Medway, *The Lure of the Sinister*, p. 225.

> covered his walls with inverted crosses and images of Satan. But that all came to an end when, one night, Geezer saw, or imagined he saw, a figure at the end of his bed inviting him to pledge his allegiance to the dark side or to simply stop toying with things he didn't understand. Consequently, Butler insists that Sabbath's songs – the satanic ones, at least – are a warning against Satanism.[67]

The argument that Black Sabbath were the first heavy-metal band – an argument based on both the style of music and the occult themes explored in the lyrics and expressed in their style – has been persuasively made by Jonathon Epstein and David Pratto.[68] That said, while the particular mixture of heavy rock music, lyrical content and style marks Black Sabbath out as perhaps the first heavy-metal band, Epstein and Pratto are entirely wrong in their assertion that 'Black Sabbath was the first rock band to make extensive use of Satanic symbolism.'[69] Not only was the occult very popular in late 1960s rock music, but slightly earlier bands, such as particularly the American band Coven and their British counterpart Black Widow, were making explicit use of Satanic symbolism.

Black Widow, who claimed to perform full black masses on stage, had some success with their single 'Come to the Sabbat', taken from their first album *Sacrifice* (1970) – which even got into the top forty in the British charts. Although hardly heavy metal, being a typical example of the progressive rock of the period, refrains such as 'Come, come, come, to the sabbat/ Come to the sabbat/ Satan's there,'[70] immediately established them as a key band in the emergence of what became known as 'occult rock'. They toured throughout Europe (becoming more successful in Italy, Sweden, Germany, France, Austria and the Netherlands than in their home country) and even played at the Isle of Wight festival. More significantly, they attracted enormous media attention as

---

67. Wilding, 'Lucifer Rising', p. 57.
68. See Epstein and Pratto, 'Heavy Metal Rock Music', p. 68.
69. Ibid.
70. Part of the track can now be heard at <http://hem.passagen.se/blk-widow/blacklp1.htm> (accessed 29 September 2004).

a result of their extravagant stage shows, which included the mock sacrifice of a nude woman – namely Maxine Sanders, the wife of Alex Sanders, the self-professed 'King of the Witches' and the founder of the Alexandrian tradition of witchcraft.[71] At the same time in North America, Coven were likewise becoming similarly notorious and gaining a significant cult following. Like Black Widow, their beliefs were conspicuously evident in their music and performances. For example, the final track of their 1969 debut album, *Witchcraft Destroys Minds and Reaps Souls*, is a thirteen-minute 'satanic mass', and the gatefold sleeve of the album shows the band engaged in the ritual, the naked female lead singer, Jinx Dawson, serving as the 'altar of flesh'. Similarly, in 1972, Jamra[72] released their album *The Second Coming*, a series of live invocations, the cover of which reproduced the Church of Satan's 'Sigil of the Baphomet' over an inverted crucifix.[73]

As for this fascination with performing live black masses,[74] it can perhaps be traced back to LaVey, who, in 1968, caused a minor sensation when he recorded a live black mass at the Church of Satan and released it as an album, *The Satanic Mass*.[75] Within twelve

---

71. Photographs and details of the band, which still has a cult following, can be found at <www.blackwidow.org.uk> (accessed 12 October 2004).
72. Jamra, about which there is very little information available, seems to have been an early 1970s occult commune. However, the name is interesting, in that the reference to Satan is Islamic. It refers to three stone pillars in Mina that symbolically represent the locations where *Shaytan* (Satan) sought to tempt Ibrahim (Abraham) away from the worship of Allah. During the *hajj*, the pilgrim symbolically stones these pillars in remembrance of Ibrahim's victory over temptation.
73. Jamra, *The Second Coming* (Stygian, 1972). See also P. H. Gilmore, 'The History of the Origin of the Sigil of Baphomet and Its Use in the Church of Satan': <www.churchofsatan.com/Pages/ BaphometSigil.html> (accessed 18 June 2005).
74. On the history and nature of 'the Black Mass', see Medway, *The Lure of the Sinister*, pp. 380–388.
75. Church of Satan, *Satanic Mass* (1968; re-released on CD by Amarillo Records, 1996).

months the live black mass had entered certain popular music sub-cultures. Indeed, it is arguable that the contemporary fascination with Satanism within rock music can be directly linked to the media impact of LaVey and the Church of Satan, which brought to life the occult spiritualities portrayed in the horror films of the 1960s and particularly in the popular novels of Dennis Wheatley. For those disillusioned with, or simply not attracted to, the Eastern turn of the 1960s hippy culture,[76] LaVey and the teachings of and myths surrounding Aleister Crowley offered a true counter-cultural alternative. For example, both the Rolling Stones and Led Zeppelin found this type of spirituality attractive during the late 1960s and early 1970s. Indeed, Led Zeppelin's guitarist, Jimmy Page, even went so far as to purchase Boleskine House (Crowley's former home) – which he owned until 1991 – and 'employed a man solely to attend auctions in search of Crowleyana'.[77] He even briefly ran his own occult shop in London's Kensington High Street, which he called Equinox after the journal edited by Crowley, and 'formed a publishing house to propagate Crowley's work'.[78] However, the point is that, as Michael Moynihan and Didrik Søderlind comment, 'simultaneously with the ascension of the Rolling Stones to world fame, other . . . rock groups entered the scene, bringing with them even more elements of the occult and black magic'.[79] Apart from the more obvious bands who cultivated a satanic image at a theatrical and superficial level, such as Black Sabbath (listen particularly to their debut 1970 album *Black Sabbath*, and see the cover of their 1973 album *Sabbath Bloody Sabbath*), we have seen that there were a number of other bands whose commitment to satanic mythology was more involved.

---

76. For more on the Easternization of the West, see C. Partridge, *Re-Enchantment of the West*, 1, ch. 5. On Easternized popular music in the 1960s, see pp. 151–156.
77. J. Hotten, 'Antichrist Superstar', *Classic Rock* 31 (September 2001), p. 67.
78. Ibid.
79. Moynihan, *Lords of Chaos*, p. 3.

This commitment to such themes coalesced by the end of the 1970s, when Venom formed in 1979, in Newcastle, UK, in that this is the group that is widely regarded as the first satanic metal band and, as such, the founders of the 'black-metal' genre. While being musically distinct from contemporary black metal – being closer to punk rock than to metal – they provided an exaggerated exposition of satanic mythology that points very clearly to the future evolution of the genre.[80] Their 1981 debut album, *Welcome to Hell*, for example, had as its cover illustration a close copy of the Church of Satan's 'Sigil of the Baphomet'. Indeed, it resembles the cover of *The Satanic Mass*, designed by LaVey (using the pseudonym Hugo Zorilla). However, the point is that, with the title of Venom's second album, *Black Metal*,

> a future style of Satanic music had found a name. The record also carved in stone some of genre's essential features. Primary among these would be an open policy of violent opposition to Judeo-Christianity, endless blasphemy, and the abandonment of all subtlety in favour of grandiose theatre which teetered over an abyss of kitsch and self-caricature.[81]

Although the band members were no more involved in the Satanist subculture than were Black Sabbath, this does not really matter. Their personal beliefs were, in the final analysis, 'altogether irrelevant for listeners who could revel in the statements found on their album sleeves' and in their lyrics.[82]

While many black-metal bands are, like Black Sabbath, not theologically interested in demonology, during the 1990s bands that were more spiritually and ideologically committed began to emerge. That is to say, artists who were personally committed to the development of some form of Satanism explicitly used their music to articulate their beliefs. Akercocke, for example, who formed in

80. See P. Schwarz, 'Boys From the Black Stuff: A Brief History of Black Metal. Part One: The Foundations', *Terrorizer* 128 (2005), p. 128.

81. Moynihan, *Lords of Chaos*, pp. 12–13.

82. Ibid., p. 13. See also Schwarz, 'Boys from the Black Stuff: Part One'.

London in 1990, became well known, not only for their suits and formal dress, but also for their explicit Satanism, exaggerated blasphemy and deliberate offensiveness.[83] Their second album, *The Goat of Mendes* (2001), is a good example of this type of material and, for many fans, is a classic example of contemporary, ideologically driven black metal. Similarly, another British black-metal band, The Reign of Erebus, has devoted itself to a blend of Satanism, misanthropy and vehement anti-Christian ideology, without, they claim, the posturing typical of many musicians within the genre.[84] Indeed, common themes, which have direct links to the crude Satanist doctrine of the survival of the fittest, are those of complete disregard for others and devotion to the satisfying of one's own desires and appetites, particular those of a sexual nature. In particular, aggression in the service of the self or, indeed, Satan, is thus a common lyrical theme. This is evident in the names of many of the bands: Bestial Warlust, Deathchurch, Black Pain, Dismember, Blood Ritual, Misanthrope, Bloodbath, Shadow Cut, Blood Red Throne, Torn to Pieces, Scar Symmetry, Trauma and Cannibal Corpse.

Particularly worrying, however, are those *ad hoc* Satanists who have so immersed themselves in Satanism's social Darwinism and extreme right-wing ideologies, that, rather than adhering to the guidelines of organized Satanism, they have engaged in criminal activity. This trajectory has been a particular cause of concern in Scandinavia. For example, the Norwegian black metal bands Burzum, Mayhem and Emperor have been linked to a series of church-burnings and graveyard desecrations between 1992 and 1994, a craze which eventually spread to Sweden and parts of central Europe in 1995.[85] The first church-burning took place on 6

---

83. See their website: <www.akercocke.com> (accessed 5 July 2005).
84. See their website: <http://reignoferebus.com/flash.html> (accessed 5 July 2005).
85. See Wilding, 'Lucifer Rising', p. 59; G. Strachan, 'Boys From the Black Stuff: Part Two' , *Terrorizer* 128 (2005), p. 37; 'European Legions: Eastern Europe', *Terrorizer* 128 (2005), p. 39; O. Badin, 'European Legions: France', *Terrorizer* 128 (2005), pp. 38–39; Kahn-Harris, 'Meaning of Strife'.

June at, it was claimed, 6.00am – i.e. the sixth day of the sixth month at six o'clock (666). Photographs of the burned ruins were also included on the Burzum EP *Aske* (meaning 'Ashes'). More worrying still were developments during the 1990s which witnessed a confluence of Satanism and far-right politics, in that a few bands began explicitly to articulate neo-Nazi ideology, Satanic mythology, right-wing Odinism and violence.[86] For example, the lead singer of Burzum, Kristian Vikernes (who had changed his given name to 'Varg' and also adopted the pseudonym Count Grishnackh[87]), as well as conducting arson attacks, also murdered a former band member and friend, Mayhem guitarist Euronymous (Øystein Aarseth).[88] 'The two', says Wilding, 'had conflicting philosophies: Euronymous was alleged to be a Satanist, while Vikernes was into Paganism and racial purity . . . Vikernes is currently serving a 21 year jail sentence, and has changed his name once again to Vara Quisling (after the infamous Norwegian Nazi collaborator).'[89] Similarly, Eithun, from the band Emperor, is also serving a life sentence for murder.

---

86. See A. Dyrendal, 'Media Constructions of "Satanism" in Norway 1988–1997', *FoafTale News* 43 (February 1998), pp. 2–5.
87. 'I couldn't stand [the name Kristian],' says Vikernes, 'which means Christ and Christian. The word *Varg* has a great meaning for me. I could speak about this matter for an hour. Anyway, briefly, if you make a diagram of this word, you'll see that it's the combination of the vertical and the horizontal of the words *Amor* (the strongest feeling), *Roma* (the centre of the world), and *Grav* (grave). [In other words, *Varg* is an acronym of *Varg, Amor, Roma, Grav.*] Besides, *Varg* derives from an archaic Nordic language and means wolf.' V. Vikernes, quoted in Moynihan, *Lords of Chaos*, p. 137.
88. Vikernes played bass on Mayhem's *De Mysteriis Dom Sathanas* (Century Media/Grind Core: 1994). Another musician, Blackthorn (Snorre Ruch), was also charged for being an accomplice in the murder of Euronymous.
89. Wilding, 'Lucifer Rising', p. 59. On the influence of Vidkun Quisling, the fascist Norwegian politician, see Moynihan, *Lords of Chaos*, pp. 162–165.

While it is difficult to determine the exact numbers involved, such extreme right-wing black metal does seem to be a growing phenomenon.[90] For example, Burzum is one of several bands that belong to an emerging movement known as National Socialist Black Metal (NSBM). According to NSBM's literature:

> The extremes of musical passion attract fascist ideologies in a time when Judeo-Christian moral values have caused humanity to poison the earth and sky and waters, destroy ancient cultures and adulterate their races, enslave many to the tedium of a society motivated by commerce, and remove all desire for individuality in existence. National Socialist black metal is aurally hateful music that diminishes the listener and saturates them with isolationist and ancient mystical beliefs, separating the tribes so we may have our peoples remain unique and unmarketable.[91]

They promote Hitler's thought: 'the first four chapters of *Mein Kampf*, the 25 points with which he addressed the German people, and his wartime correspondence with Goebbels have been highly influential in the NSBM movement.'[92] More than that, as the following statements make clear, the movement encourages ethnic cleansing:

> If you know black metal, you know that Christians and Jews are not welcome with us . . . Some NSBMers are full believers in the Nazi promise and even extend it further to 'clearing the world of all Jews, Hispanics, Congoids, Gypsys and Slavs' as a process of restoring the white homeland. Most are more immediately concerned with establishing white homelands, preserving white culture, and most of all, educating white children and preparing them for a challenging world on intellectual, academic, physical, spiritual and racial levels.[93]

---

90. See for example, the numerous bands on the 'black metal.com' website: <www.blackmetal.com> (accessed 8 July 2005).
91. <www.nsbm.org/> (accessed 6 August 2004).
92. <www.nsbm.org/faq/index.html> (accessed 6 August 2004).
93. Ibid.

These are worrying developments, for, as Guy Strachan comments, 'despite . . . the contempt with which the Nazi regime is held in Eastern Europe, the amount of bands who have leanings in this direction often seems to outweigh the number that don't'.[94] Satanist social Darwinism, the misanthropy of demonology, and the self-focused nature of Western culture reached perhaps their logical conclusion in extreme, far-right black metal, with each dark trend stimulating and feeding the other.

The very nihilism and countercultural nature of such subcultural ideologies mean that they prefer to exist on the periphery of society. To stand outside the mainstream, to be unpopular and to be misunderstood is precisely why many devotees find black metal attractive.[95] Hence, it is interesting that, while many of these bands, particularly those with extreme-right leanings, have remained underground, in recent years black metal seems to be crawling out of the shadows and into the mainstream. While groups such as Cradle of Filth, which signed to Sony, and Satyricon, which signed to Capitol, have been accused of 'selling out' by many within the subculture,[96] for them it is a natural progression. On the one hand, they're getting older and want to make money (something many black metallers see precious little of) and, on the other hand, some want to take their dark gospel to a larger audience.[97] That there is a larger audience to take it to, and that major record labels are keen to have black metal on their books, says something about the continuing fascination of demonology and satanic mythology for the Western mind.

---

94. Strachan, 'European Legions', p. 39.
95. See Purcell, *Death Metal Music*, pp. 163–169.
96. I have spoken to both fans and musicians who are contemptuous of Cradle of Filth, despite the latter's black-metal credentials.
97. See J. Hinchliffe, 'Soaring on Blackened Wings: The Rise of the Black Metal Mainstream', *Terrorizer* 129 (March, 2005), pp. 42–43.

Conclusion

It is, of course, not surprising that in a culturally Christian society the symbolism of Christian demonology and the embracing of taboo ideologies, such as Satanism, have become significant religious and cultural resources for those wanting to tread counter-cultural and anti-establishment paths. Certainly, as we have seen, it is within the traditionally anti-establishment milieu of rock music that such demonology has found some of its most devoted supporters.

Moreover, as I have argued elsewhere,[98] this fascination with demonological themes and even explicit belief in Satan challenges strong theories of secularization that posit the collapse of supernatural belief in Western societies. Although hardcore satanic belief may represent a minority of the overall heavy-metal subculture, the dissemination of demonological and broadly occult ideas is widespread. While we are not, for the most part, dealing with institutional religion here, we are also not dealing with the secular mind. Indeed, even if the world is not literally sacralized for some of the artists themselves (such as Ozzy Osbourne), their music is helping to re-enchant it for some of their fans, particularly when the demonic becomes iconic. In other words, that dark spirituality and the paranormal are enormously successful in marketing bands is in itself significant.

Finally, I am certainly not suggesting that interest in heavy metal and its subculture, with all that this symbolically entails (in fashion, language and iconography) leads to institutional Satanism or explicit occult spirituality. That would be ridiculous. Many fans of the genre, like most young people, are hedonists, more concerned with enjoying themselves day to day, offending their elders, impressing their peers and establishing an identity than they are with religion and spirituality. Black metal, inverted crucifixes and

---

98. See C. Partridge, 'Alien Demonology: The Christian Roots of the Malevolent Extraterrestrial in UFO Religions and Abduction Spiritualities', *Religion* 34 (2004), pp. 163–189; Partridge, *Re-Enchantment of the West*, 2, ch. 6.

dark culture are merely trends that, as with much else, will run their course and be replaced by other trends.[99] What I am suggesting, though, is that such trends should not be ignored by sociologists, scholars of religion and indeed theologians as they seek to understand the contemporary Western milieu. They provide significant insights into approaches to the spiritual and the paranormal in a culture that is often thought to be secular. Furthermore, that traditional Christian themes in music fail to accrue much, if any, subcultural capital, whereas satanic (or indeed, Eastern, pagan, mystical) themes are invested with enormous subcultural capital, has significant implications for those seeking to understand religion in the West. Outside Christianity, that which is allied to 'the occult' and which articulates popular demonology is far more 'cool' than that which is identifiably Christian.[100]

---

99. 'Call black metal's dress code and arcane semantics an addictive power fantasy for rejects, but it required a special rarefied sensibility for fans to don shirts depicting giant blazing pentagrams and memorize long lyrical lines of barely audible blasphemy. Constant shout-outs to Satan were distracting and distressing to the unassimilated ear, but, like most youth ideologies, mock devil worship merely expressed the desire to smash societal restraints and carve a space for unfettered fun.' I. Christie, *Sound of the Beast: The Complete Headbanging History of Heavy Metal* (New York: HarperEntertainment, 2004), p. 116.
100. It should perhaps be noted that, in the USA, there is increasing evidence that Christian themes are, if not 'cool', at least not harming an artist's profit margins. For example, in 2005 around 38 million Contemporary Christian music albums were sold. That said, many Christian bands, according to John Pauley, are still 'afraid to be ghettoized into the genre of Christian music and onto Christian radio stations'. Cf. B. Westhoff, 'God: Chart Topper. It's Suddenly Cool Again for Pop Music to Include Spirituality', *Harvard Divinity Bulletin* 34/2 (Spring 2006), <www.hds.harvard.edu/news/bulletin_mag/articles/34–2_westhoff.html> (accessed 5 October 2006).

13 NOT JUST HALOS AND HORNS: ANGELS AND DEMONS IN WESTERN POP CULTURE

Amy Summers-Minette

Meet Aziraphale and Crowley. Continuing the great tradition of mismatched pairings *à la* Felix and Oscar (*The Odd Couple*) or Bert and Ernie (*Sesame Street*), these two characters from Neil Gaiman and Terry Pratchett's book *Good Omens* have been reluctant friends for years. Aziraphale is a rare-book dealer who enjoys a nice glass of wine and crossword puzzles. Crowley is a gentleman of leisure who enjoys fast driving and taking naps. One likes classical music while the other likes Queen. Oh, and one – Aziraphale – is an angel of God, while the other – Crowley – is a demon who fell from grace eons ago.[1] The two have been odd acquaintances since the beginning – the 'in the beginning' beginning – and have a thousand-year-old arrangement not to interfere with each other's work. They even occasionally go so far as to help each other out

1. In his defence Crowley comments that 'he hadn't meant to Fall. He'd just hung around with the wrong people.' Neil Gaiman and Terry Pratchett, *Good Omens* (New York: Workman Publishing Company Inc., 1990; New York: Ace Books, 1996), p. 12.

with that work whenever it just makes good time-management sense.[2]

Within the pages of *Good Omens*, first published in 1990, Aziraphale and Crowley find themselves going beyond the occasional errand. As the forces of heaven and hell prepare for the great fight which will accompany the rise of the Anti-Christ, the pair teams up to stop the Apocalypse. Wondering what right and wrong really mean, Aziraphale and Crowley choose to help save the world they have both come to enjoy. Through their world-saving adventures, Aziraphale comes to appreciate that Crowley has a spark of goodness within him and Crowley observes that Aziraphale was 'just enough of a bastard to be worth liking'.[3] Rather than serving as embodiments of absolute good and evil, Aziraphale and Crowley are a touch more ambiguous. With witty, insightful and irreverent observations about the supernatural, *Good Omens* introduces characters which draw upon and then challenge traditional Western views about angels and demons.

This book is not alone. Over the last two decades, Western pop culture has seen a rise in books, television series and films with characters that do not fit into the traditional angelic or demonic mould. These moulds hold that angels are holy messengers and warriors for God who give human beings a hand in a tough spot. Demons are fallen angels who aligned themselves with the Devil – the greatest fallen angel – and spend their time tempting and tormenting humans. The angel on one shoulder encourages you on the benefits of being good, while the demon-devil on the other whispers just how good bad could be.

With this current trend in pop culture, you are not guaranteed easily identifiable good and bad guys when you pick up a book or watch a movie involving such supernatural creatures. Rather you may find demons with pointed horns choosing to do good while angels in white robes have halos that are more than just a little bit

---

2. As Crowley explains, they were 'both of angel stock, after all. If one was going to Hull for a quick temptation, it made sense to nip across the city and carry out a standard brief moment of divine ecstasy.' Ibid., p. 31.

3. Ibid., p. 329.

crooked. Within a world where many people believe in angels and demons,[4] the understanding of what and who angels and demons are has been shifting away from what much of Western religious and cultural tradition has held.

The average Westerner's basic understanding of angels and demons does not come from one sacred text or significant artistic work alone. The traditional Western concept of angels and demons has strong roots within the Judeo-Christian tradition and has taken many centuries and sources to form.[5] Angels begin in this tradition as simple messengers of God; the Greek and Hebrew words translated in English as 'angel' literally mean 'messenger'. In word and in deed, biblical angels brought both pleasant and painful divine messages to humans. Demons trace their roots to evil spirits in the Hebrew canonical texts that become creatures who know Jesus and can be banished by him in the New Testament. These demons spend time possessing and tormenting humans. They have also been known within the Judeo-Christian tradition as angels that rebelled against their creator, becoming fallen angels.

The very idea of two distinct classes of angels and the great rebellion and subsequent fall that separated them has a complicated history. The idea stems from two different biblical texts – Genesis 6:1–4 and Isaiah 14:12–16 – neither of which was originally about angelic or demonic beings. These two texts were first combined into one narrative and reinterpreted as addressing good and evil angels within the collection of apocalyptic texts commonly referred to as 1 Enoch.

---

4. According to recent Gallup polls, 78% of Americans say they believe in angels while 70% believe in the most infamous demon, the devil (25 May 2004). Canada and Britain have their share of believers in angels – 56% and 36% of the respective populations believe – while only 37% of Canadians and 29% of Britons believe in the devil (16 November 2004).
5. It is important to note that the Judeo-Christian tradition has been influenced by the cultures within which it has existed. For example, many credit the Greek mythological creature Pan with being the inspiration for key demonic characteristics such as horns.

1 Enoch

1 Enoch – one of the several non-canonical apocalyptic writings that sprang up within the Jewish community during the Hellenistic era – follows the story of Enoch, son of Seth, who has a vision in which he sees supernatural beings taking human women as wives. This vision is drawing upon a similar story in Genesis 6:1–4; yet, where the biblical text calls these beings only 'sons of God,' (Gen. 6:2, New Revised Standard Version), 1 Enoch makes the interpretative move to identify these sons of God as angels – those he also calls 'Watchers'.[6] Led by the angel Azazel, a group of angels choose to give in to lust and mate with human women. Angels mating with humans is a transgression, to be sure, one that results in the conception and birth of giants who then beget a race called the Nephilim. These offspring of angels and humans go about trying to devour the earth and all its inhabitants until humanity cries out for help. In Enoch's vision, good archangels come to the aid of the humans at God's command and imprison the fallen angels within fiery depths.

While 1 Enoch's interpretation of the sons of God narrative as being about angels is a part of our cultural lexicon,[7] it is the connection of Isaiah 14:12–16 to the story of fallen angels which has had perhaps the greatest impact. The Isaiah text – which is contextually referring to the king of Babylon – speaks of someone identified as 'Day Star, son of Dawn' (Isa. 14:12, NRSV), having such pride in the heart as to dream of ascending to God's throne.

---

6. This interpretation became such a part of accepted Jewish tradition that in the version of the Septuagint (the Greek translation of the Hebrew texts) used by Philo of Alexandria (20 BC–AD 40) *bĕnê hĕ-ĕlōhîm* ('sons of God' in Hebrew) was translated as *angeloi*, 'angels', in Greek. J. B. Russell, *The Devil: Perceptions of Evil from Antiquity to Primitive Christianity* (Ithaca: Cornell University Press, 1977), p. 188 n. 15.
7. In the 1998 film *City of Angels*, starring Nicholas Cage and Meg Ryan, Cage's character falls (literally) from his angelic state for the love of Ryan's character. Thomas E. Sniegnoski's book series *The Fallen*, made into a 2006 TV movie for ABC Family, also draws upon this mythology.

God responds to this prideful act with promises of bringing down this figure into the Pit. 1 Enoch alludes to this passage several times when referring metaphorically to the fall of the angels. The narrator sees the angels as stars falling from heaven and stars being bound, thrown down, and burning in fire.[8] This allusion to Isaiah 14 begins a history of reinterpreting what was originally an indictment against a foreign king as an indictment against prideful angels – particularly the one called Lucifer.[9] This pride and longing for power begin to be understood as the reason for the rebellion and fall. The New Testament book Revelation, and other apocalyptic literature of the same period which pick up on this tradition, also suggest that this warfare is not over. From the perspective of these texts, the rebellion and fall constitute the beginning – not the end – of the story.

The theologian with perhaps the greatest influence on the Western world's inherited view of angels and demons also drew connections between Isaiah's proclamations against the king of Babylon with the fate of fallen angels. Augustine, the venerated saint of the Roman Catholic Church and esteemed theologian for the Protestants, did more than simply continue this connection; he made the theological claim that, unlike humans, the angels who fell are forever tied to their original sin and can never be redeemed.[10] It is from this theological assertion that the understanding of demons as personifications of absolute evil, and of angels as absolute good, truly begins to flourish. Thanks to Augustine, the Western world firmly envisioned angels as always

---

8. See 1 Enoch 85:2, 21.

9. The Vulgate (late fourth century AD) uses the Latin word *lucifer* for 'Day-Star'. As the tradition connecting the Isaiah text with fallen angels grew stronger, 'Lucifer' became a common name for the figure of the devil. The King James Version of the Bible, published first in 1611 and still used by many Christians today, translates the text into English but keeps 'Lucifer' as a proper name, so Isa. 14:12 reads, 'O Lucifer, son of the morning'.

10. J. B. Russell, *Satan: The Early Christian Tradition*, (Itacha: Cornell University Press, 1981), p. 207.

good, and demons forever bad, without hope of changing their destinies.[11]

The tradition begun in 1 Enoch is certainly not the only perspective on the origin of angels and demons. Another popular thought about these supernatural beings is that humans can become either angels or demons depending on their actions – for example Clarence and his hopes of earning wings in *It's A Wonderful Life* (1946). Those who were truly righteous on earth are transformed into beings of absolute good in heaven, and those who were truly wicked become beings of absolute evil. Later writings about Enoch hold that the son of Seth was one such as these, becoming the angel Metatron – the voice of God.

The Middle Ages

The origin and nature of angels and demons remained a matter of interest for theologians across the generations at the same time as it caught the interest and imagination of poets and playwrights, artists and musicians. The artistic fascination truly began its heyday during the Middle Ages. During this period popular English mystery plays which portrayed biblical stories included the non-biblical story of the creation and fall of Lucifer and his minions. Morality plays of the same period explored the idea that God gave each human an angel to lead the soul to righteousness and a demon to tempt toward wickedness. An angel dressed in white and a demon decked out in red would stand behind a person and each would use every trick in his book to win the soul for his camp.[12]

---

11. Thomas Aquinas, another key theologian in Western tradition, contends that the first act of goodness by an angel forever connects that angel to God and good; the fallen angel's choice to sin forever connects that angel to sin. From that moment on, it cannot choose to be anything else. See *Summa Theologica* Q64, Articles 2 and 3.
12. One such play is *Castle of Perseverance*. See V. F. Hopper and G. B. Lahy (eds.), *Medieval Mystery Plays, Morality Plays, and Interludes* (Great Neck, NY: Barron's Educational Series, Inc., 1962) for this and other plays.

The well-known image of an angel and devil sitting on a person's shoulders fighting for influence stems from this tradition.

As these morality plays explored the inner battles angels and demons instigated within humans, the belief in greater warfare between the forces of heaven and hell – the warfare Aziraphale and Crowley would have been expected to participate in – became extremely popular. Paintings depicting beautiful angels with swords fighting horned beast-like fallen angels – as well as sinners meeting their eternal demonic fate – appeared in churches and prayer books. People saw their souls and the world around them as battleground for these warring forces.[13] This fascination was still present when John Milton wrote his seminal and influential work *Paradise Lost.*

This poem about the fall of both angels and humans has inspired artwork, music and other written works since it was first published in 1667. Some of the more recent inspirations have included musical and operatic versions.[14] Among his other influences, Milton used 1 Enoch and its inspired traditions as source material. The artistic and cultural expressions, which were inspired by *Paradise Lost*, were also influenced by and thus helped spread – often unknowingly – the vision of angels and demons found within the Enoch tradition beyond church walls and into the mainstream culture.

Western popular culture

The vision of absolute good angels and evil demons fighting for human souls and the world is what is being questioned by Western pop culture today. While the traditional concept of angels and demons is still present within pop culture – the film *Angels in the*

---

13. See S. P. Revard, *The War in Heaven* (Ithaca: Cornell University Press, 1980), p. 108.
14. For further information see *Paradise Lost: The Musical* at <http://paradiselostthemusical.com> and *Paradise Lost: Opera Electronica* at <http://paradiselosttheopera.com>.

Outfield (1994) and the TV series *Supernatural* (2005–)[15] are two recent examples of traditional representations – the last two decades have introduced angelic demons and demonic angels who challenge the notion of absolutes. The darkening of an angel's character ranges from the 1996 film *Michael*'s depiction of its title character (John Travolta) as an overweight angel who enjoys smoking and drinking – the movie's tag line 'He's an angel, not a saint' says it all – to the portrayal of a dangerous and deadly Gabriel by the perfectly creepy Christopher Walken in *The Prophecy* (1995). Demons seem less evil when played by likeable actors such as Jason Lee in Kevin Smith's 1999 film *Dogma*, and downright good when they occasionally save the world, as with the title character in Mike Mignola's Dark Horse comic series turned 2004 Columbia film release *Hellboy*.

In movies, television series and books across the Western world, angels and demons struggle with living out their destinies as prescribed by tradition. Reflecting a culture where one's origins do not determine one's future, many angels and demons refuse to stay in the dark – or the light, as the case may be. The reasons these supernatural beings chose to go against their prescribed natures and fates vary.

Angels sometimes find themselves doing evil not because they start out wicked but because they are driven to it. In his fourth film, *Dogma*, writer/director Kevin Smith tells the story of two angels who almost undo creation in their search for a way home. Loki (Matt Damon) and Bartleby (Ben Affleck) were angels of God. After killing the Egyptian first-born at God's request, Loki

---

15. Disney's *Angels in the Outfield*, directed by William Dear and starring Danny Glover and Christopher Lloyd, is a remake of a 1951 film of the same name, where angels assist a down-on-their-luck baseball team. It should also be noted that this chapter is only assessing the portrayal of demons within the first season of *Supernatural*, the Warner Brothers series starring Jensen Ackles and Jared Padalecki, about two demon-fighting brothers. Other examples of traditional representations of demons include the films *Fallen* (dir. Gregory Hoblit, with Denzel Washington, Warner Bros., 1998) and *Frailty* (dir. Bill Paxton, Lions Gate, 2001).

is convinced by Bartleby to lay down his sword of divine justice. This resignation gets them banished to a place worse than hell – Wisconsin – for the span of human history. Years later the two angels discover a loophole in God's divine proclamation. If they enter through the door of a newly rededicated church in New Jersey as humans – something they may become if they remove their wings – and then die without sinning, God will have to let them back in. What Loki and Bartleby do not know is that if they do manage to die as sin-free humans they will be proving God wrong, something which would undo creation. To prevent this, a motley crew, including Smith's most-beloved characters Jay and Silent Bob (Jason Mewes and Smith), is sent to stop them.

Though they speak foully – a Smith standard – and inspire crises of faith in nuns, Bartleby and Loki do not stray too far from their angelic roots until – that is – they discover this group is after them. Bartleby, who begins the movie as the less violent angel, becomes enraged when he discovers that agents of God are after them. He rants to Loki about God's patience and mercy with humans – how unfair it is that humans should receive such patience when they did not. He would rather kill those sent to kill him than forget his dream of going home. By the end of the film the angel who once convinced his friend to lay down his sword snaps and goes on a slaughtering spree.[16]

Struggling with both their own and humans' place in God's eyes is a popular reason for angels to dance on the dark side. Dimension's 1995 release *The Prophecy*, written and directed by Gregory Widen, introduces audiences to the archangel Gabriel (Walken in classic form) as a short-tempered killer who does not appreciate people using the Lord's name in vain. Gabriel is the leader of a second heavenly war fought over God's affection

---

16. Neither Bartleby nor Loki achieves the goal of going home. Following his rampage – which includes killing Loki – and becoming human, Bartleby ascends the steps of the church to have his sins cleansed, when God (Alanis Morissette) appears. In the presence of God, Bartleby gives up his plan and allows God to destroy him without being freed from his sin.

for humans – or 'talking monkeys' as the angel calls them. The movie is peppered with gory scenes of angels brutally fighting one another. As an angel who fights against Gabriel remarks, because of this war, 'heaven isn't heaven anymore'. Gabriel is willing to turn heaven into hell to keep humans – God's favourites – out.

The angel Gabriel takes another dark turn in *Constantine*, the 2005 Warner Brothers' film based on the DC Comics/Vertigo comic series *Hellblazer*. The film, directed by Francis Lawrence, follows John Constantine (Keanu Reeves) who spends his life fighting demonic forces in hopes of earning God's grace lost to him years ago. His normal routine of exorcising half-demons is interrupted when Constantine learns someone is trying to raise Mammon – Satan's son – in order to bring hell to earth. By the end of the film, Constantine learns that this someone is not an earth-bound evildoer or even Satan himself but the archangel Gabriel – played as a well-dressed androgynous being without much empathy by Tilda Swinton. Gabriel sees humans as creatures enormously unworthy of their special place in God's eyes. Rather than keep these humans away from heaven, as Walken's Gabriel would do, Swinton's Gabriel chooses to refine them with the fires of hell. 'I will bring you pain, I will bring you horror . . . so that those of you who will survive this reign of hell on earth will be worthy of God's love.'

Angels also appear devilish when they seem to be doing the will of God – and not just what they think God should want. The British cult television series *Hex*[17] features a villain named Malachi (Joseph Beattie), son of Azazeal (Michael Fassbender) – the leader of the fallen angels the series calls Nephilim – and a human teenager named Cassie (Christina Cole). Malachi's enemy and part-time love interest is a centuries-old witch named Ella (Laura Pyper). Ella's mission is to destroy the devilish Malachi and she is guided in this mission by the forces of good. Her mentor is the archangel Raphael (Antole Taubman) who, as one character notes,

---

17. Though *Hex* (2004–5) aired for only eighteen episodes on Sky One, it made quite an impression in those few episodes.

is 'slightly darker in real life' ('You Lose' 2.10).[18] Ella's relationship with her mentor ends when he tries to seduce her in the shower, telling her creepily: 'God has decreed that you serve me.' The forces of good no longer seeming so good, Ella strikes out on her own.

Angels are not the only beings which transcend their traditional roles in pursuit of doing what they think is best – God's will or not. The CBS television series *Touched by an Angel* (1994–2003) – a show which was known for its excessively angelic angels – had Jasmine Guy guest-star for three episodes as a fallen angel named Kathleen. In the final episode she appears in ('Clipped Wings' 3.19), Kathleen tries to get the angel Monica (Roma Downey) demoted. When she fails in her mission she becomes the fired one. Kicked off the devil's team, she receives redemption when she accepts Monica's invitation to turn back to God. Augustine's 'Once rotten, always rotten' theology of the fallen angels is not accepted by this series, which focuses a great deal on God's overwhelming love.

Not all those who have fallen rise above their state by such an easy act as accepting an invitation. Drawing on the tradition of humans becoming supernatural beings as well as on Jewish mythology about Adam's wife before Eve, SciFi Picture's *Darklight* (2004), directed by Bill Platt, tells the story of Lilith, an ancient demon who is recruited to save the world. Lilith (Shiri Appleby) begins the film not knowing her origins as Adam's first wife who became a demon. As she discovers her dark past, she becomes burdened by guilt and must decide what to do with the demonic powers that have caused so much destruction over the ages. With the help of a man whose son she had killed, Lilith chooses to join the fight against another demon in order to save humankind. Even as she makes this choice, Lilith discovers that her road to redemption will be a difficult one. She bears marks of her past sins upon her arm, marks which can only be removed by great acts of self-

18. All quotes from 'You Lose' (2.10) taken from episode synopses found at 'Hex', *AfterEllen*, <www.afterellen.com/TV/hex.html> (accessed 1 September 2006).

lessness and sacrifice. The removal of each mark – a task which involves a good amount of physical suffering – brings her one step closer to redemption.

Other demons resist their traditional roles for reasons other than atonement. The film *Hellboy*, directed by Guillermo del Toro, opens and closes with the same question: 'What is it that makes a man a man?' The journey of the title character, played by Ron Perlman, seeks to answer that question. Hellboy, or HB as he is affectionately called, comes into this world from a hell dimension in 1944. Though the Russian villain Rasputin (Karel Roden) brings HB to earth for purposes of destruction, he is captured/rescued by Allied Forces who do not force that role upon him. Raised as a son by Professor Trevor Bruttenholm (John Hurt), HB is a traditional-looking demon complete with red skin, a stone hand, and horns – which he sands down to 'fit in' – but he does not act like one. With a soft spot for cats, Baby Ruths and a girl named Liz Sherman (Selma Blair), Hellboy fights other demons to protect the world.

Though Hellboy spends his whole life going against the demonic grain, he is pulled into what some consider his true nature when Rasputin reappears. Rasputin has HB's father killed and then leads him to a place where he can follow his supposed destiny – opening the portal to hell and letting loose scary tentacled beasts called Ogdru Jahad. By threatening the life of another person Hellboy loves – Liz – and forcing Hellboy to speak his demonic name, Anug Un Rama, Rasputin succeeds in bringing out the demon in Hellboy. As the lovable HB transforms into a true child of hell, his red skin glows even brighter and the horns he sands down grow both long and pointy, fire swirling all around them. Just as this demon is about to open the doorway to hell with his stone hand – the right hand of doom – his friend John Myers (Rupert Evans) throws the crucifix the Professor always wore into Hellboy's hand, reminding him that his father gave him a choice. Strengthened by his father's memory, Hellboy breaks off his newly grown horns and returns to his non-bent-on-destroying-the-world state. When an outraged Rasputin asks Hellboy what he has done, Hellboy replies, 'I chose.' The movie ends with an answer to the question it opened with: 'What makes a man a man? The choices he makes – not how he starts things but how he decides to end them.'

The notion that a demon is more than his or her origins is explored in epic depth by Joss Whedon in his critically acclaimed television series *Buffy the Vampire Slayer* (1997–2003) and its spin-off *Angel* (1999–2004). A reworking of Whedon's 1992 Twentieth Century Fox film of the same name, *Buffy* introduces audiences to a pretty, blonde teenager named Buffy (Sarah Michelle Gellar), who fights the forces of darkness even as she tries to not flunk history. The worldview of 'demons bad, people good' ('New Moon Rising' 4.19) does not last long for this professional demon-fighter. In Whedon's universe, everyone has a touch of dark and light within them. Buffy – who one never really doubts is on the side of good – discovers that even she has a bit of darkness; the powers which enable her to fight the forces of evil as the Slayer are demonic in origin ('Get It Done' 7.15).

During the show's first season, Buffy learns that her boyfriend Angel (David Boreanaz) is a vampire – a creature who in *Buffy* mythology is of demonic origin ('Angel' 1.7). Buffy asks her Watcher – not an angelic Watcher as in the Enoch tradition but certainly a guide and guardian – if a vampire could ever be a good person. Giles (Anthony Stewart Head) replies that a vampire is 'demon at the core, there is no halfway', equating being a demon with being evil. While the perspective on demons as being pure evil is one held by the many around her, Buffy finds nothing is that simple. 'It's different with different demons,' she explains to a demon-equals-bad thinker years after she first discovers that Angel is a vampire. 'There are creatures – vampires for example – who aren't evil at all' (4.19). As it turned out, this demon named Angel had been cursed with a soul – which in the *Buffy* universe acts much like a conscience – and could indeed be good, though it was not always easy. Angel struggles with the sins of his past as he seeks to rise above them first on *Buffy* and then his own series.

This vampire with the ironic name is not the only vampire with sparks of goodness. Spike (James Marsters) is a vampire introduced during *Buffy*'s second season as a lover of wreaking havoc. He is also a vampire who has genuine love for others – first for another vampire, named Drusilla (Juliet Landau), and then for

Buffy herself. It is his love for Buffy that leads Spike into doing acts many would label 'good'. While still soulless, Spike offers Buffy genuine, even if awkward, compassion after she discovers that her mother is sick ('Fool for Love' 5.7), suffers torture to keep Buffy's sister safe ('Intervention' 5.18), and fights alongside Buffy's friends to keep the world protected from evil even after the Slayer has – temporarily – died ('The Bargaining, Part 1' 6.1). Even with all his moments of genuine goodness, Spike knows he can never fully be the man Buffy could love without something more. Thus the vampire suffers a series of challenging and painful trials in order to get what he believes will make him a truly good being – his soul ('Grave' 6.22).[19] This souled vampire ends his tenure on *Buffy* by sacrificing his life to save the world ('Chosen' 7.22).

Along with vampires who have souls, Whedon's universe contains many other demons who do not live the evil lives their origins would suggest. One of the main characters on *Angel* is a green-skinned, red-horned demon named Lorne (Andy Hallet). Lorne, a friend of Angel's, is a reluctant fighter for good – not because he wants to fight for evil, but because he would much rather sing show tunes than swing a sword. Another demon who fights a little reluctantly is Anya (Emma Caulfield). Anya first appears on *Buffy* as a thousand-year-old vengeance demon who loses her powers during a face-off with Giles ('The Wish' 3.9). Without her powers, Anya becomes a human teenager and eventually falls in love with one of Buffy's friends, Xander (Nicholas Brendon). Anya spends several years as a human before a painful break-up with Xander leads her back to her vengeful ways ('Hells Bells' 6.16). Anya soon discovers that vengeance just isn't what it used to be. Anya explains her struggles with being a vengeance demon to Willow (Alyson Hannigan) saying: 'Causing pain sounds really cool, I know, but turns out, it's really upsetting. Didn't use to be, but now it is' ('Same Time, Same Place' 7.3). This demon who once found her identity in the vengeance she inflicted willingly

---

19. Another demonic figure who seeks to become good for the sake of love is Cole (Julian McMahon) – a demon in love with a good witch – from the TV series *Charmed* (1998–2006, created by Constance M. Burge).

gives up her powers ('Selfless' 7.2) and eventually meets her death fighting against the same apocalypse Spike died to prevent (7.22).

Whedon has frequently been quoted as suggesting that the demons on *Buffy* are metaphors for experiences in life. Along with addressing issues of being a teenager and becoming an adult, these demons illustrate that life is not a struggle between two clearly distinguishable forces of good and evil. *Buffy* puts into story the truth of the world – that it is not a simple place where 'the good guys are always stalwart and true, the bad guys are easily distinguished by their pointy horns or black hats' ('Lie To Me' 2.7).

In the Western world, where most absolutes have become extinct, where what is wrong may look right and right wrong, the angels and demons, which once represented the distinct separation between what is good and what is evil, now often represent moral ambiguity. Those who once represented the two choices in life – be good or be bad – are now simultaneously liberated and burdened by choices themselves. Just as people are not bound to the situation within which they are born, angels and demons are no longer bound to behave in any particular way. Anya and Angel, Hellboy and Gabriel, Aziraphale and Crowley – these figures in Western pop culture stand as a reminder that you cannot view the world in black and white – or red and white as the case may be. Good and evil may still exist, but the simple appearance of a halo or horns no longer clearly indicates whether it is good or evil at work.

APPENDIX A: SPIRITS, GOOD AND EVIL, IN TRADITIONAL AFRICAN RELIGIONS

Tribe/group /region	Spirit /ancestor name	Spirit area of influence
Yoruba	Olodumare	Supreme being
Yoruba	Orisa-Nla	Supreme divinity
Yoruba	Orunmila	Oracle divinity associated with *ifa* divination
Yoruba	Esu	Mischief-maker
Yoruba	Ogun	Hunter and warrior
Yoruba	Sango	Natural disasters
Yoruba	Sopona	Earth divinity and associated with smallpox
Igbo	Alusi	Divinities – powerful spirits
Igbo	Chukwu	Supreme Being
Igbo	Ala	Earth goddess
Akan	Abosom	Divinities – powerful spirits
Xhosa	umTyholi	Creator of evil things
Dinka	Deng	Sky with rain
Dinka	Abuk	Garden and crops

Tribe/group /region	Spirit /ancestor name	Spirit area of influence
Dinka	Garang	Heat of sun and body
Dinka		
Dinka	Macardit	Kills people; other misfortunes
Dinka	Flesh	Beneficent spirit whose presence is sought
Lugbara		
Herero		
Gikuyu		
!Kung		
MoLuba		
Shona	Mhondoro	Royal ancestors
Shona	Ngozi	Spirit possessing humans
BaKongo		
Turu		
Luba		
Lovedu		
Mandari	Nyok	Spirits of slain animals, deformed babies, homicide victims
Mandari	Jok	Spirits that cause illness
West Africa	Bori	Spirits associated with natural forces which afflict, possess and protect
Bakossi	Ngoe	Primeval ancestor
Fang	Evus	Possessing spirit: source of power and witchcraft
Atuot		
Nuer		
Kalabar	Fenibaso	Spirit possessing priest of Soku
North East Africa	Zar	Spirits that attack causing ailments
Segeju	Shetani	Spirits causing women's illnesses
Sidamo	Shatana	Spirits causing ailments
Nguni		Spirits causing possession illness known as *ukuthwasa*
Mende		
Kimbu		

Tribe/group /region	Spirit /ancestor name	Spirit area of influence
Nyamwezi		
Ganda	Balubaale	Divinities – powerful spirits
Ganda	Mukasa	Lord of Lake
Nyoro	Bacwezi	Spirits of legendary ancestors

APPENDIX B: GODS GOOD AND EVIL, IN HINDUISM

Category	Name/ sub-category	Characteristic features
Pan-Indian deities	Brahman	The impersonal, ultimate reality.
	Brahma	One of the Trimurti, or Trinity of the supreme gods of Hinduism: Brahma, Vishnu and Shiva. A personification of the impersonal Brahman.
	Vishnu	A supreme god of Hinduism, whose function is particularly to preserve and save the world from danger. He has incarnated in the world ten times for this purpose.
	Shiva	One of the supreme gods, he is known as the destroyer of the universe. A god known for his austere looks and endurance in meditation.
Sura	33 million gods	A term that includes the minor gods and goddesses and demigods of Hinduism.
	Demigods	Gods who are partly divine and partly

Category	Name/ sub-category	Characteristic features
	(including sons of gods such as Arjuna and Bhima)	human, such as the Pandavas, who were created as the sons of Kunti, wife of Pandu, by gods as a result of a boon from the sage Durvasa. Gods who are in charge of natural forces and rivers, etc., are also considered to be demigods. Examples are Vayu, god of wind, and Ganga, goddess of the river Ganges.
	Regional gods such as the Ayyappan and Muttappan of Kerala	Dravidian gods of Kerala who later came to be identified as a fusion of the supreme gods Vishnu and Shiva of Hinduism. Their abodes at Shabarimala and Parassinikatavu respectively in Kerala have become popular centres of pilgrimage and worship.
	Various celestial beings like Gandharvas, Kinnaras (celestial musicians), Apsaras (celestial nymphs)	Gandharvas , Kinnaras and Apsaras are celestial beings, usually living in heaven, whose duty is to entertain the gods and goddesses through music and dance. Chitraratha is considered to be the king of Gandharvas. Urvashi and Menaka are well-known apsaras, strikingly beautiful and skilled in dance. Kinnaras are gifted in singing and dancing and have the heads of human beings but the bodies of birds or horses.
	Theriomorphic deities: Airavata the elephant, Nandi the bull, Garuda the eagle, and Sesha the serpent	These are demigods who are in animal form, and are usually the vehicles of gods and demigods. Garuda, for example, is the vehicle of the supreme god Vishnu.
Asuras		Asuras are considered in later Hinduism to be the evil counterparts of Suras or gods, and in Hindu mythology there is a constant struggle between the Suras and Asuras.
	Rakshasas, e.g. Sukeshin	Rakshasas are asuras who are particularly known for their horrific form and evil doings. Their abode is usually portrayed

Category	Name/ sub-category	Characteristic features
		as the forests of South India. Some of them are great scholars, such as Sukeshin, who taught virtue and *sanatana dharma* (the eternal righteousness) to demons. Many of them are devotees of the supreme gods, from whom they obtain boons which they put to evil use. Ravana for example, King of Lanka (Sri Lanka), was a rakshasa with ten heads and twenty arms who was a devotee of Shiva and, with the powers granted to him by the god, terrorized heaven and the demigods.
	Yakshas	Yakshas are nature spirits who inhabit forests, woods and lakes and are generally benevolent and harmless. But there are evil Yakshas who can waylay travellers and drink their blood like vampires in European legends.
	Yakshis	Female counterparts of Yakshas, generally malevolent and known for drinking human blood like vampires. Usually said to reside in trees and palms.
	Bhutas	Horrible-looking spirits guarding the abode of Shiva and some other gods. The term is also applied to ghosts of evil human beings.
	Bali	In Hindu mythology (Vishnu Purana) Bali is an asura and the king of Kerala in South India, whose reign is considered to be the golden age of Kerala. He was so able and virtuous that people adored him and sidelined the demigods who became jealous and feared their extinction as objects of worship by human beings. They sought the help of Vishnu, who appeared in the form of a Brahmin child and, by a ruse, pushed Bali to the nether world, where as an asura he rightfully belonged.

Category	Name/ sub-category	Characteristic features
	Indra	In Hindu mythology Indra is the king of the demigods and ruler of heaven and the demigod in charge of thunder and rain. His weapon is the dreaded thunderbolt.
	Varuna	A great asura who later joined the suras is said to be the guardian of the moral order, being the conserver of Rta (cosmic law and truth).
	Agni	The god of fire is the medium through which human beings communicate with the gods.
	Soma	God associated with a hallucinogenic drink derived by pressing the plant soma that was used in sacrificial rituals and also drunk to obtain visions and religious experience by ancient Hindus.
	Mithra	Another name for Varuna. Literally a friend, this god is also featured in the Indo-Iranian religion known as Mithraism.
	Hiranyakashipu	The evil asura king, father of Prahlada, a devotee of Vishnu.
	Prahlada	Virtuous son of Hiranyakashipu, an asura king, Prahlada was a devotee of Vishnu and refused to give up worshipping Vishnu when ordered by his father on pain of death.
	Shukra	Grandson of Hiranyakashipu, he was the teacher of all the demons. He lost one eye in an encounter with Vishnu, the supreme god.
	Yama	The god of death in Hinduism.
	Mahisha	An asura in the form of a fierce bull, he terrorized the demigods until killed by Durga, the warrior-goddess of Hinduism.